3 50

TEACHING

TEACHING
A Psychological Analysis

C. M. FLEMING

M.A., Ed.B., Ph.D.
University of London Institute of Education

METHUEN & CO LTD
11 NEW FETTER LANE LONDON EC4

First published October 3, 1958
Reprinted with minor corrections 1959
Reprinted in this size 1964, 1965
This edition 1968
Reprinted 1969
S.B.N. 416 03260 5
2.2

First published as a University Paperback 1964
Reprinted 1965
This edition 1968
Reprinted 1969
S.B.N. 416 29650 5
2.2

Printed in Great Britain by
Billing & Sons Limited, Guildford and London

Distributed in the U.S.A. by
Barnes & Noble Inc.

TO ALL
YE WHO TEACH

PREFACE

A SOCIAL APPROACH to human beings, admitting their need for appreciation and participation. A liberal-minded attitude to the processes of education, with awareness of the significance of insight and the part played by learners' concepts of themselves. Careful analysis of subject-matter, recognizing the importance of thoroughness in its study. Acceptance or rejection of the desirability of these determines the success of those who seek to influence others at any level and in any sort of situation – in homes, in schools, within industry, and on the councils of the nations. Much of the evidence indicative of their importance is, however, not yet readily available; and echoes of other viewpoints still linger to reduce the effectiveness of action. An attempt is therefore here made to indicate the origins of these interpretations and assess their relevance to day-to-day problems in what may well be the most typical situation – that of a 'teacher' within a school.

Teachers play many parts and to an understanding of these they bring all the wisdom accumulated in the totality of their living. Some study of motivation, of learning, and of growth is a necessary preliminary to a consideration of the work they do as technical experts in the presentation of topics or the assessment of personality or progress. To this must be added some concern with their requirements as administrators responsible for human relationships, as agents in the maintenance of public morale, and as explorers of the effectiveness of methods as yet untried.

Under such headings the matters commonly included in the discussion of school life and work may usefully be considered; and they are here presented in this form. The revised edition takes special account of additional findings in fields such as the programming of material, the social determinants of learning at home and in the classroom, methods of teaching, the contribution of non-selective (comprehensive) schools and intellectual and personal development as indicated in long-term studies.

C. M. FLEMING

CONTENTS

in more open-ended situations of a variety of types. Changes in data language and the design of experiments

LIST OF TABLES

PART I

INTRODUCTORY

I

THE TEACHER IN
THE ACT OF TUITION

TEACHING MAY BE studied in any situation in which a certain excess of skill or prestige prompts a human being to try to pass on to another something of his competence – in knowledge (belief), feeling (appreciation), purpose (value), or action. The contact may be between two adults or two children. It may be between a child and an adult, an employer and an employee, a parent and a child, or an officially appointed teacher and a pupil. The phrasing may differ in different circles. 'I'll show you.' 'I think I am right in supposing . . .' 'I guess that's so.' 'Take it from me.' The response is surprisingly similar in all. 'Do you know what you are talking about?' 'Is that style of play any good?' 'Is your taste to be trusted?' 'Are those values relevant?' These questions may be asked by those who are being 'taught'. They may occur to the teachers themselves as they 'teach'. Always they imply an inquiry as to personal qualifications and commonly they are followed by some form of search for professional skill. 'How can this teaching be done?' 'What method is the best?'

Conscious concern with such questions is behind the centuries-old belief in teacher-training exemplified in the gathering of disciples round a Master in Galilee. It found modern elaboration in the writings of Erasmus, Ignatius, Mulcaster, Comenius, Pestalozzi, and Herbart; and it reached institutional form in the eighteenth-century seminaries of Halle and Stettin, and the nineteenth-century training colleges of many lands.[1] The standard of competence required from professional teachers may vary from country to country and its content may be differently interpreted in different social settings. General awareness of its importance is indicated by the provision which is made not only for initial preparation but for continued education through 'refresher courses', 'in-service training', quinquennial testing by national teachers' examinations and the like.[2]

3

The studies relevant to such professional skill were offered in earlier centuries through philosophic appraisals of the teacher's art. Now they are to be found chiefly in the interpretations of psychologists who have accepted the challenge of the educators and have sought to study the processes of learning and teaching in experimental investigations and through observational records of long-term development in various fields.[3]

Prior to entrance to a school most teachers have thus deliberately made some attempt to answer the two questions:

(a) Have I something to teach? (Do I know the subject?)
(b) How can the teaching best be done? (How do I propose to present my subject?)

Upon beginning to teach a change occurs. The door of a classroom opens. Fifteen to fifty pairs of eyes are focused upon the newcomer. There is a silence laced with expectancy; and self-examination as to knowledge of content and method drops into insignificance before the more immediate challenge: 'Can I win and hold their attention?' 'Will they follow me, like me, obey me?' 'What sort of person will be successful in this situation?' 'Am I that sort of person?'

Classroom procedures and good teaching

On this topic, could the prospective teacher pause to study it, a considerable amount of evidence is available.[4] In its simplest form it is to be found in the answers given by pupils to direct questions of the type: 'What sort of teacher do you like best?' 'What, in your opinion, are the qualities of a good teacher?' Replies differ somewhat from school to school; and the range of available adjectives is very wide. Birchmore, for example, in a recent London inquiry collected from three hundred and forty pupils statements which included one hundred and five good qualities and sixty-four bad qualities. These could be grouped under such headings as order and discipline, knowledge, personal attributes, ways of handling class-work, and ways of dealing with boys; but there remained a wide variety of opinion within the general framework of an emphasis on the importance of decency and kindliness on the part of the teacher as a human being – friendliness and an absence of fussiness and bossiness.[5]

More subtle methods have been used by those who, interviewing boys and girls, have extracted by incidental means evidence as to the

4

accepted stereotypes of good or bad teachers held by groups of pupils in differing circumstances.[6] Similar material has been collected through the analysis of pupils' essays on superficially neutral topics.[7]

From all of this a composite picture may be painted. Pupils declare that they prefer teachers who conform to something like the following pattern:

has no favourites,
has patience,
goes out of his way to help backward pupils,
is fair and considerate,
does not punish the whole class because of one boy,
admits when he is wrong,
does not get angry when asked to explain,
can explain a difficult subject simply,
does not control the class by fear,
does not snoop,
has a thorough knowledge of his subject.[8]

Most of this, it will be noted, is in terms of what good teachers do and say. It is a matter of general procedures rather than of personal characteristics.

A similar descriptive approach has been followed in many studies made by adult observers. These are in direct succession to the philosophic fiction of Rousseau and the didactic prescriptions of Pestalozzi and Froebel; but they now offer an analysis of actual happenings supported by photographic and sound recordings and elaborated by techniques derived from nineteenth-century reports on the speech development of infants.[9] The latter were admittedly concerned with the observation of one child at a time and they encouraged too rigid a labelling of individuals as egocentric,[10] socially blind, independent, dependent, unresponsive, self-assertive, submissive, and the like.[11] About the third decade of the present century, however, interest began to be taken in the responses of children to the attitudes and actions of their parents and teachers; and a beginning was made in what can now be described as the scientific study of the teaching process.

Four books are of importance here. Bühler in the 1920s broke new ground by her use of methods of concentrated observation by trained observers and her classification of their recordings under predetermined headings (contacts in approach and response according to observable purposes—social, pedagogical, organizational, charitable or economic, and expressive either of friendly or unfriendly intentions).[12] A not dissimilar classification was offered by Murphy in a descriptive reproduction of the sayings and doings of nursery school pupils in their relationships with one another;[13] and the relevance of such methods to the observation of relationships between teachers and older pupils was next made clear by several investigations reported by Lewin and his students in the fourth decade. Bühler had shown that the observational methods currently used by anthropologists could be applied to the observation of children. Murphy had drawn attention to the variations of behaviour of the same children in differing groupings. It was left to Lewin to add methods of controlled experiment adapted from experimental psychology. In a series of studies reported subsequently under several variants of his first title: *Patterns of . . . Behavior in Experimentally-created 'Social Climates'* [14] he showed that a high measure of reliability could be established as between one observer and another; and that the behaviour of ten-year-old boys in a club situation varied with the words and attitudes of their leaders.

Lewin's descriptive categories are of considerable interest. He gave definitions of leadership in terms of its authoritarian, democratic or *laissez-faire* character; and he analysed his detailed records of words and actions under headings such as the giving of orders, non-constructive criticism, guiding suggestions, praise and approval, jovial and confident behaviour on the part of the leaders; and friendly remarks, aggressive behaviour, discontent, group-mindedness (thinking in terms of 'we' rather than 'I') or demands for attention on the part of the club members.

More elaborate experiments of a similar type were organized by Anderson some years later. In these the subjects were children working under routine conditions in school; and an attempt was made to describe the sayings and doings of their teachers by classifying them under approximately twenty-nine headings in terms of dominative or integrative behaviour – with and without evidence of conflict and with and without evidence of working together.[15] Illustrative of these are some of the commonplaces of classroom intercourse. 'Hurry up', 'Sit still', 'We haven't time now', 'I told you so', 'Someone is not attending', 'I want you to read this', 'I hope you are using your minds', 'I think we are ready', 'I'll show you', 'That's better',

'Who would like to do it?', 'I want to see how very well you can do it', 'Can anyone help him?', 'She has been so kind as to offer', 'I think we all enjoyed it', 'I'm sorry', 'Yes! I saw it too'. Intonation and gesture were involved as well as words. Very similar phrases might be used in a relationship describable as 'domination with evidence of conflict' ('I'm busy now' – a direct refusal) and in one which fell into the category 'domination with evidence of working together' ('I'm busy now' – an implied promise of later action). 'Good for you' (as an approval of prescribed work) might be said in a situation in which the teacher was dominant or as an acceptance of an unsolicited contribution in a situation characterized as 'integration with evidence of working together'.

In recording in terms of these categories and in observation of pupils' responses (making contributory remarks, seeking help, offering services, telling experiences, looking up from work, and so on), Anderson and his co-workers in Illinois succeeded in demonstrating considerable consistency as between one observer and another. They confirmed Lewin's findings that the behaviour of the same children differed in response to teachers whose classroom behaviour was markedly different. They showed that there were similarities in the behaviour of children of different ages under similar sorts of treatment; and they supported the conclusion that more satisfactory responses were won by teachers who used a democratic approach.

Other inquiries of comparable nature have more recently been reported by Withall, by Baxter, and by Bush in studies of teacher-pupil relationships, by Higginbotham in the recording of leaderless group discussions, and by Arbuckle in the discussion of the comparative effect of teaching of different sorts.[16]

The significance of such work is twofold. It is important as a contribution to the developing science of psychology through its addition of a polished tool of descriptive analysis to the psychologist's armoury of interviews and questionnaires – of questions asked orally in a face-to-face situation or instructions given in printed form in tests to be answered by pencil on paper. It is significant because its evidence confirms other findings as to the effectiveness of an attitude which can be described as democratic. Pupils prefer teachers who treat them in friendly fashion. Teachers who permit initiative and co-operativeness evoke more satisfactory reactions from their pupils.[17]

These recent recordings have also added depth to the meaning of the word 'democratic'. In the two most detailed analyses so far

7

available – that of Lewin and that of Anderson – the democratic or integrative attitude was shown to include decision as well as trust, and the giving of directions along with courtesy. To borrow a phrase which has significance in many other contexts, a democratic approach 'has more in common with' a dictatorial approach than has often been supposed. It is not *laissez faire*. It does not represent abdication on the part of the teacher nor an advocacy of self-expression or complete freedom for pupils without regard to the requirements of others and without recognition of the necessity for technical advice from adults.[18] The difference in social climate is to be found in a point of view expressed in attitude or intonation rather than in any specific form of words or actions. To the dictator his subjects seem other than himself – of lesser breed and incapable of responsibility and decision. To the guide his clients are potentially of like quality to himself though admittedly of lesser skill. To the company of the guides, good teachers seem to belong both from the point of view of their own pupils and from that of adult observers of the teaching process.

Findings such as these go far to answer the question as to the sort of procedures which have been found successful in establishing good relationships in a classroom. They do not help the new teacher to answer the other questions which arise on actually encountering pupils. 'Have I the correct sort of personality?' 'Will I be able to win and hold their attention?'

The wording of these questions, it will be noted, is in itself indicative of some recognition of the complexity of the situation. The first formulation: 'Have I the correct personality?' implies a looking in on the individual – a consideration of the teaching personality as an entity in itself. The second phrasing: 'Will I be able to win attention?' is already an admission of a relationship to pupils.

Three issues are involved: a study of the personality of the successful teacher (What are good teachers like?), the assessment of that personality, and an understanding of the nature of human motivation (How can pupils be reached and held?). To the first, further consideration may now be given. The others are deliberately reserved for later chapters.

Personal qualities and good teaching

On this topic the Sophists and Socrates had their views; and echoes of their arguments are still to be heard in pronouncements from platform, pamphlet or press.[19] A good teacher is adaptable, attractive, careful, considerate, co-operative, dependable, enthusiastic, forceful, healthy, honest, industrious, neat, open-minded, original, and progressive as well as well-informed. The picture is one of a hypothetical human being with certain fixed and rather clearly defined attributes in the form of personal qualities such as optimism, fairness, and self-control, professional qualities such as knowledge of subject-matter and techniques of teaching, and social qualities such as sympathy, understanding, and skill in judging the reactions of others.[20]

Certain changes in wording may, however, be traced down the decades. The philosophic rationalists of the mid-nineteenth century put emphasis on strength of character, clarity of thinking, firmness of discipline, intelligence, and scholarship.[21] By the late nineteenth and early twentieth century there was more talk of tough-mindedness, extraversion, and gifts in the management of people.[22] Emphasis was next put on organizing ability, and on skill in the arrangement of conditions contributory to the establishment of correct habits. This was supported by a concern for clarity of analysis of the content of the curriculum, perseverance in drill, and clearness in presentation.[23]

The writers of the late 1920s asked for an interest in citizenship. The good teacher was one who, participating in the concerns of the community, understood the social relevance of the curriculum – one whose projects were therefore related to the frequency of similar activities in the adult life in which pupils might later be expected to participate.[24]

By the 1930s attention was turning to the significance of attitudes. The good teacher was one who showed gifts of leadership, discrimination in assessment of the seriousness of misdemeanours along with a certain flair for the treatment of behaviour disorders, supplemented by professional skill in the use of standardized tests and the diagnosis of individual difficulties in the learning of the basic subjects.[25]

In the 1940s there were signs of a fuller appreciation of the adult who showed attractiveness and persuasiveness – ability to win attention as well as command support.[26]

More modest in range are the descriptions attempted in recent inquiries into methods of assessing teaching ability [27] – supported by investigations into procedures suitable for selecting students for training [28] and into reasons given for entering the teaching profession.[29] From analysis of these it is possible to extract published findings on the qualities which correspond most closely to reputed skill in teaching. These again vary from ratings in open-mindedness (in the sense of an originality, adaptability, and tolerance which permit participation on the part of the pupils), a businesslike approach in the organization of class activities, impartiality, calmness, consistency, sociability, and attractiveness (Ryans), intelligence and the willingness to use it in the classroom situation, to scores in objective tests of resourcefulness, social participation, and interest in teaching (Evans).[30] Findings differ somewhat from one College to another, with variations in the size of the group under instruction, the type of subject, the age of the pupils, and the nature of the classroom organization. It seems, therefore, possible to say with considerable confidence that there is no reason to suppose that any one type of personality pattern has monopoly of the claim to be regarded as that of the potentially successful teacher.[31]

Teachers take stock of their pupils

The door has opened and closed. Fifteen to fifty pairs of eyes have focused on the teacher.

'Pupils react to the procedures of their teachers.' 'Many different sorts of personalities are found among good teachers.'

A slight movement breaks the silence. Something must be done and done rapidly. The teacher passes from thoughts of subject matter, method, or personal suitability, to concentration upon massed figures and faces. 'What sort of boys or girls are these?' 'How can these pupils be reached and held?'

Impressions are at first of the group as a whole. Clean, tidy, expectant, bright, dishevelled, unkempt, sullen, dull. The teacher begins to speak; and individuals come into view. Some responsive. Some interrogative. Some quizzical. Some friendly. Some indifferent. Some attentive. Some make offers of help. Others ask questions with surprising assiduity. Some whisper to their neighbours. A few seem busy with their own affairs. On first encounter there is, however, an air of general attentiveness and an orderliness which the new teacher happily attributes to personal attractiveness and competence. Little by little, learning of names takes place. Details become clearer; and the new teacher applies the methods in common use in day-to-day assessment of personality:[32]

(a) observation of physical characteristics;

10

(b) interpretation of general appearance and speech;

(c) identification of actions;

(d) analysis of expressive movements in gesture, voice, eyes, or carriage.

Before the end of the first hour, clearly defined labels have been attached to many children (intelligent, unresponsive, co-operative, confident, well behaved); and the adult is tempted to suppose that allies and opponents have taken recognizable form and that the main attributes of the group have been discerned.

Social patterns in a class

Enlightenment comes only too rapidly. On second encounter few pupils react in exactly the same fashion. The self-assertive are unaccountably quiet. The mouselike are surprisingly arresting. The teacher is driven to the realization that ratings of personal attributes in terms of observable performance have not given an answer to the question as to how any pupil is likely to behave.

To the eyes of the new teacher the class appears to be an organized whole into which he has to insert himself, or a series of well-knit groups which are waiting to take action in co-operation with him or against him. Only by degrees is it realized that the social pattern of a class is more complicated than it at first appears and that responsiveness to teachers is related not merely to the teacher's personal qualifications and ability to satisfy the known requirements of the pupils in terms of knowledge or skill, but to the currents of friendliness or dislike, admiration or disdain, among the pupils themselves. Some information on these currents is obtainable through the close attention to small cues which forms part of the acquired wisdom of a skilled teacher. Glances, gestures, sitting positions – expressive movements of various kinds – are pointers to the assessment of group relationships in a sense as real as that in which they contribute to the assessment of individual personalities. 'Which pupil supports which pupil?' 'Who creates a diversion if a certain child makes a mistake?' 'Which are the leaders?' 'Who fails to win supporting laughter when he makes a joke?' 'Who rarely offers an audible contribution?'

Fuller examination of such inter-group relationships is one of the special contributions made by the psychological findings of the last few decades. Its further consideration forms part of the subject-matter of this book. Meanwhile it is sufficient to note that it is from some such experiences as these in the actual encounters of teachers with their pupils that there comes the selection of topics relevant to an understanding of the psychology of teaching.

What sort of beings are they who engage in teaching and learning?
Why do they do those things which they do?
What are the processes involved in learning and in teaching?
What are the relationships discernible in both?
What changes occur as pupils grow towards maturity?
What are the reactions of pupils as they learn?
What are the mutual influences of members of teaching and learning groups?
What are the technical skills which the teacher must acquire?

In more formal phrasing:

The study of Motivation, Learning, and Growth.
The Pupil in the School Situation.
The Teacher as Technician, as Craftsman, and as Administrator.
The Therapies of Membership of Groups.

Under these headings there may be subsumed most of the issues essential to an understanding of the teaching and learning situation – its relationships, its difficulties, and its delights. Their consideration will take the reader far from the actual classroom; but always return can be made to the human problems implicit in the teacher's thoughts:

Do I know my subject?
How can my subject best be taught?
What sort of person will be successful here?
Am I that sort of person?
What kinds of boys and girls are these?
How can they as pupils be reached and held?

REFERENCES

1. BOYD, W., *The History of Western Education.* Lond.: Black. 1921.
   RICH, R. W., *The Training of Teachers in England and Wales during the Nineteenth Century.* Cambridge: C.U.P. 1933.
2. Discussion of the general problem of the qualifications and training desirable for teachers are to be found in such books as:
   RUGG, H., *The Teacher of Teachers.* N.Y.: Harper. 1952.

RICHARDSON, C. A., BRULÉ, H., and SNYDER, H. E., *The Education of Teachers in England, France and U.S.A.* U.N.E.S.C.O. 1953.

RYANS, D. G., *Measuring the Intellectual and Cultural Backgrounds of Teaching Candidates.* N.Y.: Co-operative Test Service I.I. 1941.

3. FLEMING, C. M., *Bull. Educ.* **29.** 9–11. 1952.

FLEMING, C. M., *Brit. J. Educ. Studies.* **3.** 1. 17–23. 1954.

4. EVANS, K. M., *A Study of Teaching Ability at the Training College Stage.* Ph.D. Thesis. London. 1952. See also:

PHILLIPS, A. S., *An Examination of Methods of Selection of Training College Students.* M.A. Thesis. London. 1953.

EVANS, K. M., *Educ. Res.* **I.** 3. 22–36. 1959.

EVANS, K. M., *ibid.* **II.** 1. 3–8. 1959.

EVANS, K. M., *ibid.* **IV.** 1. 67–80. 1961.

MORI, T., *J. Educ. Psychol.* **56.** 4. 175–83. 1965.

5. BIRCHMORE, B., *A Study of the Relationships between Pupils and Teachers.* M.A. Thesis. London. 1951.

See also:

TIEDEMAN, S. C., *J. Educ. Res.* **XXXV.** 9. 657–64. 1942.

BROOKOVER, W. B., *ibid.* **XXXIV.** 4. 272–87. 1940.

BOLLINGER, R. V., *J. Exper. Educ.* **XIII.** 4. 153–73. 1945.

LEEDS, C. H., and COOK, W. W., *ibid.* **XVI,** 2. 149–59. 1947.

COOK, W. W., and LEEDS, C. H., *Educ. and Psychol. Measurement.* **7.** 3. 399–410. 1947.

DANG, S. D., *A Study of Co-operation in Certain Secondary Schools.* M.A. Thesis. London. 1949.

6. JAMES, H. E. O., and TENEN, C., *The Teacher was Black.* Lond.: Heinemann. 1953.

7. BOOK, W. F., *Pedagog. Sem.* **XI.** 204–32. 1904.

BOOK, W. F., *ibid.* **XII.** 239–88. 1905.

FINCH, I. E., *A Study of the Personal and Social Consequences for Groups of Secondary School Children of the Experience of Different Methods of Allocation within Secondary Courses.* M.A. Thesis. London. 1954.

8. BIRCHMORE, B., loc. cit. [5].

SYMONDS, P. M., *J. Educ. Res.* **XL.** 9. 652–61. 1947.

WITTY, P., *ibid.* **XL.** 9. 662–71. 1947.

9. MCCARTHY, D., in CARMICHAEL, L., *et al., Manual of Child Psychology.* N.Y.: John Wiley. 1946 and 1954; and MCCARTHY, D., in BARKER, R. G., *et al., Child Behavior and Development.* N.Y.: McGraw-Hill. 1943.

10. In direct succession to these are:

PIAGET, J., *The Language and Thought of the Child.* N.Y.: Harcourt Brace. 1926.

PIAGET, J., *Le Développement des Qualités chez l'Enfant.* Neuchâtel: Delachaux et Niestlé. 1941.

PIAGET, J., *La Formation du Symbole chez L'Enfant.* Neuchâtel: Delachaux et Niestlé. 1945.

11. BÜHLER, C., in MURCHISON, C., *A Handbook of Child Psychology.* Worcester, Mass.: Clark U.P. 1933.

ISAACS, S., *Social Development in Young Children.* Lond: Routledge. 1933.

12. BÜHLER, C., loc. cit. [11].

BÜHLER, C., *The Child and His Family.* N.Y.: Harper. 1939.

13. MURPHY, G., MURPHY, L. B., and NEWCOMB, T. M., *Experimental Social Psychology.* N.Y.: Harper. 1937, and MURPHY, L. B., *Social Behavior and Child Personality.* N.Y.: Columbia U.P. 1937. MURPHY, L. B., in BARKER, R. G., *et al.* loc cit. [9]. 1943.

MURPHY, L. B., in HUNT, J. MC. V. (ed.) *Personality and the Behavior Disorders.* N.Y.: Ronald Press. 653–90. 1944.

14. LEWIN, K., LIPPITT, R., and WHITE, R. K., *J. Soc. Psychol.* 10. II. 271–99. 1939.

See also: LIPPITT, R., in WATSON, G. (ed.). *Civilian Morale.* Boston: Houghton Mifflin. 1942.

LIPPITT, R., and WHITE, R. K., in BARKER, R. G., *et al.,* loc cit. [9]. 1943.

LIPPITT, R., and WHITE, R. K., in NEWCOMB, T. M., and HARTLEY, E. L. (ed.). *Readings in Social Psychology.* N.Y.: Henry Holt. 1947.

15. ANDERSON, H. H., *et al., Applied Psychol.* Monographs Amer. Psychol. Assoc. 6. 8. 11. 1945. 1946.

WITHALL, J., *J. Exper. Educ.* XVII. 3. 347–61. 1949.

16. BAXTER, B., *Teacher–Pupil Relationships.* N.Y.: Macmillan. 1950.

HIGGINBOTHAM, P. J., *An Investigation into the Use of Leaderless Group Discussions.* M.A. Thesis. London. 1949.

ARBUCKLE, D. S., *Teacher Counseling.* Cambridge, U.S.A.: Addison-Wesley. 1950.

OESER, O. A. (ed.), *Teacher, Pupil and Task.* Lond.: Tavistock Publications. 1955.

BUSH, R. N., *The Teacher–Pupil Relationship.* N.Y.: Prentice-Hall. 1954.

17. For a discussion of the educational relevance of findings as to differences in social climate see:

FLEMING, C. M., *The Social Psychology of Education.* Lond.: Kegan Paul. 1944, 1959 and 1961.

FLEMING, C. M., *Adolescence.* Lond.: Routledge. 1948, 1955 and 1963.

OTTAWAY, A. K. C., *Learning through Group Experience.* Lond.: Routledge. 1966.

See also: DAVIS, C., *Room to Grow: A Study of Parent–Child Relationships.* Toronto: Univ. of Toronto Press. 1966.

18. See, for example, the definition in operational terms (i.e. in terms of what they do) of the authoritarian, the democratic, and the *laissez-faire* leader in LIPPITT, R., and WHITE, R. K., loc. cit. [14]. 1943.

19. On Socrates and the Sophists see: BOYD, W., loc. cit. [1].

More recent views are exemplified in: CHARTERS, W. W., and WAPLES, D., *The Commonwealth Teacher-Training Study.* Chicago: Univ. of Chicago Press. 1929.

See also: CATTELL, R. B., *Brit. J. Educ. Psychol.* **I.** 1. 48–72. 1931.

20. JENSEN, A. C., *J. Exper. Educ.* **XX.** I. 79–85. 1951.

    See also: DOMAS, S. J., and TIEDEMAN, D. V., ibid. **XIX.** 2. 101–218. 1950.

    FLANAGAN, J. C., *Psychol. Bull.* **51.** 4. 327–58. 1954.

    EVANS, K. M., loc. cit. [4]. 1952.

    VERNON, P. E., *Yearbook of Education.* Lond.: Evans. 51–75. 1953.

21. SULLY, J., *The Teachers' Handbook of Psychology.* Lond.: Longmans. 1886.

    GARLICK, A. H., *A New Manual of Method.* Lond.: Longmans. 1896.

22. WELTON, J., and BLANDFORD, F. G., *Principles and Methods of Moral Training.* Lond.: Univ. Tutorial Press. 1909.

    DARROCH, A., *The Place of Psychology in the Training of Teachers.* Lond.: Longmans. 1911.

    WITHAM, E. C., *J. Educ. Psychol.* **V.** 4. 267–78. 1914.

    SPRAGUE, H. A., *Pedagog. Sem.* **XXIV.** 72–80. 1917.

23. KENT, R. A., *J. Educ. Res.* **II.** 802–7. 1920.

    BROOKS, S. S., ibid. **IV.** 4. 255–64. 1921.

    THOMSON, G. H., *J. Exper. Ped.* **6.** 2. 75–82. 1921.

24. MEAD, A. R., *J. Educ. Res.* **XX.** 4. 239–59. 1929.

    See also: FLEMING, C. M., *Research and the Basic Curriculum.* Lond.: Univ. of London Press. 1946 and 1952.

25. RINSLAND, M. A. O., *J. Exper. Educ.* **VI.** 3. 307–17. 1938.

26. JACKSON, V. D., ibid. **VIII.** 4. 422–74. 1940.

    BROOKOVER, W. B., ibid. **XIII.** 4. 191–205. 1945.

    VON HADEN, H. I., ibid. **XV.** 1. 61–84. 1946.

    STRANG, R., *Every Teacher's Records.* N.Y.: Teachers' College, Columbia Univ. 1936 and 1947.

27. EVANS, K. M., *Brit. J. Educ. Psychol.* **XXI.** II. 89–95. 1951.

    EVANS, K. M., loc. cit. [4]. 1952.

    EVANS, K. M., *Education for Teaching.* 50–4. Nov. 1954.

28. For surveys of work on the selection of teachers see also:

    BUTSCH, R. L. C., *Rev. Educ. Res.* **I.** 2. 99–107. 1931.

    SANFORD, C. W., and TRUMP, J. L., in MONROE, W. S. (ed.), *Encyclopaedia Educ. Res.* N.Y.: Macmillan. 1390–6. 1950.

    BARR, A. S., *Rev. Educ. Res.* **X.** 3. 185–90. 1940, and ibid. 1946, 1949, 1952, 1955.

29. EVANS, K. M., *A Study of Attitude towards Teaching as a Career.* M.A. Thesis. London. 1946.

    EVANS, K. M., *Brit. J. Educ. Psychol.* **XXII.** 63–9. 1952.

    EVANS, K. M., ibid. **XXIII.** 58–63. 1953.

30. RYANS, D. G., *J. Exper. Educ.* **XX.** I. 67–77. 1951.

    LOVELL, K., *An Investigation into Factors Underlying Teaching Ability in Primary and Secondary Modern Schools.* M.A. Thesis. London. 1951.

    SKINNER, W. A., *An Investigation into Assessment of Teaching Ability in Teachers of Technical Subjects.* M.A. Thesis. London. 1949.

    EVANS, K. M., loc. cit. [4]. 1952.

31. CHURCH, C. C., *Pedagog. Sem.* **XXVI.** 41–8. 1919.
   GRIEDER, C., and NEWBURN, H. K., *J. Educ. Res.* **XXXV.** 9. 683–93. 1942.
   BUSH, R. N., ibid. **XXXV.** 9. 645–56. 1942.
   RETAN, G. A., ibid. **XXXVII.** 2. 135–41. 1943.
   SYMONDS, P. M., ibid. **XLIII.** 9. 688–96. 1950.
   LAMKE, T. A., *J. Exper. Educ.* **XX.** 2. 217–59. 1951.
   See also: HAMPTON, N. D., ibid. **XX.** 2. 179–215. 1951
   With this may be compared the variety of attributes among leaders. For a summary of work on this see: SHERIF, M., and SHERIF, C. W., *Groups in Harmony and Tension.* N.Y.: Harper. 1953.
   BEWSHER, L. G., *A Study of Attitudes and Incentives amongst a Group of Students training to be Teachers.* M.A. Thesis. London. 1965.
32. VERNON, P. E., *The Assessment of Psychological Qualities by Verbal Methods.* Lond.: H.M.S.O. 1938.
   ALLPORT, G. W., *Personality.* N.Y.: Henry Holt. 1937.
   VERNON, P. E., *Personality Assessment.* Lond.: Methuen. 1964.
   See also: FLEMING, C. M., loc. cit. [17]. 1944, 1959 and 1961.
   ALLPORT, G. W., *Pattern and Growth in Personality.* N.Y.: Holt, Rinehart and Winston. 1963.

PART II

THE TEACHER AS A
STUDENT OF MOTIVATION

II

UNDERSTANDING HUMAN NATURE: PHILOSOPHY, EXPERIMENTAL PSYCHOLOGY, BIOLOGY AND SOCIOLOGY

ALL TEACHERS IN their day play many parts. They are students of human behaviour. They are organizers of differing forms of human learning and inevitably they are engaged as technical experts in the assessment of the effect of their endeavours. They may do these things wittingly or unawares and with varying degrees of willingness or competence; but whatever attitude they adopt their skill is directly related to the views they hold as to the nature of human beings and the reasons for their behaving as they do. These opinions may be mere reproductions of earlier assumptions or beliefs more soundly based upon the best evidence available today. Whichever form they take, their implications can be fully understood only in the light of some knowledge of what went before. No apology is therefore offered for pausing in this book at various points to remind the reader of the contributions made by certain influential thinkers of the past.

This chapter is essentially such a reminder. It is unorthodox in structure – of the nature of a summary rather than a survey – and its contribution may be indicated quite briefly by saying that in the study of human motivation a progression can be traced from an emphasis on mental processes to a concern with conflicting instincts and from that to a preoccupation with social influences. The study of individuals was thus succeeded by more direct concern with human beings as members of society; and, from that, the step was later taken to inquiries into the meaning of intimate human relationships. In 1860 psychology was still a sub-section of philosophy. By 1880 the new psychology was experimental. In 1900 it was 'dynamic';

and by 1920 many workers were looking to sociology rather than to biology for the key to unlock the secrets of the mind.[1]

These dates present a rough approximation for which, however, documentary evidence can be adduced (see Table I). The writings to which they correspond are so well known that it is not necessary to reproduce their content here. It is sufficient to remark that the word psychology is relatively recent,[2] that the beginnings of its

TABLE I

Successive Viewpoints in the Study of Motivation

	The Study of Individuals		The Study of Members of Groups	
Period	−1895	−1920	−1935	—
Contributory disciplines	Philosophy Experimental psychology	Biology Physiology	Sociology Anthropology	Social psycho- logy A phenomeno- logical approach
Emphasis	Mind Reason	Body Emotions	Society Social circumstances	Intimate groups Human relationships
Key to interpreta- tion	Faculties Conflict of ideas	Instincts Conflict of impulses	Attitudes Influence of society	Needs Changes in self-picture
Educational aim	Instruction Mind-training	Non-interference Self-expression	Social matur- ing Citizenship	Guidance Self-discovery
Explanation of failure	Badness Laziness	Frustration Inhibition	Rejection Neglect	Defeat Exclusion
Exponents*	Herbart 1816 Wundt 1863 Bain 1878 Ward 1880 Sully 1886 Wm. James 1890	Freud 1901 Stanley Hall 1904 McDougall 1908 Binet 1910 Thorndike 1911 Adler 1911 Jung 1912	Terman 1925 Burt 1925 Thrasher 1927 Mead 1928 Moreno 1934	Suttie 1935 Lewin 1939 Rogers 1942 Allport 1943 Sherif 1947 Jersild 1952

* The dates given are those of a major publication in mid-life. Fewer are shown for the last two periods since consideration of these forms the main subject-matter of this book.

acceptance can be traced in the influence of Herbart and of Wundt,[3] that Bain still wrote as a philosopher while Sully and William James were mediators between the old and the new, and that Freud, Stanley Hall, and McDougall belonged to the generation which was deeply moved by Darwin's *Origin of Species* (1859), with its discussion of instincts and his *Descent of Man* (1871), with its concern with the development of mental powers in man and in animals.[4]

The challenge to Freud's theories came through workers like Adler, Jung, Fromm, and Karen Horney who had doubts related to the individualism of his approach;[5] and the more general challenge to the facile use of the word 'instinct' followed through the reports of anthropologists as to cultural variations in different parts of the world.[6]

The work of the biological psychologists was significant in its reminder of the complexity of human behaviour, of the possibility of ambivalence (the close intermingling of opposites such as loving and hating), and of the element of apparent irrationality and unexpectedness in human reactions. Their influence may be traced in books on educational psychology in the first three decades of the century; and their echoes may be heard in many phrases which have passed into popular use; resistance, conflict, the unconscious, sublimation, repression, and the like.[7]

The transition to a concern with social background may be illustrated from two notable English books – Burt: The *Young Delinquent* (1925), and Burt: *The Backward Child* (1937). In these he presented a pioneering series of life-histories in their setting of socio-economic level, broken homes, poverty, and irregular school attendance. In 1925 there was still much to be said about instincts. By 1937 the word had almost passed from the vocabulary in which discussion was offered as to the backwardness of the individual child.

Changes in the connotation of terms

In the 1920s it was not realized that this sociological emphasis offered a major clinical challenge both to psycho-analytic interpretations and to other forms of biological psychology. On retrospect, however, it can be seen that while those trained in psycho-analysis continued to practise psycho-analysis as a procedure in the sense of protracted inquiries into the content of early experience – carried out in explorations of the ideas associated with memories produced

21

by patients for the sympathetic interpretation of their analysts – psycho-analysis as a theory became progressively less adequate as a description of human functioning.[8]

On retrospect also it is worthy of note that the word 'instinct' passed into disuse among psychologists in proportion to their recognition of the significance of environment and their consequent realisation of the unsuitability of a term which by its implications discouraged a study of the antecedents and concomitants of human behaviour. Even in the field of comparative psychology the word is now used with considerable caution in discussion of experimental studies of animal learning; and much of what used to be thought of as the manifestation of specific inborn patterns is studied as a process of development in an environment of a particular kind.[9]

In the case of those writers on human psychology who continued to favour metaphors of biological origin, the connotation of the term 'instinct' can also be seen to have altered almost insensibly. What began as an explanatory concept emphasizing the unlearned, the irrational, and the passionate, ended as a mere reference to a potentiality or 'tendency to action' modifiable through experience and intelligence into a disposition in favour of a certain procedure.[10] In this more limited interpretation it seems justifiable (in paraphrase of MacLeod and Bronfenbrenner) to remark that certain of these master-craftsmen half a century ago produced designs resembling in some respects the latest models in personality theory.[11] Their procedures were argumentative rather than observational and they accepted the individualistic postulates of their day; but within their discussion of dispositions and sentiments there lurked phrases whose import is only now beginning to be realized (see Chapter IV below).

In spite of these foreshadowings, their main contributions cannot, however, be fully reconciled with the deeper insight of more recent studies. The older theories carried materialistic and hedonistic undertones which permitted the painting of one side only of the picture; and many recent attempts to reach a general 'theory of action' by combining them with modern learning theory and modern social psychology have foundered in this gulf between the decades.[12] A removal of the animistic terminology of Freud (his *ego*, *id*, warring instincts, censor, *super-ego*, and the like),[13] a modification of McDougall's stress on innate endowment and an enlargement of the connotation of sociological descriptions of home or street cannot

22

suffice of themselves to take full measure of the subtleties of human motivation. Like the philosophers' still earlier emphasis on reason, they require supplementation by certain later interpretations which are both more adequate and more purely psychological in viewpoint.

Why do those boys and girls behave as they do?

'When they understand what they are to do they will do it.'
'They are getting pleasure out of it. That's why they do it.'

These were among the answers of the philosophers:

'He's over-sexed. He can't help it.'
'She was born that way.'
'That satisfies his Unconscious. He must do it.'

This was the special contribution of the biological psychologists.

'It's their home background. What else can you expect?'

This was the further comment of those who favoured a socio-logical approach.[14]
Each added something to the teacher's understanding of his charges. None provided an adequate solution to his problem.

REFERENCES

1. SCHWEGLER, A., *Handbook of the History of Philosophy.* 6th ed. Edinburgh: Edmonston. 1877.
   FLUGEL, J. C., *A Hundred Years of Psychology. 1833–1933.* Lond.: Duckworth. 1933.
   BRETT, G. S., *A History of Psychology.* Lond.: Allen & Unwin. 1921.
2. HAMILTON, W., *Lectures on Metaphysics. (Given in 1836–1837.)* 5th ed. Edinburgh: Blackwood. 1870.
3. For a historical survey of these controversies see:
   TITCHENER, E. B., *Systematic Psychology: Prolegomena.* N.Y.: Macmillan. 1929.
   BOYD, W., *The History of Western Education.* Lond.: Black. 1921.
4. BAIN, A., *Education as a Science.* Lond.: Kegan Paul. 1878.
   SULLY, J., *The Teachers' Handbook of Psychology.* Lond.: Longmans. 1886.
   See also: MORGAN, C. LLOYD, *Psychology for Teachers.* Lond.: Arnold. 1894.
   HALL, G. S., *et al.*, *Aspects of Child Life and Education.* N.Y.: Appleton. 1907.

BALDWIN, J. M., *Mental Development in the Child and the Race*. N.Y.: Macmillan. 1894.

HALL, G., *Educational Problems*. N.Y.: Appleton. 1911.

For reproductions of much of this earlier work see:

DENNIS, W. (ed.), *Readings in the History of Psychology*. N.Y.: Appleton. 1948.

FREUD, S., *Introductory Lectures on Psycho-Analysis*. Lond.: Allen & Unwin. 1922.

FREUD, S., *New Introductory Lectures on Psycho-Analysis*. Lond.: Hogarth Press. 1933.

FREUD, S., *An Autobiographical Study*. Lond.: Hogarth Press. 1935.

FREUD, S., *The Psycho-Pathology of Everyday Life* (1901). Lond.: Penguin Books. 1938.

FREUD, S., *An Outline of Psycho-Analysis*. Trans. J. STRACHEY. Lond.: Hogarth Press. 1949.

See also: FREUD, S., 'Psycho-Analysis' in *Encyclopaedia Britannica*. 14th ed. 1929.

FRIEDLANDER, K., *The Psycho-Analytic Approach to Juvenile Delinquency*. Lond.: Kegan Paul. 1947.

HOLLITSCHER, W., *Sigmund Freud: An Introduction*. Lond.: Kegan Paul. 1947.

5. ADLER, A., *The Neurotic Constitution* (1912). Lond.: Kegan Paul. 1921.

ADLER, A., *Understanding Human Nature*. Lond.: Allen & Unwin. 1930.

ADLER, A., *Social Interest. A Challenge to Mankind*. Lond.: Faber. 1938.

See also: GANZ, M., *The Psychology of Alfred Adler and the Development of the Child*. Lond.: Routledge. 1953.

WAY, L., *Alfred Adler: An Introduction to his Psychology*. Lond.: Penguin Books. 1956.

JUNG, C. G., *Modern Man in Search of a Soul*. Lond.: Kegan Paul. 1933.

JUNG, C. G., *Essays on Contemporary Events*. Lond.: Kegan Paul. 1947.

JUNG, C. G., *The Development of Personality*. Lond.: Routledge. 1954.

See also: GOLDBRUNER, J., *Individuation*. Lond.: Hollis & Carter. 1955.

FROMM, E., *The Fear of Freedom*. Lond.: Kegan Paul. 1942.

HORNEY, K., *New Ways in Psycho-Analysis*. Lond.: Kegan Paul. 1939.

HORNEY, K., *The Neurotic Personality of our Time*. N.Y.: Norton. 1937.

HORNEY, K., *Our Inner Conflicts*. Lond.: Kegan Paul. 1946.

HORNEY, K., *Neurosis and Human Growth*. Lond.: Routledge. 1951.

6. BERNARD, L. L., *Instinct*. Lond.: Allen & Unwin. 1924.

MALINOWSKI, B., *Sex and Repression in Savage Society*. Lond.: Kegan Paul. 1927.

SUTTIE, I. D., *The Origins of Love and Hate*. Lond.: Kegan Paul. 1935.

See also: MEAD, M., *Sex and Temperament in Three Primitive Societies.* Lond.: Routledge. 1935.

MEAD, M., *From the South Seas.* N.Y.: Morrow. 1939.

BENEDICT, R., *Patterns of Culture.* Lond.: Routledge. 1935.

KARDINER, A., *et al.*, *The Psychological Frontiers of Society.* N.Y.: Columbia U.P. 1945.

MURDOCH, G. P., and WHITING, J. W. M., in SENN, M. J. E. (ed.), *Problems of Infancy and Childhood.* N.Y.: Josiah Macy Jr. Foundation. 1951.

7. GREEN, G. H., *Psychanalysis in the Classroom.* Lond.: Univ. of London Press. 1921.

ISAACS, S., *The Children we Teach.* Lond.: Univ. of London Press. 1932.

8. ZILBOORG, G., in EISSLER, K. R. (ed.), *Searchlights on Delinquency.* 329–37. Lond.: Imago Publishing Co. 1949.

PFISTER, O., in EISSLER, K. R., ibid. 35–49.

LUCHINS, A. S., *J. Consult. Psychol.* XII. 6. 417–25. 1948.

See also: LINTON, R., *The Cultural Background of Personality.* N.Y.: Appleton. 1945.

KARDINER, A., *et al.*, loc. cit. [6].

SHERIF, M., *An Outline of Social Psychology.* Harper. 1948.

9. MOSS, F. A., *et al.*, *Comparative Psychology.* N.Y.: Prentice-Hall. 1934 and 1942.

SCHNEIRLA, T. C., in SENN, M. J. E. (ed.). *Problems of Infancy and Childhood.* N.Y.: Josiah Macy Jr. Foundation. 1951.

ALLEE, W. C., NISSEN, H. W., and NIMKOFF, M. F., *Psychol. Bull.* 60. 5. 287–97. 1953.

CRUIKSHANK, R. M., in CARMICHAEL, L. (ed.). *Manual of Child Psychology.* 2nd ed. N.Y.: John Wiley. 1954.

BEACH, F. A., *Psychol. Rev.* 62. 6. 401–10. 1955.

10. THOMSON, G. H., *Instinct, Intelligence and Character.* Lond.: Allen & Unwin. 1924.

11. KRECH, D., and KLEIN, G. S., *J. of Personality.* XX. 1–23. 1951.

PARSONS, T., SHILS, E. A., *et al.*, *Towards a General Theory of Action.* Cambridge, Mass.: Harvard U.P. 1951.

Cf. MACLEOD, R. B., in ROHRER, J. H., and SHERIF, M., *Social Psychology at the Cross-roads.* N.Y.: Harper. 215–41. 1951.

BRONFENBRENNER, U., 'Personality'. *Annual Rev. Psychol.* 4. 157–82. 1953.

12. SEARS, R. R., *Survey of Objective Studies of Psychoanalytic Concepts.* N.Y.: Social Sciences Research Council. 1943.

MOWRER, O. H., and KLUCKHOHN, C., in HUNT, J. MCV. (ed.), *Personality and the Behavior Disorders.* N.Y.: Ronald Press. 1944.

PARSONS, T., and SHILS, E. A., *et al.* loc. cit. [11].

See also: ADAMS, A. K., *et al.*, *Learning Theory, Personality Theory and Clinical Research.* N.Y.: John Wiley. 1954.

SHAFFER, L. F., and SHOBEN, E. J., *The Psychology of Adjustment,* 2nd ed. Boston: Houghton Mifflin. 1956.

13. BRONFENBRENNER, U., in BLAKE, R. R., and RAMSEY, G. V., *Perception: An Approach to Personality*. N.Y.: Ronald Press. 1951.

14. Illustrations of certain of these viewpoints are to be found in MCLELLAND, D., *Studies in Motivation*. N.Y.: Appleton. 1955.

See also: BARBU, Z., *Brit. J. Sociol.* **III.** 1. 64–76, 1952.

HALL, C. S., and LINDZEY, G., *Theories of Personality*. N.Y.: John Wiley. 1957.

BISCHOF, L. J., *Interpreting Personality Theories*. N.Y.: Harper. 1964.

III

UNDERSTANDING HUMAN NATURE: SOCIAL PSYCHOLOGY AND THE CONCEPT OF NEED

AN AWARENESS OF the part played by social relationships came relatively late in the history of experimental psychology.[1] Not until the 1920s was serious attention given to the possibility that performance in a laboratory might vary with the degree of proximity of other human beings;[2] and even when the testing of individuals was followed by the testing of groups it was not at first realized that responses might be related to the impression produced by the tester. (Individual tests were commended as a means of discovering the abilities and attributes of actual children or adults – in contrast to the more generalized picture of humanity then offered by theorists. Group tests were accepted as an aid in the assessment of teachers' competence.)[3] By the end of the third decade of the twentieth century it had, however, been noted that not only have the words used by an investigator an effect upon the responses obtained,[4] but that the influence of an observer or a co-worker may be genuine even when neither is visible to the testee.[5] With this recognition of the social implications in the test situation part of the foundation had been laid for social psychology, in the present connotation of that term.

Child Guidance Clinics

Another contribution came in the educational field from contemporary inquiries in certain Child Guidance Clinics. The clinics had had their immediate origins in the apparently fortuitous improvement in spelling, reading or arithmetic which followed upon the use of single pupils as subjects for investigation.[6] (Dora had the honour of 'going to the University'. Her reading in school unexpectedly

27

improved. Tom went to 'The Laboratory'. His errors in arithmetic became less frequent. George was shown the wonders of a tachisto-scope. He began to take an interest in spelling.) Earlier attempts by Galton, Bryant, Cattell, Witmer, and others to secure scientific measurement of school children had also prepared the way for the acceptance of research workers;[7] and the findings of extensive school surveys of arithmetic and reading in the early twentieth century had lent psychological support to teachers' awareness of the existence of a wide range of individual differences at every age. Teachers were no longer unwilling to admit that 'problem' pupils existed (as they had had to be in the years when 'payment by results' was an accompaniment of the belief that only inefficient teachers had unsuccessful pupils).[8] The publicity given to psycho-analytic treatment of hysteria in the First World War had given further encour-agement to the belief that psychologists might be able to help teachers with children who showed behaviour difficulties as well as with pupils who failed to learn; and for all these reasons an increasing number of Educational and Child Guidance Clinics had been established in the 1920s in North America and Western Europe. At the time a distinction was not drawn between psycho-analytic theory and psycho-analytic procedures; but it was realised that 'problem' pupils were helped by contact with workers in clinics; and, while the reasons given for successful treatment were not those which would now be acceptable, it can be seen on retrospect that the mere exis-tence of the first clinics was a testimony to what would now be described as the significance of favourable human relationships.[9]

In many other respects the work of Child Guidance Clinics tended towards the preservation of a belief in the personal character of human difficulties. Attention was deliberately directed to the indi-vidual;[10] and in many clinics it was considered unnecessary or even undesirable for the psychologists to see either the parents or the teachers in their actual contacts with the child. As in the case of patients receiving psycho-analytic treatment in the same decades, the personality of the pupil was still thought of as a somewhat encap-sulated entity with fixed attributes whose manifestations could be altered only by prolonged and expert individual treatment by a psychologist or a psychiatrist.[11]

The immediate effect of this upon the schools was to deflect attention from experiments with new methods of teaching and to foster an interest in the classification of children – in terms of levels of ability, stages of growth, types of backwardness or kinds of misdemeanours. Teachers were encouraged to reorganize their schools in groups homogeneous in attainment and intelligence:[12] and they were invited to look for the symptoms of certain sorts of behaviour problems suitable for referral to Child Guidance Clinics. It was within this setting that an attempt to collect statistics as to the frequency and incidence of such problems led directly to the next notable step in the recognition of the significance of social relationships.

In 1924 and 1925, in an investigation sponsored by child guidance groups in Minneapolis and Cleveland, Wickman had set out to discover the relative number of problem pupils of different kinds.[13] Answers to his first questionnaire suggested the possibility that teachers had clearly formulated attitudes as to the relative seriousness of certain behaviour disorders. These he later compared with the attitudes of psychologists in Child Guidance Clinics with the intention of convincing teachers that they should attach less importance to overt and noisy forms of misdemeanour than to anti-social fears and timidities. The title of Wickman's monograph – *Children's Behavior and Teachers' Attitudes* – and certain of his findings directed attention, however, to the fact that the nature and frequency of problems differed from teacher to teacher and suggested the possibility that children's behaviour might vary with the attitudes of their teachers. Meanwhile somewhat similar conclusions were being drawn from other extensive psychometric and sociological inquiries into the home background, the out-of-school activities and the earlier school history of problem children.[14] Wickman's work had served to challenge facile generalizations as to absolute numbers of culprits of different kinds; and his published results contributed to the dawning realization that similarities of social setting or socioeconomic level are not always followed by similarities of reaction in classroom or playground, and that the meaning of common relationships such as that of teacher to pupil or parent to child has not a universal content but may differ according to the behaviour of the adult and the accompanying past and present experiences of the child. The concepts of what is now called social psychology thus began to be recognized as relevant not only to the testing of subjects in laboratories or clinics but to educative processes as they are carried out in schools or homes by teachers or parents.[15]

Closely associated with this has been an awakening concern with the personal requirements or 'needs' of members of such human groups; and the next step in the interpretation of motivation was the almost unnoticed insertion of this new concept into the discussion. To understand its significance it is necessary to look once more at the biological emphasis of the latter part of the nineteenth century.

The work of the biologists had been in part a protest against contemporary belief in the passivity of human learning with its theory of 'impressions' made upon a mind conceived of as a wax tablet. They had reaffirmed the recalcitrant and resistant character of human 'nature' with unlearned instinctive reactions and demands for sensual satisfactions; and they had thought of human beings as self-centred and anti-social – entering into civilized living in terms of a 'social contract' in which, for the attainment of greater ultimate pleasure, certain of the natural instinctual and physical satisfactions were set aside. This formulation, as has been noted, carried echoes of many earlier versions of hedonistic individualism; and its influence has survived in the thinking of those psychologists who write of 'socialization' with emphasis on the primacy of behaviour which is both self-centred and self-seeking.[16] It was criticized not only by psychologists who were interested in variations in human behaviour but by those who supported a return to an emphasis on environment (the characteristics acquired through learning) rather than on inheritance (the reactions which might be attributed to the original nature of man). The evidence submitted by Thorndike and by Watson has been more often discussed in relation to learning than to a consideration of human motivation (see Chapter V below). Their work served, however, to bring into clear relief a restatement of the environmentalist position in both fields.[17]

Drives – primary and secondary

In partial reaction against both Thorndike's theory of habit formation and the generalizations of the instinct theorists there came from Woodworth in 1918 the suggestion that the word 'drive' might be more appropriate than the word 'instinct' to account for the element of something akin to purpose which it seems necessary to admit in explanation of the observable fact that neither human beings nor animals always respond in a mechanically or automatically identical fashion to stimuli which (to an observer) appear the same in character and in intensity.[18]

This word has been accepted by many subsequent workers. It has, however, often been used in support of continued concentration on the individual to the neglect of the social; and it has been assumed (contrary to the intentions of Woodworth) that the primary motivations (primary drives) are the physical urges or tensions of hunger, thirst, fatigue or sex. A purely secondary or derived status has been given to the social and more characteristically human satisfactions; and these 'secondary' drives have been supposed to appear only through a process of association with responses to stimuli originally attractive as a means of satisfying more primitive bodily needs for relief.[19] On retrospect, it can be seen that to some extent this limitation of meaning was a consequence of the unformulated undertones carried by the mechanistic implications of the word 'drive'. A 'drive' tends to be thought of as an impulse of limited character travelling in a predetermined direction towards a somewhat narrowly defined objective (the driving belt of an engine, the 'drive' of a golf ball, and the like). The word is therefore most suitably applied to the more individual and physical human promptings; and its use comes most happily to those who deliberately confine their observations to that which can be inferred from externally observed reactions – eating, drinking, resting, sleeping, mating, and the like.

It was probably on account of this limited connotation that there came almost unawares into the vocabulary in which motivation was discussed an alternative to the word 'drive', in the form of a new word 'need'. This was used by certain writers almost interchangeably with the words 'drive' or 'primary motivation';[20] but its most characteristic contribution can now be seen to lie in its admission of the coexistence of the social and the individual aspects of man's nature. Because of this it has proved attractive not only to theorists in the field of learning but (with a slightly different interpretation) to social psychologists and to workers in Child Guidance Clinics.[21]

Needs – physiological and psychological

The word 'need' carries implications of a certain mutuality of reference. It is commonly used in circumstances in which there is assumed to be both an object or organism with certain requirements and an environment or a society which can contribute to the satisfying of these requirements. It is therefore peculiarly suited to the description of the motivational functioning of human beings in their relationships with other members of human groups.

The theory of psychological needs thus fills the gap left by criticisms of the word 'instinct' and by some realization of the inadequate connotations of the word 'drive'. It makes no claims for universality and identity in the means taken by human beings to secure satisfaction. It does not unduly focus attention upon the inheritance of hypothetical animal instincts (with the inference that the growth of personality is the unfolding of a biologically pre-determined pattern). It does not lend support to the alternative view that behaviour is completely determined by an environmental establishment of habits. It is, however, significant in that it permits recognition of the fundamentally social nature of human experience. The formulation of a list of needs suggests that their satisfaction may be looked for within the range of ordinary living. The recognition of unsatisfied needs makes more definite the formulation of action which may be taken to help human beings in distress.

This interpretation in terms of needs, it is to be noted, is an interpretation of human behaviour at a level of which human beings are unaware. It is more profound than that offered by theories such as psycho-analysis or McDougall's dynamic psychology, since it takes account not merely of individual attributes but of the essential inter-relationships of human beings with one another. For reasons such as these the concept has proved more fruitful and more encouraging to educational endeavour than earlier interpretations in terms of the expressing of instincts, the fixing of habits, the training of faculties, or the disciplining of the will.

The word is admittedly unsatisfactory because of the temptation it offers to loose thinking. Correctives to this can be found only in its limitation in this context to those psychological requirements which are common to all human beings by virtue of their humanity. The most significant of these appear to be:

the receiving of appreciation or affection,
  (experiences of being beloved)
the sharing in co-operative endeavour,
  (opportunities of making a contribution or participating)

and the conditions contributory to growth – the meeting of new experiences, the chance to attain some measure of understanding or insight, and the exposure to suitable tuition in informational or other educational experiences (see Figure I).

The concept is admittedly a hypothesis – an inference from certain observable data. Its significance requires, however, to be judged not

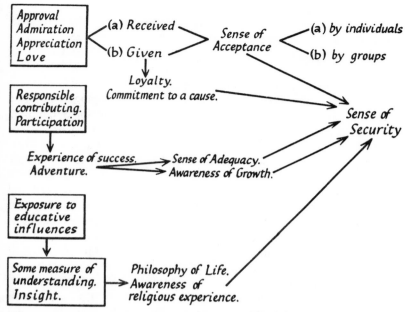

Figure I. Chart illustrating forms of expression and experiences associated with psychological needs.

merely through an appraisal of the assumptions as to human functioning which its acceptance or rejection can be seen to involve, but in terms of the evidence which it attempts to subsume. To the latter – the objective findings which can be cited in its support – some consideration may now be given.[22]

Evidence from case-histories

Much relevant material is to be found in psycho-analytic records in which the word 'need' occurs only incidentally. Powdermaker, Levis, and Touraine, for example, writing in 1937, noted that among delinquent adolescent girls those most resistant to treatment appeared to be those who had been unwanted or rejected in early childhood. They had had no opportunities for forming libidinal relationships; and in later years they showed little or no ability to make emotional attachments ('transferences') either to persons or to groups. They could therefore not be reached by those who tried to help them. Their development had been thwarted by lack of satisfaction of the need to give and to receive tenderness (to use Suttie's phrase of contemporary date); and this deprivation had been followed by an exaggerated emphasis on substitute satisfactions – the lust for power, for pleasure or for possessions.[23]

Similar findings were reported by Bowlby some years later in a discussion of forty-four juvenile thieves referred to a Child Guidance Clinic. These, when compared with a control group of like number, age and sex, showed a greater proportion of 'affectionless' children (fourteen as against none) along with a greater proportion of children separated for six months or more from their mother or foster-mother during their first five years (seventeen as against two). The degree of overlap between an absence of emotional response and delinquency, and a history of separation and disturbed mother-child relationships was again suggestive of the reality of the need for continued contact with human beings who were believed to be loving and appreciative.[24] Comparable weaknesses in development have been recorded in case-histories of children who have had excessive experience of reputed inadequacy or obvious failure [25] and children who have been denied the opportunity of contributing at the level of their ability – the over-protected, the under-exercised, the unduly-sheltered.[26] While deprivation of affection appears to lead to anxiety and inability to make contact with others, the denial of the opportunity of making an adequate contribution tends to be followed by irresponsibility and rebellion.[27]

These findings are admittedly descriptive and anecdotal rather than experimental; but their accumulation over recent decades lends impressive support to an emphasis on the significance of the social rather than the biological origin of much human behaviour. While the childhood memories of adolescents or adults who are recognizably psychotic, promiscuous or over-prejudiced may carry a certain measure of distortion related to their present condition, the nature of their fantasies has in many case-studies been shown to be related to recorded interruptions in the stability of their personal experiences of co-operative living in an atmosphere of acceptance.[28]

Observation of present circumstances

Evidence pointing in the same direction is to be found in analyses of the present wishes, hopes, and fears of human beings. Mention has been made of pupils' admiration for teachers who are friendly and trusting. This may readily be interpreted in terms of the need both to receive appreciation and to make some contribution to the classroom group. A similar longing for recognition, new experience, security, and response was noted in the late 1910s by Thomas in a study of the wishes of groups of young prostitutes whose delinquencies he dared to explain not in terms of perverted personal characteristics – physical or psychological – but as a sequel to the failure of society to make their adjustment possible through the satisfaction of their basic human requirements.[29] At the time this was a surprising formulation. Down the decades it has, in one wording or another, become a commonplace in the interpretation of delinquency.[30] Down the decades also evidence has come of a pervasive human yearning both for appreciation and for what has in recent years been described as participation (to use Allport's word) or co-operative activity (in the phrase favoured by Mayo)[31]. Mother and child from the earliest days need to give and receive in the partnership of the 'nursing couple'.[32] Even the most unsuccessful parents confess to longings for co-operation in the family,[33] and boys and girls not only desire co-operation with their teachers [34] but reach out perpetually towards co-operation with one another.[35] Findings such as these are supported by studies of the unsatisfactory personal and intellectual development of children who for longer or shorter periods have experienced emotional deprivation in institutions, as refugees under evacuation or in hospitals,[36] and it is therefore now generally acknowledged that the need for confident, friendly, and co-operative relationships with others is basic to man's nature. Only through the satisfaction of this composite requirement both to give and to receive can wholesome human development be effected or mental health be established and maintained.

Long-term studies

Long-term studies contributory to the same interpretation are to be found in the field of emotional and social development, in experimental variations of classroom or institutional procedures, in records of remedial treatment in the field of child guidance, and in inquiries into the development of morale in the forces and in industry. From all of these it seems justifiable to draw the same conclusions. Adolescents under observation in the Californian Adolescent Study reacted favourably to opportunities to contribute in a responsible fashion to the welfare of their groups; and they blossomed physically as well as socially under appreciation from adults and contemporaries.[37] An increase in the stability and the tenderness of personal contacts was followed by improved emotional and intellectual development in children in institutions and day nurseries.[38] Boys and girls who were allowed to learn under co-operative procedures in the Eight-Year Study compared favourably both in social and academic maturity with their contemporaries who had been handled in more formal and dictatorial fashions.[39] Pupils in classrooms where friendly associations were encouraged improved in attitudes towards learning and held their own in tests of scholastic attainment as compared with control groups in whose schooling an emphasis had been placed on individual achievement and personal success.[40] Morale in civilian life, in industry, and in the forces was highest in the case of those who had most opportunity for the satisfaction of their need for personal appreciation and understanding as well as for an awareness of the significance of the contribution they were making to the well-being of a friendly group.[41]

Further reference will be made in later chapters to the educational relevance of these findings. It is sufficient here to note that through them there has come a fuller connotation to the concept of psychological need and its expansion from the somewhat individualistic concern of the psycho-analysts with the maternal-care received by the infant in the first few months or years to an appreciation of the quite parallel and contemporary requirement for an opportunity of making a contribution – participating as well as receiving – in the day-to-day contacts of ordinary human living. In the language of the philosophers, altruism or co-operativeness can be said to be as primary as egotism or self-seeking. In support of this position it is, however, now possible to cite not merely philosophic opinion but an accumulation of evidence from studies of human beings in a variety of situations and at all ages. Psycho-analysts in the study of the life histories of pathological patients made an important contribution through their emphasis on the relationships of parents and children. Too exclusive an attention to what was given to infants in nursing, weaning, habit-training, and the like and too close a concentration on the physical aspects of this treatment (continuity of care by the biological parent) tempted them, however, to an undue neglect of the modifications in attitude and in behaviour which are effected through social influences at every age, and led also to a disregard of the active contribution which even little children make to the groups of which they form a part. It is reasonable to suppose that every experience leaves its traces.[42] Consideration of available evidence from older or more normal human beings suggests, however, that the psycho-analytic interpretation was an over-simplification which accepted too readily the presuppositions of a hedonistic individualism current in Viennese circles in Freud's younger days. In correction of this position it is important also to note the accumulating evidence from anthropological studies as to the apparently wide range of human flexibility in adaptation to very different conditions.[43] Much has been made by Bowlby and others of the biological analogy of a critical moment in developmental history at which traumatic experiences acquire special significance. Recent findings of social research with adults as well as with children suggest the desirability of caution in the use of this comparison as applied to personal and social behaviour. It is possible to trace a series of stages in the developmental tasks allotted to human beings, as they mature in any given society.[44] There is, however, little observational or experimental support for the supposition that human beings can not at any age be helped by the ordinary agencies of group living (in home and school and church) to overcome early calamities and master distressing present situations. In contrast to the essential pessimism of the Freudian interpretation there seems reason to believe that modifiability rather than fixity is an essential characteristic of human development.[45] This is most obviously true in the case of physical health, which is admittedly related to variations in the satisfying of physical needs (for suitable food, rest, warmth, and the like); but in quite comparable fashion healthy mental and personal functioning has been shown to depend on the satisfying of the psychological requirements of appreciation, participation, and insight.

Withdrawal of adequate nutrition, shelter, and relaxation at any age is followed by physical destruction of greater or lesser degree. Lack of the psychological support given by the receiving of admiration, the making of a contribution and the attainment of some measure of understanding goes far to account for deviations in behaviour which would otherwise be incomprehensible. Fry's correction of Bowlby's title: *Maternal Care and Mental Health*, into the more comprehensive wording: 'Child Care and the Growth of Love'[46] is a pointer to the indestructible human faith in the possibility of re-education. It is also an asseveration of the equal primacy of the individual and the social and the inescapable interdependence of both. To some recognition of this interdependence the concept of basic psychological needs owes its origin and from it much of its usefulness is still derived.

REFERENCES

1. For a lucid expression of this point of view see: BONNER, H., *Social Psychology*. N.Y.: American Book Co. 1953. See also: FLEMING, C. M., *Brit. J. Educ. Studies*. 3. 1. 17–23. 1954.

2. ALLPORT, F. H., *Social Psychology*. Boston: Houghton Mifflin. 1924.
   DASHIELL, J. F., in MURCHISON, C. (ed.), *A Handbook of Social Psychology*. Worcester, Mass.: Clark U.P. 1935.
   See also: MURPHY, G., *et al.*, *Experimental Social Psychology*. N.Y.: Harper. 1937.
   SPROTT, W. J. H., *Social Psychology*. Lond.: Methuen. 1952.

3. THORNDIKE, E. L., *Individuality*. Boston: Houghton Mifflin. 1911.
   RUSK, R. R., *Introduction to Experimental Education*. Lond.: Longmans. 1912.
   RICE, J. M., *Scientific Management in Education*. Lond.: Harrap. 1915.
   See also: 14th, 15th, and 17th *Yearbooks* of the National Society for the Study of Education. 1915, 1916, 1918.

4. DASHIELL, J. F., loc. cit. [2].

5. ALLPORT, F. H., loc. cit. [2].
   DASHIELL, J. F., loc. cit. [2].

6. FERNALD, G. M., and KELLER, H., *J. Educ. Res.* IV. 354–77. 1921.
   HINCKS, E. M., *Disability in Reading and its Relation to Personality*. Cambridge, Mass.: Harvard U.P. 1926.

7. RUSK, R. R., loc. cit. [3].
   SANDIFORD, P., *The Mental and Physical Life of School Children*. Lond.: Longmans. 1913.
   See also: MERRILL, M. A., *J. Consult. Psychol.* XV. 4. 281–9. 1951.

8. RICE, J. M., loc. cit. [3].
   STARCH, D., *Educational Measurements*. N.Y.: Macmillan. 1916.

9. SAYLES, M. B., and NUDD, H. W., *The Problem Child in School*. N.Y.: Commonwealth Fund. 1925.
   ELLIS, M. B., *The Visiting Teacher in Rochester*. N.Y.: Commonwealth Fund. 1925.
   CLEUGH, M. C., *Psychology in the Service of the School*. Lond.: Methuen. 1951.
   For studies based on work in Glasgow University Educational Clinic from 1926 onwards see: FLEMING, C. M., *A Survey of Reading Ability*. Ph.D. Thesis, Glasgow. 1930. and FLEMING, C. M., *Individual Work in Primary Schools*. Part III, 96–123. Lond.: Harrap. 1934.

10. A useful description of traditional child guidance procedures is given in: STEVENSON, G. S., and SMITH, G., *Child Guidance Clinics*. N.Y.: Commonwealth Fund. 1934.
    BURBURY, W. M., BALINT, E. M., and YAPP, B. J., *An Introduction to Child Guidance*. Lond.: Macmillan. 1945.

11. For later suggestions towards treatment of the child in his group see: ROGERS, C. R., *The Clinical Treatment of the Problem Child*. Boston: Houghton Mifflin. 1939.

PLANT, J. S., *Personality and the Cultural Pattern*. N.Y.: Commonwealth Fund. 1937.

BOWLBY, J., *Human Relations* II. 2. 123-8. 1949.

See also: FLEMING, C. M., *Adolescence*. Ch. XII. Lond.: Routledge 1948, 1955 and 1963.

LUCHINS, A. S., *J. Consult. Psychol.* XII. 6. 417-25. 1948.

HUNT, J. MCV., ibid. XIII. 2. 69-81. 1949.

12. NUNN, T. P., *Education: Its Data and First Principles*. Lond.: Arnold. 1920.

TERMAN, L. M., *Intelligence Tests and School Reorganization*. Lond.: Harrap. 1923.

13. WICKMAN, E. K., *Children's Behavior and Teachers' Attitudes*. N.Y.: Commonwealth Fund. 1928.

14. BRILL, J. G., and PAYNE, E. G., *The Adolescent Court and Crime Prevention*. N.Y.: Pitman. 1938.

15. Representative of Lewin's contribution are:

LEWIN, K., in MURCHISON, C. (ed.), *A Handbook of Child Psychology*. Worcester, Mass.: Clark U.P. 1933.

LEWIN, K., *A Dynamic Theory of Personality*. N.Y.: McGraw-Hill. 1935.

LEWIN, K., *Principles of Topological Psychology*. N.Y.: McGraw-Hill. 1936.

LEWIN, K., *et al.*, *J. Soc. Psychol.* **10**. 2. 271-99. 1939.

LEWIN, K., *Resolving Social Conflicts*. N.Y.: Harper. 1948.

LEWIN, K., and CARTWRIGHT, D., *Field Theory in Social Science*. N.Y.: Harper. 1951.

16. Cf. FREUD, S., *Introductory Lectures on Psycho-Analysis*. Lond.: Allen & Unwin. 1922.

JONES, E., *Papers on Psycho-Analysis*. Lond.: Baillière, Tindall & Cox. 1912.

MARTIN, W. E., and STENDLER, C. B., *Child Development*. N.Y.: Harcourt Brace. 1953.

Contrast VALENTINE, C. W., *Psychology and its Bearing on Education*. Lond.: Methuen. 1950.

17. THORNDIKE, E. L., *Educational Psychology*. N.Y.: Teachers' College, Columbia Univ. 1913.

WATSON, J. B., *Psychol. Rev.* **20**. 158-77. 1913.

WATSON, J. B., *Behaviorism*. N.Y.: Norton. 1924.

18. WOODWORTH, R. S., *Dynamic Psychology*. N.Y.: Columbia U.P. 1918. For later development of similar concepts see the discussion of the functional autonomy of motives in: ALLPORT, G. W., *Personality*. N.Y.: Henry Holt. 1937.

19. For an accessible statement see: HULL, C. L., in MCCONNELL, T. R., *et al.*, The Psychology of Learning. 41st *Yearbook* of the National Society for the Study of Education. Part II.

See also:

MILLER, N. E., and DOLLARD, J., *Social Learning and Imitation*. New Haven: Yale U.P. 1941.

20. HULL, C. L., *Principles of Behavior*. N.Y.: Appleton. 1943.
    HULL, C. L., *Essentials of Behavior*. New Haven: Yale U.P. 1951.
    HULL, C. L., *A Behavior System*. New Haven: Yale U.P. 1952.
21. BHALLA, S., *The Psychological Needs of Children*. M.A. Thesis. London. 1949.
22. FLEMING, C. M., The Concept of Need. Unpublished Lecture. London. 1950.
    BOWLBY, J., *Maternal Care and Mental Health*. Geneva: World Health Organization Monograph, Series No. 2. 1951.
    See also: BOWLBY, J., edited and abridged by M. FRY, *Child Care and the Growth of Love*. Lond.: Penguin Books. 1953.
23. SUTTIE, I. D., *The Origins of Love and Hate*. Lond.: Kegan Paul. 1935.
    POWDERMAKER, F., LEVIS, H. T., and TOURAINE, G., *Amer. J. Orthopsychiat*. VII. 58–71. 1937.
    See also: LEVY, D. M., *Amer. J. Psychiat*. 94. 1. 643–52. 1937.
    GOLDFARB, W., *Amer. J. Orthopsychiat*. XIV. 1. 162–6. 1944. Also XV. 2. 247–55. 1945.
    GOLDFARB, W., *Amer. J. Psychiat*. 102. 1. 18–33. 1945.
    For a good summary of findings on parental rejection see: SYMONDS, P., *The Psychology of Parent-Child Relationships*. N.Y.: Appleton. 1939.
    HAMLEY, H. R., et al., *The Education of Backward Children*. Lond.: Evans. 1936.
    FIELD, H. E., *Yearbook of Education*. 866–82. Lond.: Evans. 1936.
    For a general discussion see: RIBBLE, M. A., in HUNT, J. MCV. (ed.), *Personality and the Behavior Disorders*. N.Y.: Ronald Press. 1944.
24. BOWLBY, J., loc. cit. [22].
    BOWLBY, J., *Forty-four Juvenile Thieves*. Lond.: Baillière, Tindall & Cox. 1946.
    SKODAK, M., and SKEELS, H. M., *J. Genet. Psychol*. 66. 21–58. 1945.
    PRATT, D., *Psychiatry*. 15. 2. 179–88. 1952.
25. PLANT, J. S., loc. cit. [11].
26. MOODIE, W., *The Doctor and the Difficult Child*. N.Y.: Commonwealth Fund. 1940.
    BARKER, R. G., and GUMP, P. V., *Big School, Small School*. Stanford: University Press. 1964.
    LEVY, D. M., *Maternal Overprotection*. N.Y.: Columbia U.P. 1943.
27. PLANT, J. S., loc. cit. [11].
    FLEMING, C. M., *Internat. J. Soc. Psychiat*. IV. 3. 214–20. 1958.
28. BOWLBY, J., loc. cit. [22]. 1951.
    ADORNO, T. W., et al., *The Authoritarian Personality*. N.Y.: Harper. 1950.
29. THOMAS, W. I., *The Unadjusted Girl*. Boston: Little, Brown. 1920.
    See also: THOMAS, W. I., *Social Behavior and Personality*. N.Y.: Social Science Research Council. 1951.
30. HEALY, W., and BRONNER, A. F., *New Light on Delinquency and its Treatment*. New Haven: Yale U.P. 1936.
    PLANT, J. S., loc. cit. [11].

PARTRIDGE, E. D., *Social Psychology of Adolescence*. N.Y.: Prentice-Hall. 1939.

See also: *Making Citizens*. Lond.: H.M.S.O. 1945, and BRILL, J. G., and PAYNE, E. G., loc. cit. [14].

FLEMING, C. M., *Adolescence*, loc. cit. [11], ch. XVI.

31. ALLPORT, G. W., *Psychol. Rev.* **52**. 3. 117–32. 1945.

ROGERS, M., *Sociometry*. IX. 4. 352–71. 1946.

FRASER, RUSSELL, *The Incidence of Neurosis among Factory Workers*. Lond.: H.M.S.O. 1947.

LINE, W., *Brit. J. Med. Psychol.* XXIV. 1. 42–8. 1951.

32. MIDDLEMORE, M. P., *The Nursing Couple*. Lond.: Hamish Hamilton. 1941.

33. BOWLBY, J., loc. cit. [22]. 1951.

GARSIDE, A., *A Study of the Wishes as to Their Children's Development Expressed by a Group of Parents of Primary School Children*. M.A. Thesis. London. 1956.

34. DANG, S. D., *A Study of Co-operation in Certain Secondary Schools*. M.A. Thesis. London. 1949.

Cf. JERSILD, A. T., *Child Psychology*. 3rd ed. N.Y.: Staples Press. 1947.

See also: BUSH, R. N., *The Teacher-Pupil Relationship*. N.Y.: Prentice-Hall. 1954.

35. MEEK, L. H., *The Personal-Social Development of Boys and Girls*. N.Y.: Progressive Education Association. 1940.

36. On children in institutions see: BÜHLER, C., in MURCHISON, C., *A Handbook of Child Psychology*. Worcester, Mass.: Clark U.P. 1933.

BÜHLER, C., *From Birth to Maturity*. Lond.: Kegan Paul. 1935.

GOLDFARB, W., loc. cit. [23]. 1943.

BURLINGHAM, D., and FREUD, A., *Infants without Families*. Lond.: Allen & Unwin. 1944.

ISAACS, S., *Childhood and After*. Lond.: Routledge. 208–38. 1948.

For a convenient summary of references on evacuees see:

FLEMING, C. M., *The Social Psychology of Education*. Lond.: Kegan Paul. 21. 1944, 1959 and 1961.

WOLF, K. M., *Psycho-Anal. Study of Child*. 1. 389–404. 1945.

On children in hospitals see: EDELSTON, H., *Genet. Psychol. Monogr.* **28**. 3–95. 1943.

SPENCE, J. C., *The Purpose of the Family*. Convocation Lecture. Lond.: National Children's Home. 1946.

SPITZ, R. A., *Psycho-Anal. Study of Child*. 1. 53–74. 1945.

FISCHER, L. K., *Amer. J. Orthopsychiat.* XXII. 522–33. 1952.

PRUGH, D. G., *et al.*, ibid. XXIII. 70–106. 1953.

37. MEEK, L. H., loc. cit. [35].

JONES, H. E., *Development in Adolescence*. N.Y.: Appleton. 1943.

WIDDOWSON, E. M., *Lancet*. 1. 24. 1316–1318. 1951.

38. BURLINGHAM, D., and FREUD, A., loc. cit. [36].

FLINT, B. M., *The Child and the Institution: A Study of Deprivation and Recovery*. Toronto.: Univ. of Toronto Press. 1966.

39. See: AIKIN, W. M., *The Story of the Eight Year Study*. N.Y.: Harper. 1942.

For a summary see: HEMMING, J., *Teach Them to Live*. Lond.: Heinemann. 1948.

40. GARDNER, D. E. M., *Long-Term Results of Infant School Methods*. Lond.: Methuen. 1950.

RICHARDSON, J. E., *An Experiment in Group Methods of Teaching English Composition*. M.A. Thesis. London. 1948.

HALLWORTH, H. J., *A Study of Group Relationships among Grammar School Boys and Girls*. M.A. Thesis. London. 1951.

STAINES, J. W., *A Psychological and Sociological Investigation of the Self as a Significant Factor in Education*. Ph.D. Thesis. London. 1954.

WILKIE, J. S., *A Study of Some Effects of the Free Choice of Certain Activities and of Companions for Group Work*. M.A. Thesis. London. 1955.

PEARCE, R. A., *Co-operation in the Classroom*. M.A. Thesis. London. 1956.

GARDNER, D. E. M., *Experiment and Tradition in Primary Schools*, Methuen. 1966.

41. ANGELL, R. C., *The Family Encounters the Depression*. N.Y.: Scribners. 1936.

WATSON, G., in WATSON, G. (ed.), *Civilian Morale*. Boston: Houghton Mifflin. 1942.

See also: PATERSON, T. T., *Morale in War and Work*. Lond.: Max Parrish. 1955.

For a relevant symposium see: SOROKIN, P. A. (ed.), *Explorations in Altruistic Love and Behavior*. Boston: Beacon Press. 1950.

See also: ANDERSON, H. H., in CARMICHAEL, L., *et al.*, *Manual of Child Psychology*. N.Y.: Wiley. 1954.

STOUFFER, S. A., *et al.*, *The American Soldier*. Princeton: Princeton U.P. 1949.

42. PENFIELD, W., *Proc. Fourteenth Internat. Congress Psychol*. 47–69. 1955.

43. ORLANSKY, H., *Psychol. Bull*. 46. 1–48. 1949.

PINNEAU, S. R., *Child Development*. 21. 4. 203–28. 1950.

LEWIS, H., *Deprived Children*. Lond.: O.U.P. 1954.

DAVID, M., Unpublished report. U.N.E.S.C.O. 1952.

For discussion of these findings see: BOWLBY, J., in SENN, M. J. E. (ed.), *Problems of Infancy and Childhood*. N.Y.: Josiah Macy Jr. Foundation. 1954.

PINNEAU, S. R., *Psychol. Bull*. 52. 5. 429–52. 1955.

WALL, W. D., *Education and Mental Health*. U.N.E.S.C.O. 1955.

See also: MURDOCH, G. P., and WHITING, J. W. M., in SENN, M. J. E. (ed.), *Problems of Infancy and Childhood*. N.Y.: Josiah Macy Jr. Foundation. 1951.

WHITING, J. W. M., and CHILD, I. L., *Child Training and Personality*. New Haven: Yale U.P. 1953.

MEAD, M., and WOLFENSTEIN, M., *Childhood in Contemporary Cultures*. Chicago: Univ. of Chicago Press. 1955.

STOTT, D. H., *The Lancet*. 624–8. May 5, 1956.

BOWLBY, J., *et al.*, *Brit. J. Med. Psychol.* **XXIX**. 3 and 4. 211–47. 1956.

44. HAVIGHURST, R. J., *Human Development and Education*. N.Y.: Longmans. 1953.

45. KLEIN, M., and RIVIÈRE, J., *Love, Hate, and Reparation*. Lond.: Hogarth Press. 1937.

In contrast to this may be placed such a statement as that in ESTES,

S. G., *J. Consult. Psychol.* **XII**. 2. 76–81. 1948.

PARKER, R. A., *Decision in Child Care*. Lond.: Allen and Unwin. 1966.

AXLINE, V. M., *Dibs: In Search of Self.* Gollancz. 1964 and 1966.

46. BOWLBY, J., edited by M. FRY. loc. cit. [22]. 1953.

See also: MAYS, J. B., *The Young Pretenders*. Lond.: Michael Joseph. 1965.

FLINT, B. M., loc. cit. [38].

IV

UNDERSTANDING HUMAN NATURE: SOCIOMETRY AND THE CONCEPT OF THE SELF

MENTION HAS ALREADY been made of the sensitivity of group members to the attitudes and the directives of their leaders. From recognition of the significance of such social relationships and awareness of the contribution made by the satisfaction of primary needs it was an easy step to a concern with the subtleties of response consequent on members' awareness of the presence of one another. If human beings have been so made that co-operativeness is a primary attribute, and if without the emotional satisfaction of appreciation from other human beings they neither develop in wholesome fashion from infancy nor respond in satisfactory ways to human approaches at later ages, it seems reasonable to suppose that what is happening in groups is more complicated than the experiences to which attention is directed in those discussions which stress the type of social climate produced by teachers, leaders or supervisors. The part played by the leader or teacher is demonstrably significant. The part played by pupils or members is also crucial. Recognition of this has come slowly over the last three decades; and its relevance to teaching and learning is as yet rarely emphasized.

The character of a group was known by the philosophers to exercise an influence on the behaviour of its members; and discretion in the choice of one's friends has won commendation from many fathers both before and since the days of Polonius. The step was not, however, often taken from generalizations as to the influence of bad (or good) companions to a belief that a lively concern with the cross-currents of friendship is desirable on the part not only of parents within families but of teachers, club-leaders or employers in fields which are commonly still thought of in purely intellectual, manipulative or economic terms.

Something akin to present awareness of the significance of membership of friendly groups seems on the surface indicated by a few questionnaires issued at the turn of the century by psychologists working within what was then called the Child Study Movement. 'What kind of chum do you prefer?'[1] 'How many friends have you?' 'How many friends would you wish to have?' 'Whom would you like to resemble?'[2] Such questions might have proved the starting-point of research into the effect of group contacts on individual members, but no such development occurred. Answers were classified. Lists were prepared and filed. Statements were made as to the moral qualities admired and the size of group preferred by boys and girls at various ages. There the matter ended. No questions were asked as to the connexion between the number and nature of a pupil's friends and the actual behaviour of the pupil. Still less was any attempt made to use information on friendships as a means to the understanding of a classroom situation.

Clearer formulation of the extent to which human beings are sensitive to the actions and the personalities of their companions came in the 1920s from certain writers who had been in more direct contact with boys and girls. Thrasher and Moreno, for example, at about the same time directed attention in differing fashions to the flow of feeling between members of gangs (in Chicago)[3] and between boys and girls at play (in the gardens of Vienna).[4] Thrasher was concerned to describe the mutual interpretation of subtle signs by which the purposes of the group are conveyed from one member to another. Moreno, from observations of impromptu dramatizing, came to believe that emotional responses are more spontaneously made when adults or children are permitted to work or play together in groups of their own choosing. Both realized something of the extent to which children and adolescents are actively engaged in judging one another; and both used this knowledge as a means of effecting changes in the behaviour of groups. Thrasher's work prepared the way for the situational and social treatment of delinquency (modifying the meaning of the behaviour of a gang rather than removing individuals from contact with their friends). Moreno succeeded in demonstrating that by encouraging friendly groupings it was possible to improve the morale of displaced adults in new settlements, of pupils in day schools, and of adolescent girls in residential institutions.

Moreno was both a doctor and an actor. He was committed as a psychiatrist to the therapeutic treatment of human beings in distress; but he delighted in the study of the evolution and organization of groups and his interest turned at an early age from analytic interviews with single patients in consulting rooms to group methods of therapy through what he later called psychodrama (creating, acting out, and sharing with others the spontaneous drama of a personal problem) and sociodrama (the acting out by a group of their problems in role playing, inter-group relations, and beliefs collectively held).[5] This aspect of his work makes him one of the founders of the group psychotherapy which reached widespread notice in the 1940s[6] (see Chapter XVIII below). More directly relevant to the situation of the pupil in the classroom was his development of 'sociometry' – a method of discovering, describing, and evaluating the relations of members to one another within a group. This was attempted by what, on retrospect, seems a very simple device. He asked each member to write in order of preference the names of a specified number of persons with whom he would wish to be associated in a certain situation – sitting at meals, working in a laundry, sharing living quarters and the like. (To this could be added the names of any whom the writer particularly desired to avoid.) From the information so obtained Moreno claimed that it was possible to make quantitative recordings of the social currents within groups, the extent of acceptance or rejection, and the relative leadership status of members. Groups so analysed could then be studied for scientific purposes by those interested in the dynamics of group structure: and in the light of the same data opportunities could also be provided for changes in the pattern of interaction between one person and another. Classification by friendship thus became one of the means open to therapists and to teachers in the educative treatment of groups.[7]

Sociometric techniques

Sociometric techniques are not to be used lightly. They are in essence very different from the somewhat detached and impersonal questionnaires characteristic of the Child Study Movement and its successors in the field of mental measurement. In origin they belong to the very real and somewhat desperate situation of Moreno as the doctor at Mittendorf, who contributed to the development of a co-operative community out of some ten thousand refugees by avoiding the separation of friends and encouraging some choice in the matter of buildings. A similar urgency and reality may be discerned in the circumstances in which sociometric questions were introduced into America in prisons, reformatories, and public day schools some years later.[8] It was again essential that genuine preferences should be expressed; and it was important that action should be taken in response to the wishes indicated. In similar fashion, in the equally poignant setting of ordinary classroom relationships, it is necessary for teachers to keep faith with their pupils both by adapting classroom conditions in such a way that some account is taken of the desires formulated and by regarding as confidential any information which they obtain. Only if this is done is it probable that pupils will make genuine choices; and only in response to sincere statements can pupils be given the help they require. In the decades since Moreno first expounded sociometric techniques his methods have been tried both with adults and children in many lands. Abundant evidence is now available as to the improvement in attitude and in attainment which follows from the satisfaction which the sociometric procedure gives to the pervasive human need for affection and approval.[9] Equally significant is the insight it provides into the varying levels of friendliness among members of any group.

As an aid to the study of these relationships Moreno at an early date made the proposal that they could be charted in spatial diagrams reminiscent of the geographer's mapping of a region or the geometrist's illustration of an argument. In Figure II below such a 'sociogram' is shown for the recorded first choices of a group of pupils to whom an invitation had been given to choose companions for two different pursuits. Arrows indicate the direction of choices; and groupings show the general pattern of inter-relationships.

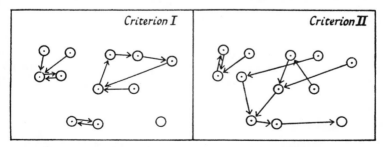

Figure II. Chart showing choice of companions for two different pursuits.

Observation of these preferences shows certain differences among pupils. Some are stars (with many choices directed towards them). Some are isolates rejecting all or perhaps rejected by all. Some form members of chains – A choosing B, B choosing C, and C choosing D. Some are linked in pairs by mutual preferences. The exact pattern of cohesiveness within a group may change for different purposes and at different times,[10] but only rarely is information as to its subtleties available to teachers through ordinary teaching contacts. One of the benefits conferred by the use of sociometric questions has therefore been the vividness of the reminder they give of the discriminative interest shown by pupils in their assessment, both of the degree of their kinship to other members of their groups and of the values (consolation, comfort or assistance) to be obtained from contacts with selected individuals.

Guess-Who? techniques

Another way of discovering what pupils think of one another was provided by the Guess-Who? Test suggested by May in the Character-Education Enquiry and elaborated by Tryon in the Californian Adolescent Study.[11] It consists of presenting to pupils a series of more or less detailed descriptions of boys and girls – accompanied by instructions to the effect that they are to write the name of the pupil to whom the description most aptly refers.

'Someone who is shy; who does not like being watched.'
'Someone who takes life easily and calmly; who does not worry and get upset.'
'Someone with a lot of friends.'
'Someone who is very upset when scolded or blamed.[12]

Questions of this sort can be introduced as part of a series of games with groups of pupils who know one another well. Their usefulness, like that of the sociometric techniques, depends on the relationship between pupils and teacher, and they are genuinely informative only when pupils are convinced of the sincerity and friendliness of their teachers.

Discriminative dramatizing

Another procedure is that used by Butler and by Higginbotham. In this an outline of a play was given and pupils were asked to suggest which of their fellows would best fit into each part.

FINISH THE PLAY

A game for people with imagination

On the next page you will find the story of a play which is not quite finished.

I want you to fill in some spaces on the last sheet which will tell how you think the story might finish.

To do this you will have to consider what sort of people the story is about and how they would behave.

Next, I want you to imagine that your class is going to act this play. Anyone in the class, including yourself, can be chosen to act a part.

Write on the last sheet the name of the boy or girl who would be the best actor for each character. Also fill in whom you would choose for the producer – the person who takes charge of the play and decides the details of action and dress. No one else in the class will see your answers, so put down your own personal choices.

'*Stranded*'

Scene 1. The deserted seashore of an island in the Indian Ocean. On the stage is an air liner which has just crashed. Though badly damaged in the front, the aeroplane has not caught fire and the passengers are climbing out.[13]

Analysis of responses to such questions (like analysis of answers to sociometric questions) may draw attention to qualities unsuspected by teachers; and often the group of boys and girls seen from within presents a very different picture from that which is visible to an adult, however experienced.

Essay writing

Information of a kind more difficult to analyse can be obtained by setting pupils to write essays on relevant topics such as 'My Form' ('My Class'), 'What I Like about My School'. The usefulness of these essays depends again on the precautions taken to convince pupils that their confidences will not be betrayed; but there is reason to believe that groups of pupils known to differ in type of class-room relationship produce composite pictures very different in detail.[14]

49

Both essay-writing and direct questioning thus support the finding that pupils look in friendly or unfriendly fashion upon one another, and that they form definite judgements about one another in terms not dissimilar to those used by adults.

Group members take stock of themselves

Insight into the complexities of the classroom situation requires, however, an awareness not merely of the psychological needs of teachers and pupils, and of the attitudes of pupils towards one another, but also some understanding of the part played by pupils' views about themselves.

'What sort of person am I?'
'How do I compare with others?'
'What do other people think I am like?'
'What do I wish to be like?'

Recognition of the significance of such issues appears to have had three sources: the infiltration into psychological discussions of sociological concepts such as status and role; the interpretation of human motivation in terms of needs; and a developing sensitivity to the content of conscious thinking in various fields (see Table II).

Self-reference as to status and role

An emphasis on external observation – on 'evidence' rather than on 'theory' – had been part of the psychologists' programme when in the late nineteenth century they made clear the respects in which psychology as a science differed from philosophy.

Philosophers down the ages had discussed the self and the not-self, the self as known and the self as knower[15]; and, in protest, most psychologists had deliberately repudiated the use of these phrases. Mention of the concepts may still be traced in relatively early writings such as those of Titchener, of William James, and of Stout;[16] but by the turn of the century it was with apologies that any reference was made to the knower; and McDougall in 1908, like William James in 1890, deliberately deflected attention to the empirical self – the sum-total of all that man can call his own.[17] To this he added an emphasis on the processes by which there is organized round the idea of the self a system of emotional and conative tendencies or dispositions which he described as 'the master-

TABLE II

Contributory Strands in the Recognition of Self-reference

Self-reference as to Status and Role	Psychological Needs and the Development of the Self-Picture	Ego-psychology (the Psychic-Surface) and the Content of Conscious Thinking
William James: the empirical self. 1890	Rogers and Axline: self-reference in therapy. 1942. 1947	A. Freud: mental mechanisms and the Ego. 1937
Shand: the self-regarding sentiment and outgoing tenderness. 1896	Allport: psychometric study of opinions as to oneself. 1928	Kris: the psychic surface. 1951
McDougall: self-display and self-abasement. 1908	Rogers: self-acceptance in remedial treatment. 1948	Sutherland: a modified Freudianism. 1953
Genetic psychology and the vocabulary of self-awareness. 1930s and 1940s	Jersild: the concept of the self and child development. 1954	Allport: conscious thinking. 1953
Sherif: self-reference and ego-involvement. 1936		
Snygg and Combs: the preservation and enhancement of the phenomenal self. 1949		
Allport: participation. 1945		

sentiment of self-regard', acquired in the experience of the individual by constant interplay between self and society.

This use of the word 'sentiment' is of some importance. It had been introduced by Shand in 1896 and elaborated by Stout a few years later in connexion with growth in awareness of a distinction between the self and the not-self (the child himself and the world of things and people).[18] Shand had emphasized the complexity of the combination of the principle of self-love (the self-regarding sentiment) and the system of parental love or outgoing tenderness towards others (of self-respect and respect for others). McDougall, on the contrary, was concerned to show some continuity in development from the primary instinctive dispositions that man has in common with the animals to the highest types of human will and character.

Thus, while stressing the primacy of the self-regarding sentiment, he interpreted its growth in terms of self-centredness and concern with personal status – with the twin instincts of self-display or self-assertion (whose affective aspect he called the emotion of positive self-feeling) and self-abasement or submissiveness (with negative self-feeling as its associated emotion).

McDougall's book was published in 1908; and at the time little attention appears to have been paid to his sections on the formation of sentiments. Contemporary interest still centred on the mechanics of associative learning and the implications of the theory of evolution. Behaviourists and other workers in the field of general psychology found common ground in continued concentration on the study of the obvious responses discernible in a controlled situation. Psycho-analysts discouraged any expression of concern with the significance of one's thoughts about oneself and emphasized the potency of conflicting instinctual forces at a level of which human beings were, by definition, unaware. Both behaviourists and psycho-analysts thus united in a neglect of the self as known (the self in the sense of something known) while the self as knower (the self in the sense of something which knows) functioned only as the receiver of stimuli from the external world. (In this limited sense it continued to have a certain technical standing through the use by English-speaking psycho-analysts of the Latin word 'ego' – 'I' – in the trilogy which they had translated as id, ego, and super-ego. Scanty attention was however given to its content.)

Meanwhile, in the fields of genetic psychology, experimental psychology, and social psychology, evidence was accumulating which, after a silence of about thirty years, contributed to an extension of psychological insight through an emphasis upon the ubiquity of self-reference in the forming of personal and social attitudes.

Genetic psychology and self-awareness

Studies of the vocabulary of infants in the eighteenth and nineteenth centuries had included some records of the use of the personal pro-nouns: 'mine', 'me', 'I', 'we', and 'our'; but no particular significance had been attached to their occurrence. Binet at the turn of the century had experimented with structured interviews designed to uncover the growth of vocabulary and possible differences in mental functioning; and his work had been continued by Piaget some decades later. It was not, however, until the 1930s that Piaget's use of the word 'egocentric' (to describe children's responses to certain questions) provoked a lively controversy in which Isaacs, McCarthy, and others challenged the nature of his sampling, and exposed the inadequacies of his experimental design.[19] The episode is of interest as a possible milestone on the return to an appreciation of the extent to which human beings at all ages think in terms involving reference to themselves.

A similar revival of sensitivity to self-awareness may be detected in the same decade in certain studies in the social psychology of adolescence.[20] Older boys and girls are admittedly concerned about the winning of a place in the adult world. They are uncertain of their status (the degree to which their worth is recognized) and they are unsure of the role which they are to play (the contribution which society asks them to make). It is therefore not surprising that long-term investigations in this field made a notable contribution to the collection of material [21] from which at a later date illustrative episodes could be extracted in support of the thesis that in the learning of social attitudes there is continual dependence on all related experience both present and past; and that this total 'frame of reference' has a certain resistance to change which can best be understood as attributable to the 'universal human tendency to maintain and enhance the established constellation of attitudes which constitutes the ego or the self'.

Experimental psychology and ego-involvement

In the early exposition of this interpretation the work of Sherif was outstanding. Writing on the Psychology of Social Norms and (with Cantril) on the Psychology of Ego-Involvements he marshalled evidence in illustration of the contribution made by self-reference to perception as well as to the developing awareness of status which occurs in social maturing.[22] Even in superficially impersonal experiences such as autokinesis (the apparent movement of a stationary spot of light observed in a completely dark room) perception is judgemental and selective – affected both by suggestion from others and by reference to previously established individual standards. This notion of a persisting frame of reference may be traced in earlier studies such as those of Henri on the localization of skin stimulation (1897), of Wertheimer on alterations in the visual field seen in a slanting mirror (1925), of Duncker on frames in induced movement (1929), of Bartlett on the influence of established schemata on recollection (1932), and of Luchins on modifications in the perception of complex drawings (1945). The special contribution of the 1940s lay in the connecting of this admission of 'ego-involvement' with contemporary interpretations in terms of human needs. As looked at from the outside, human beings appear to have been so made that they need appreciation and the chance to participate. As seen from within they are (in Sherif's phrase) striving to anchor themselves through attitudes towards objects or persons which satisfy their basic need for belongingness as an acceptable member of a group.

It is to be noted that this emphasis on the crucial significance of the 'preservation and enhancement of the phenomenal self' (the self of which the human being is aware) as presented by Sherif and Cantril and expounded later by Snygg and Combs [23] was, like McDougall's discussion of the self-regarding sentiment, suggestive of a concern with status rather than with role. It permitted a preoccupation with the standing of an individual in relation to other persons – to the neglect of the contribution which the individual may make to the co-operative activities of a group. To this extent the interpretation of this group of workers was, like McDougall's, still under the influence of the one-sided viewpoint of earlier individualistic studies. It tended to emphasize getting rather than giving – prestige rather than service.[24]

Social psychology and personal participation

A corrective to this was meantime being offered in the general field of social psychology both through explicit formulation of the significance of the human need for participation and through emphasis on the bio-social origins of human personality.[25] Allport, writing in 1943, had surveyed the uses of the word 'ego' in contemporary psychology and had expanded his earlier discussion of the specificity of personal traits with observations on the increase in consistency of reaction consequent on 'self-involvement'. Where status or reputation is in question there tends, for example, to be sufficient regularity of response to justify a description of personality in terms of general traits. Where the 'ego' is not involved inconsistency of behaviour is often shown. In a later discussion of participation he gave an even clearer exposition of the relevance of personal participation both to the maintenance of mental health and to the preservation of morale in industry and in the armed forces.

The concept of the self as participator as well as protagonist may be discerned also in Murphy's approach to the understanding of personality with its suggestion that a sense of group identification may be a more powerful source of motivation than competitive self-assertion. This is reminiscent of earlier discussions of 'belonging-ness' offered by clinical psychologists, by industrial psychologists, and by anthropologists. It carries echoes of Suttie's emphasis on the equal primacy of giving and receiving; and it serves as a psycho-logical counterpart to the admission of the complexity of human nature inherent in the sociologists' concern with 'role' as well as with 'status' – with the desire for 'service' as concomitant to the longing for 'prestige'.

Psychological needs and the development of the self-picture

Developments in the clinical field may next be reviewed – along with the contribution of psychometrics and other educational studies to the fuller understanding of the self-picture.

Early in the twentieth century Adler had formulated certain of the personal consequences of self-despising. Two decades later Wickman had deprecated neglect of undue shyness and withdrawal; and Fromm had faced the consequences of the experience of loneliness. Plant in the late 1930s had pleaded for the twin requirements of a sense of adequacy and a sense of acceptability; and Moodie had emphasized the importance of early and effective conquest of the skills which admit a child to full membership of the human group.[26] The relevance of all this to education had been illustrated by signi-ficant studies of successful and unsuccessful students at Sarah Lawrence College.[27]

The importance of such issues to the understanding of children and adults in distress had thus been admitted in general terms; but until the 1940s descriptions of procedures and reactions both in the educational and in the clinical field had remained almost entirely at the level of general statements coupled with the personal comments of the therapist or the teacher as external observers. In this setting a notable step was taken by Rogers and by Axline through the pub-lishing of records of the actual words and movements of patients and of therapists in the therapeutic situation. From analysis of these there came the first clear recognition of the amount of articulate self-reference in the thinking of human beings.[28]

Can I do it? Am I adequate?
Do they like me? Am I acceptable?
What is it all about? Do I understand it?

The importance for therapy of this concern with the self was next established by Axline, Rogers, and other clinicians through the demonstration of observable changes in the content of the self-picture as recorded in statements made by patients before and after therapy.[29]

Records of remedial work among backward pupils hold similar findings.[30] Contact with one adult who contrives to change the self-picture of a child's inadequacy may be followed by the first step towards success. 'Of course you can.' 'She thinks I can.' 'Perhaps I can.' And – last, and triumphantly – 'I can.'[31] The content of the picture of the self is definitive for conduct; and the ultimate test for education and for therapy lies in the modifications they effect in the personal attitudes of pupils or patients.

Psychometrics and educational inquiries

Not dissimilar findings may be discerned in research studies in the field of personality. Psychometry in its beginnings had been directed to the measurement of abilities; but in the middle twenties it expanded to include the assessment of all discernible psychological qualities. Attributes such as security, confidence, submissiveness, and dominance came within its purview.[32] Testing as well as rating of personal traits was attempted; and inquiries were undertaken into values, preferences, interests, and attitudes.

Included among these were references to the opinions held by subjects about themselves. Bernreuter's neurotic inventory, Allport and Vernon's study of values, Allport's test of ascendance and submission, Davis' inquiries into confidence, and Forrester's study of the attitudes of adolescents toward their own development – all of these contained phrases relevant to the recognition of the self-picture.[33] In the interpretation of psychometric studies the insight obtained was not, however, specifically related to the content of conscious thinking. It remained as a background of research evidence concomitant with, but somewhat distinct from, the observational and more personal records accumulating through long-term studies of children and adolescents, through experiments with social climates and through analysis of the process of therapy.

Ego-psychology and the psychic surface

In a slightly different fashion there may also be noted an infiltration into psycho-analytic discussions of greater concern with the content of the ego. Much of this is attributable to Anna Freud's affirmation of the significance of personal integration and her interpretation of mental mechanisms as a means of fostering the growth of a strong 'ego' and defending a 'weak' one from assault.[34] Like many other workers in the late 1930s she had been prepared to admit the importance of a sense of security;[35] and confirmatory evidence of the desirability of this had been provided in the early 1940s through work in residential nurseries for war-orphans and air-raid victims.[36] 'She is my very own nurse – if not my mother'. 'She loves me.' 'I am worthy of love.' And so on. Some acknowledgement of the articulate nature of such thoughts is made in recent studies in 'ego-psychology', and affiliated thinkers such as Kris have not hesitated to attribute to the 'psychic surface' much that would not have been conceded by Freud himself.[37]

The usefulness of this psycho-analytic interpretation is, however, somewhat reduced by its retention of Freudian stereotypes as to adult roles and by its tendency to think in terms of a hypothetical 'real ego' the 'self-expression' of which requires to be safeguarded against the assaults of civilisation and society. Its contribution is also rendered less effective by its over-facile generalizations as to the content of mental mechanisms – rationalization (the unconscious replacement of actual motives by others which are more acceptable), super-ego formation (the internalizing of social demands), sublimation (the directing of impulses towards goals which are likely to meet with social approval or indifference), and transference (the reproduction in a new situation of attitudes acquired in an earlier relationship). These can now more usefully be described as the means by which human beings maintain continuity in their picture of themselves.

This is what I am like. Rationalization.
This is what others thought of me and how they behaved towards me. They will do the same now. Transference.
This is what I do. Super-ego formation.
This I ought to be and to do. Development of an ego-ideal.
This is what others would like me to do. Sublimation.

Through this accumulation of evidence from genetic psychology,

57

from experimental and social psychology, from clinical psychology, and from psychometrics it is now possible to examine in detail the pictures which human beings form of themselves (the 'self-picture'), the pictures which they believe are held by others (the 'looking-glass self' of Cooley or the 'other-self' of modern writers) and the picture of the 'ideal-self' to which they desire to approximate.[38]

In the development of these concepts individuals are at all times limited by their frames of reference – the totality of functionally related factors (past and present) which operate momentarily to determine perception, judgement, and attitude. The perceived or conceptualized self may be only part of the total personality as seen by others. The picture of the 'other-self' may be distorted; and the 'ideal self' may bear no relationship to attainable conduct. There is in these discrepancies a perpetual reminder of the extent to which human beings function in fashions of which they themselves are unaware. Concern with the content of conscious thought is thus supplementary to recognition of the basic psychological needs.

From the 1890s to the 1940s it was so generally considered that action was motivated by forces of which an individual can have no personal understanding that attention was directed away from inquiries into the potency of the thoughts of human beings about themselves. Ambitions, ideals, fears, and deliberate intentions were regarded as belonging to an out-moded introspectionism; and it was assumed that no statement should be taken at its face value. In the light of recent recognition that perception, cognition, and attitude have a measure of self-reference which contributes to personal continuity and consistency, psychological interpretation has now passed beyond both the dynamics of psycho-biological structure and the equally one-sided viewpoint of an emphasis on the primacy of society. Human beings are both social and individual. Through recognition of their unconscious needs for participation, appreciation, and insight and through observation of the establishment of self-concepts it is becoming more possible to understand their reactions, the structure of their personality, and the content of their behaviour in differing situations.[39]

Relevance to psychiatry

Interpretations along these lines have in recent years transformed the practice of many psychiatrists. They are obviously relevant to a variety of forms of group treatment but they are implicit also in the development of individual therapy of a client-centred or non-directive type. Very apposite here is, for example, the account given by Rogers of his own progression from exclusive concern with the influence of companions and the emotional climate of family or school to a realization of the part played by self-acceptance.[40] Analysis of follow-up studies of seventy-five delinquents in 1941 had seemed to indicate that those most susceptible to treatment were those who showed the highest measure of insight into their own attitudes and their own situation. This at the time seemed incredible; and its publication was not considered until it had been confirmed by a second series of seventy-six delinquents in 1944. By 1948 it was merely illustrative of a view for which evidence was accumulating from many sources.

Within the group who still describe themselves as psycho-analysts quite comparable changes in emphasis are occurring. In 1956 – one hundred years after the birth of Freud – special memorial volumes in his honour were published in many countries. These paid suitable tribute to the significance and the originality of his contribution; but more remarkable than the enthusiasm of the writers was the frequency with which they added comments which carried them beyond the interpretation which had been acceptable to Freud himself even in his latest books. A concern with transference rather than with instincts. Preoccupation with the 'ego' rather than the 'id' – the psychic surface as distinct from the 'depths' of the unconscious. A turning to the 'here and now' and the relations of a human being to various 'objects' in place of former concentration on the remote past and the complex states associated with too lively or too feeble a sense of guilt. An emphasis on the need for mother-love and a sense of security in contrast to discussion of the Oedipus complex, of hatred, aggressiveness or reparation.[41] In fashions such as these attention is turning to social relations rather than to biological factors and to the striving for self-actualization in place of the sublimation of life instincts. A new name is urgently needed. The newer theories are more than 'neo-Adlerian'. They are clearly no longer Freudian or psycho-analytic;[42] and the noun 'psycho-therapy' carries often the connotation of group treatment. Rogers' proposal of the term 'client-centred therapy has been countered by the comment that all therapies lie somewhere on a continuum ranging from more overt to less obvious concern with the thoughts and feelings of the patients; and his alternative of 'non-directive therapy' meets the criticism that in all forms of treatment there are some 'limits' as well as a greater or lesser emphasis on the interpretations offered or accepted by a therapist.[43]

Educational relevance

Whatever the phrase ultimately used in description of these view-points, the significance of the controversy lies in the publicity it gives to a more social approach and in the clarity of its recognition of the possibility of re-education through changes in the self-concepts held by learners. These findings are particularly relevant to the work of a teacher; and it is not without significance that some of the most interesting of the analyses of the content of the self-picture have come from within the field of educational psychology.

Havighurst and Taba in their studies of adolescent character and personality used, for example, the writing of an essay on 'The Person I would Like to be Like' as part of the basis for classifying boys and girls under selected patterns of behaviour described as self-directive, adaptive, submissive or defiant.[44] While they did not directly dis-cuss the concept of the self, their material contains suggestive examples of self-reference in different situations.

More definitive for education was the work of Jersild who supple-mented earlier inquiries into children's fears by direct search for their views about themselves. From the responses made by some thousands of pupils to the two subjects: 'What I Like About Myself' and 'What I Dislike About Myself' he found, for example, that at all ages from ten to twenty there was concern with personal attributes and social relationships, physical characteristics, clothing, home and family, recreation and ability in sport and at school.[45] There was much evidence of friendly attitudes towards other people and a marked tendency to self-disparagement in relation to school experi-ence. A willingness to co-operate and a longing to participate were prominent in the self-picture displayed.

Similar findings have come from the work of Staines. Through interviews and questionnaires he obtained statements comparable to those of Jersild; and, by asking pupils to sort these into piles as more or less true of themselves, he found it possible to obtain statistically reliable analyses of their attitudes under categories such as: physique and appearance, abilities, status, popularity, friendliness, interests, values, and goals. Re-testing after a three-months' interval showed deterioration in confidence and certainty among pupils who received treatment which tended to reduce their status in their own eyes and in those of their peers. The content of the self-picture did not vary consistently with groups of differing ages. For all it was a matter of genuine interest and concern.

From Staines' interviewing, questionnaires, and self-ratings there comes also an impressive reminder of the urgency of children's need both for personal acceptance (with the complementary fear of rejection) and for personal adequacy or participation (with its complementary dread of failure).[46] Similar conclusions may be drawn from an inquiry reported by del Solar in New York.[47] In this an analysis of interviews and questionnaires addressed to parents, teachers, and pupils showed that, in the sample of families examined, the children were convinced that acceptability would follow upon adequacy.

Conquest of subject matter and success or failure in school have always been matters of concern to teachers. Teachers are, however, often tempted to forget that boys and girls at every age are not only capable of looking with discerning eyes at one another but that, in a language of their own which may not be quite that of the teacher, they are examining themselves in terms quite relevant to the basic psychological needs whose satisfaction they require.

The fashions in which such self-perception is contributory to development may best be considered after a survey of the course taken in recent decades both by the scientific study of learning and by the experimental investigation of perceptual processes in general.

REFERENCES

1. Cited in BUHLER, C., in MURCHISON, C., *A Handbook of Child Psychology*. Worcester, Mass.: Clark U.P. p. 374, 1933.
2. BÜHLER, C., loc. cit. [1]. pp. 390–1.
3. THRASHER, F. M., *The Gang*. Chicago: Univ. of Chiago Press. 1927.
4. MORENO, J. L., *Who Shall Survive?* Washington: Nervous and Mental Disease Publishing Co. 1934.
   HENDRY, C. E., LIPPITT, R., and ZANDER, A., *Reality Practice as Educational Method*. Psychodrama Monographs. No. 9. 1944.
   SHOOBS, N. E., *Psychodrama in the Schools*. Psychodrama Monographs. No. 10. 1944.
   MORENO, J. L., *Psychodrama*. N.Y.: Beacon House. 1946.
5. MORENO, J. L. (ed.), *Group Psychotherapy: A Symposium*. N.Y.: Beacon House. 1945.

6. FLEMING, C. M., *The Social Psychology of Education*. Lond.: Kegan Paul. 1944, 1959 and 1961.

FLEMING, C. M., *Adolescence: Its Social Psychology*. Lond.: Routledge. 1948, 1955 and 1963.

7. JENNINGS, H. H., *Sociometry in Group Relatons*. Washington: Amer. Council on Educ. 1948 and 1959.

RICHARDSON, J. E., *et al.*, *Studies in the Social Psychology of Adolescence*. Lond.: Routledge. 1951.

NORTHWAY, M. L., *A Primer of Sociometry*. Toronto: Univ. of Toronto Press. 1952 and 1967.

8. MORENO, J. L., loc. cit. [4]. 1934 and 1953.

9. MORENO, J. L., *Sociom. Monogr.* 2. 1943.

MOUSTAKA, C., *A Study of Sociometric Choices in their relation to Attainments, Abilities and Attitude*. Ph.D. Thesis. London. 1959.

MOUSTAKA, C., *Internat. J. Sociom. & Sociat.* II. 1. 35–9. 1960.

BRADBURN, E., *Educ. Rev.* 12. 2. 112–24. 1960.

BLYTH, W. A. L., *Brit. J. Educ. Studies.* VIII. 2. 127–47. 1960.

EVANS, K. M., *Sociometry and Education*. Lond.: Routledge. 1962.

MOUSTAKA, C., *Attitudes, Sociometric Status and Ability in Greek Schools*. Paris: Mouton. 1967.

See also Sociometry, Sociometric Monographs, *Group Psychotherapy*, and the *International Journal of Sociometry, passim.*

10. WILKIE, J. S., *A Study of some Effects of the Free Choice of Certain Activities and of Companions for Group Work*. M.A. Thesis. London. 1955.

EDWARDS, T. L., *A Study of the Social Relationships of a Group of School Prefects with One Another and with Other Members of the School Community*. M.A. Thesis. London. 1952.

PEARCE, R. A., *Co-operation in the Classroom*. M.A. Thesis. London. 1956.

11. HARTSHORNE, H., and MAY, M. A., *Studies in the Nature of Character*. N.Y.: Macmillan. 1928–30.

See Meek, L. H., *The Personal-Social Development of Boys and Girls*. N.Y.: Progressive Education Association. 1940.

12. DAVIS, J. A. M., *A Study of Confidence in a Group of Secondary School Children*. M.A. Thesis. London. 1944.

13. BUTLER, C. D., *The Assessment of Social Attitudes of School Children*. M.A. Thesis. London. 1949.

See also: HIGGINBOTHAM, P. J., *An Investigation into the Use of Leaderless Group Discussions*. M.A. Thesis. London. 1949.

BRAY, D. H., *A Study of Personal Attributes and Roles Favoured by Boys and Girls Aged Eleven to Thirteen Years*. Ph.D. Thesis. London. 1961.

BRAY, D. H., *Educ. Rev.* 15. 1. 44–53. 1962.

14. FINCH, I. E., *A Study of the Personal and Social Consequences for Groups of Secondary School Children of the Experience of Different Methods of Allocation within Secondary Courses*. M.A. Thesis. London. 1954.

15. BRETT, G. S., *A History of Psychology*. Lond.: Allen & Unwin. 1921.

MILLER, G. A., *Psychology: The Science of Mental Life*. Lond.: Hutchinson. 1964.

16. JAMES, W., *The Principles of Psychology*. N.Y.: Holt. 1890.

TITCHENER, E. B., *Outline of Psychology*. N.Y.: Macmillan. 1896.

STOUT, G. F., *Manual of Psychology*. Lond.: Univ. Tutorial Press. 1898.

17. FULLERTON, G. S., *Psychol. Rev.* **4**. 1–26. 1897.

MCDOUGALL, W., *An Introduction to Social Psychology*. Lond.: Methuen. 1908.

18. SHAND, A. F., *Mind*. N.S. V. 203–26. 1896.

HOWIE, D., *Australasian J Psychol. Phil.* **XXIII**. 35–56. 1945.

19. ISAACS, S., *Intellectual Growth in Young Children*. Routledge. 1930.

For accessible summaries of earlier criticism of Piaget see:

MCCARTHY, D., in BARKER, R. G., *et al.*, *Child Behavior and Development*. N.Y.: McGraw-Hill. 1943.

DEUTSCHE, J. M., in BARKER, R. G., *et al.*, ibid.

HUANG, I., *et al.*, *J. Genet. Psychol.* **66**. 63–8. 1945.

HUANG, I., and LEE, H. W., ibid. **66**. 69–74. 1945.

BOUCHET, H., *L'Individualisation de l'Enseignement*. Paris: Presses Universitaries. 1948.

See also: OAKES, M. E., *Children's Explanations of Natural Phenomena*. N.Y.: Teachers' College. 1947.

OAKES, M. E., *Science Educ.* **29**. 137–42. 190–201. 1945.

LANGEVELD, M. J., *Verkenning en Verdieping*. Purmerend: J. Muusses. 1950.

BUNT, L. N. H., *The Development of the Ideas of Number and Quantity according to Piaget*. Groningen: Wolters. 1951.

SYSWERDA, A. H., *De Ruimtevoorstelling Bij Het Kind Volgens J. Piaget en B. Inhelder*. Groningen: Wolters. 1955.

RUSSELL, D. H., *Children's Thinking*. Boston: Ginn. 1956.

LANGEVELD, M. J., *Studien zur Anthropologie des Kindes*. Tubingen: Max Niemeyer. 1956.

VAN HIELE, P. M., *Development and Learning Process*. Groningen: J. B. Wolters. 1959.

KING, W. H., *Brit. J. Educ. Psychol.* **XXXI**. 1–20. 1961.

LOVELL, K., *Brit. J. Psychol.* 52. 143–53. 1961.

WALLACE, J. G., *Concept Growth and the Education of the Child*. Lond.: Nat. Found. Educ. Res. 1965.

ALMY, M., *Young Children's Thinking*. N.Y.: Teachers College. 1966.

FLEMING, C. M., *J. Christian Educ.* **8**. 3. 123–7. 1965.

FLEMING, C. M., *Learning for Living*. **6**. 1. 10–13. 1966.

20. PARTRIDGE, E. D., *Social Psychology of Adolescence*. N.Y.: Prentice-Hall. 1939.

21. MEEK, L. H., loc. cit. [11].

JONES, H. E., *Development in Adolescence*. N.Y.: Appleton. 1943.

FLEMING, C. M., *Adolescence*. loc. cit. [6].

22. SHERIF, M., *The Psychology of Social Norms*. N.Y.: Harper. 1936.

CANTRIL, H., *The Psychology of Social Movements*. N.Y.: John Wiley. 1941.

SHERIF, M., and CANTRIL, H., *The Psychology of Ego-Involvement*. N.Y.: John Wiley. 1947.

23. SNYGG, D., *Psychol. Rev.* **48**. 404–24. 1941.

SNYGG, D., and COMBS, A. W., *Individual Behavior*. N.Y.: Harper. 1949.

24. With this may be compared the sociological discussion of role as well as status. See: SARGENT, S. S. (ed.), *Culture and Personality*. N.Y.: Viking Fund Inc. 1949.

SARGENT, S. S., in ROHRER, J. H., and SHERIF, M., *Social Psychology at the Cross-roads*. 355–70. N.Y.: Harper. 1951.

PATERSON, T. T., *Morale in War and Work*. Lond.: Max Parrish. 1955.

25. ALLPORT, G. W., *Personality*. N.Y.: Henry Holt. 1937.

ALLPORT, G. W., *Psychol. Rev.* **50**. 451–78. 1943.

ALLPORT, G. W., ibid. **52**. 117–32. 1945.

ALLPORT, G. W., *Occup. Psychol.* **XX**. 2. 54–62. 1946.

MURPHY, G., *Personality*. N.Y.: Harper. 1947.

ASCH, S. E., *Social Psychology*. N.Y.: Prentice-Hall. 1952.

LINE, W., *Brit. J. Med. Psychol.* **XXIV**. 1. 42–8. 1951.

See also: SOROKIN, P. A. (ed.), *Explorations in Altruistic Love and Behavior*. Boston: Beacon Press. 1950.

STOUFFER, S. A., *et al.*, *The American Soldier*. Princeton: Princeton U.P. 1949.

26. ADLER, A., *Understanding Human Nature*. Lond.: Allen & Unwin. 1930.

ADLER, A., *Social Interest*. Lond.: Faber. 1938.

WICKMAN, E. K., *Children's Behavior and Teachers' Attitudes*. N.Y.: Commonwealth Fund. 1928.

FROMM, ERICH, *The Fear of Freedom*. Lond.: Kegan Paul. 1942.

PLANT, J. S., *Personality and the Cultural Pattern*. N.Y.: Commonwealth Fund. 1937.

MOODIE, W., *The Doctor and the Difficult Child*. N.Y.: Commonwealth Fund. 1940.

27. MUNROE, R. L., *Teaching the Individual*. N.Y.: Columbia U.P. 1942.

MURPHY, L. B., and LADD, H., *Emotional Factors in Learning*. N.Y.: Columbia. U.P. 1944.

See also: FLEMING, C. M., *Adolescence*. loc. cit. [6]. 1948, 1955 and 1963.

28. ROGERS, C. R., *Counseling and Psychotherapy*. Boston: Houghton Mifflin. 1942.

ROGERS, C. R., *Client-Centered Therapy*. Boston: Houghton Mifflin. 1951.

ROGERS, C. R., *Amer. Psychologist*. **2**. 9. 358–68. 1947.

ROGERS, C. R., *J. Cons. Psychol.* **II**. 82–94. 1949.

AXLINE, V. M., *Play Therapy*. Boston: Houghton Mifflin. 1947.

See also: AXLINE, V. M., *J. Consult. Psychol.* **XII**. 4. 209–16. 1948.

AXLINE, V. M., ibid. **XIV**. 1. 53–63. 1950.

29. RAIMY, V. C., ibid. **XII.** 3. 153–63. 1948.

LIPKIN, S., ibid. **XII.** 3. 137–46. 1948.

ROGERS, C. R., KELL, B. L., and MCNEIL, H., ibid. **XII.** 3. 175–86. 1948.

ROGERS, C. R. (ed.), ibid. **XIII.** 3. 1949.

RASKIN, N. J., ibid. **XIII.** 3. 206–20. 1949.

SEEMAN, J., ibid. **XIII.** 3. 157–68. 1949.

BERGMAN, D. V., ibid. **XV.** 3. 216–24. 1951.

GALLAGHER, J. J., ibid. **XVII.** 6. 443–6. 1953.

ROGERS, C. R., *International J. Soc. Psychiat.* **I.** 1. 31–41. 1955.

30. STAINES, J. W., *Brit. J. Educ. Psychol.* **XXVIII.** II. 97–111. 1958.

31. ADAMS, R. H., *An Investigation into Backwardness in Arithmetic in the Junior School.* M.A. Thesis. London. 1939.

BILLS, R. E., *J. Consult. Psychol.* **XIV.** 140–9. 1950.

32. VERNON, P. E., *Personality Assessment:* Lond.: Methuen. 1964.

33. ALLPORT, G. W., and ALLPORT, F. H., *The A–S Reaction Study.* Boston: Houghton Mifflin. 1928.

THURSTONE, L. L., and THURSTONE, T. G., *Personality Schedule.* Chicago: Univ. of Chicago Press. 1929.

BERNREUTER, R. G., *The Personality Inventory.* Stanford: U.P. 1935.

ALLPORT, G. W., and VERNON, P. E., *A Study of Values.* Boston: Houghton Mifflin. 1931.

DAVIS, J. A. M., loc. cit. [12].

FORRESTER, J. F., in RICHARDSON, J. E., *et al.*, loc. cit. [7].

34. FREUD, A., *The Ego and the Mechanisms of Defence.* Lond.: Hogarth Press. 1937.

35. KLEIN, M., and RIVIÈRE, J., *Love, Hate and Reparation.* Lond.: Hogarth Press. 1937.

36. BURLINGHAM, D., and FREUD, A., *Infants without Families.* Lond.: Allen & Unwin. 1944.

37. KRIS, E., *Psychoanal. Quarterly.* **XX.** 15–30. 1951.

See also: EZRIEL, H., *Brit. J. Med. Psychol.* **XXIV.** 1. 30–4. 1951.

38. COOLEY, C. H., *Human Nature and the Social Order.* N.Y.: Scribner's. 1902.

JERSILD, A. T., *Child Psychology.* 4th ed. N.Y.: Prentice-Hall. 1954.

BILLS, R., VANCE, E. L., and MCLEAN, O. S., *J. Consult. Psychol.* **XV.** 257–61. 1951.

CALVIN, A. D., and HOLTZMAN, W. H., ibid. **XVII.** 1. 39–44. 1953.

HANLON, T. E., *et al.*, ibid. **XVIII.** 3. 215–18. 1954.

OMWAKE, K. T., ibid. **XVIII.** 6. 443–6. 1954.

39. ALLPORT, G. W., *Amer. J. Orthopsychiat.* **XXIII.** 1. 107–19. 1953.

See also: ESTES, S. G., *J. Consult. Psychol.* **XII.** 2. 76–81. 1948.

ZILBOORG, G., in EISSLER, K. R. (ed.), *Searchlights on Delinquency.* Lond.: Imago Publishing Co. 329–73. 1949.

RASKIN, N. J., *J. Consult. Psychol.* **XII.** 2. 92–110. 1948.

COMBS, A. W., ibid. **XII.** 4. 197–208. 1948.

BEIER, E. G., ibid. **XV.** 5. 359–62. 1951.

LIPKIN, S., *Psychol. Monographs.* **68.** 1. 1954.

ESTAPHANOS, S. R., *A Critical and Operational Study of Interests and Preferences in Organised Groups*. Lond.: Ph.D. Thesis. 1967.

40. ROGERS, C. R., KELL, B. L., and MCNEIL, H., *J. Consult. Psychol.* **XII.** 3, 175–86. 1948.

    ROGERS, C. R., *International J. Soc. Psychiat.* **I.** 1. 31–41. 1955.

    EZRIEL, H., *Brit. J. Med. Psychol.* **XXIII.** 1. 59–74. 1950.

41. EZRIEL, H., *Brit. J. Med. Psychol.* **XXIV.** 1. 30–4. 1951.

    SUTHERLAND, J. D., in MACE, C. A., and VERNON, P. E. (ed.), *Current Trends in British Psychology*. Lond.: Methuen. 1953.

    GUNTRIP, H., *Brit. J. Med. Psychol.* **XXIX.** 2. 82–99. 1956.

42. For a survey of opinion on this see: Neo-Freudian or Neo-Adlerian? *Amer. Psychologist.* **8.** 4. 165. 1953.

43. POTTER, M., *J. Consult. Psychol.* **XIV.** 4. 250–5. 1950.

44. HAVIGHURST, R. J., and TABA, H., *Adolescent Character and Personality*. N.Y.: John Wiley. 1949.

45. JERSILD, A. T., *In Search of Self*. N.Y.: Teachers' College, Columbia Univ. 1952.

    See also: STRANG, R., *J. Educ. Psychol.* **XLVI.** 7. 423–32. 1955.

46. STAINES, J. W., loc. cit. [30].

    See also a series of theses from London University: KHATOON, U., M.A., 1958. BARAHENI, M. V., M.A., 1959. EMMETT, R. G., M.A., 1959. CHETCUTI, F., M.A., 1960. LAHIRY, M., M.A., 1960. MISTRY, Z. D., M.A., 1960.

    KAY, M. M., *Educ. Res.* **II.** 2. 149–51. 1960.

    WILKIE, J. S., *A Study of the Self-Picture and its Conçomitants in the Period from the last year of the Primary School to the first year of the Secondary School*. Lond.: Ph.D. Thesis. 1962.

    PHILLIPS, A. S., *Brit. J. Educ. Psychol.* **XXXIII.** 2. 154–61. 1963.

    EMMETT, R. G., *An Experimental Study of Personal Interaction in the Classroom with Special Reference to the Self-Concept of Student Teachers*. Ph.D. Thesis. Lond. 1964.

    BRAY, D. H., *J. Exper. Educ.* **31.** 1. 93–7. 1964.

    FLEMING, C. M., in SANDVEN, J., *The Role of Educ. Res. in Social Education*. 107–114. Oslo: Universitetsforlaget. 1963.

    WALLACE, J. G., *Concept Growth and the Education of the Child*. Lond.: Nat. Found. Educ. Res. in England and Wales. 1965.

    MUSGROVE, F., *The Family, Education and Society*. Lond.: Routledge 1966.

47. DEL SOLAR, C., *Parents and Teachers View the Child*. N.Y.: Teacher's College, Columbia Univ. 1949.

    See also: GRIFFITHS, W., *Behavior Difficulties of Children as perceived and judged by Parents, Teachers and Children Themselves*. Minneapolis. Univ. of Minnesota Press. 1952.

PART III

THE TEACHER AS A
PROMOTER OF LEARNING

V

EXPERIMENTS IN LEARNING:
ASSOCIATION THEORY
AND FIELD-THEORY

THIS CHAPTER, LIKE Chapter II above, fulfils some of the functions of a glossary. Its essence is given in Tables III and IV which offer in abbreviated form a reminder of the origins of certain phrases whose echoes still linger in market-place and home.[1] Many of these are in the tradition of the experimental studies of the 1890s; and they owe much to the philosophy and the natural sciences of the nineteenth century. Each is linked with a name now famous in the history of psychology; but the meaning of each can best be understood in the light of an awareness of the date and the order of its appearing.

An emphasis on repetition and exercise (Thorndike and Ebbinghaus) along with successful trials (Thorndike). A concern with conditioning (Pavlov and Watson).[2 Modern variants of association by stimulus and response (Guthrie, Carr, and Robinson).[3] A differentiation between responses spontaneously emitted and responses elicited (Skinner).[4] The popularizing of the notion of Gestalt (Wertheimer)[5] and the development of systematic analysis (Clark Hull).[6] Accounts of all of these are readily available and require no detailed summarizing here. They have, by their nature, little relevance to the behaviour of human beings in schools or homes or workshops. Many of them, like earlier work in the field of motivation, were individualistic in approach. They were concerned with changes in the reactions of single human subjects or animals under conditions which had deliberately been simplified and controlled; and even in the more open-ended situations of the type described by Hobhouse and by Köhler [7] there was an underestimation of the significance of social influences upon the act of learning.

TABLE III

Learning Theories Based on Experimentation with Individual Subjects in Narrowly Controlled Situations

Exponents	Notable Dates	Typical Material	Representative Phrases
Ebbinghaus	1885	Memorizing of non-sense syllables and verses from Don Juan	Retention as a function of repetition, time, and order of presentation. Oscillation of mental receptivity
Thorndike	1898 1913	Hungry cat in puzzle box. Food outside	Stimulus and response. Trial and error. Laws of readiness, exercise, and effect. Satisfiers and annoyers. Multiple responses. Associative shifting. Response by analogy
Pavlov	1899	Dogs in solitude. Measured saliva-tion in presence of food and a second stimulus	Conditioned stimulus and response. Reinforcement. Extinction. Generaliza-tion. Conditioned discrimination
Watson	1914 1924	Mazes Problem-boxes	Frequency and recency of stimulation. Covert stimulus-response sequences
Thorndike	1932 1935	Chicken in a maze. Blindfold drawing. Learning new words	After-effects of reward. Belongingness. Polarity. The spread of effect
Guthrie	1921 1942	Cat escaping from cage. Photographs Analysis of move-ments	Simultaneity of cue and response. Conditioning by contiguity. Repetitious-ness of behaviour. Move-ment-produced stimuli. Associative inhibition

TABLE III (*continued*)

Exponents	Notable Dates	Typical Material	Representative Phrases
Carr	1925	Memorizing with guidance	Activities adaptive. Responses ideational as well as motor. Motivating stimuli
Robinson	1932	Nonsense syllables	Instigating items. Instigable processes and activities. Law of assimilation. Retro-active inhibition
McGeoch	1942	Rote learning. Problem solving Motor skills, etc.	Dimensions of learning – types of situations and nature of processes
Skinner	1938	White rat in darkened sound-resisting box. Food ejected on pressing a lever	Elicited or respondent responses. Emitted or operant responses. Instrumental or operant conditioning (response instrumental in producing reinforcement)
	1953	Pigeon, neck stretching	Differential reinforcement strengthens probability of recurrence. Stimulus generalization
Hull	1940 1952	Animal's conditioned responses. Maze-learning. Human rote learning	Postulates and theorems. Primary (physical) drives or needs. Primary reinforcement. Secondary (associated) drives. Secondary reinforcement. Intervening pure stimulus act. Fractional anticipatory goal reaction. Habit-family hierarchies. Goal-gradients (gradients in the effect of reward or reinforcement). Oscillation of inhibition. A molar approach

Much has been made of differences in viewpoint between field-theorists and association-theorists; and each distinction in terminology is admittedly indicative of a special contribution to the fuller understanding of the learning process.

An emphasis on a perceptual pattern already organized in its relationships;
a concern with native structure;
attention to the immediate apprehension of wholes and the later differentiation of parts;
admission of the relevance of personal experience (awareness or idea-like processes).

These were the challenges offered by Gestalt psychologists and field-theorists to the four comparable viewpoints of the association-theorists:

A concern with external stimulation through sensory receptors;
interest in the influence of environment;
attention to the summation of elements and their later combining into wholes;
exclusive concentration on observable responses, reactions or movements.

All such comparisons are both relevant and illuminating; and to them may be added a sensitivity in field-theory to the significance of the present and the possible occurrence of sudden restructuring of the field – of insight (A-ha!) or hind-sight (Is that what it meant?) – in contrast to the associationists' emphasis on the continuity and chain-like character of habit-building and their preference for machine-like models with stresses and resistances.

Changes in data language and the design of experiments

These distinctions are, however, of less significance than the later changes which followed upon modifications in the language used in formulating problems and in the type of experiment designed for their solution. The associationists had to do with the observation of one animal or one human being put into a controlled situation and faced with a problem (an object) of a narrowly specified kind. The field-theorists worked with situations in which interest centred on the collocation of more than one object – sounds, colours or forms in juxtaposition, lines or drawings in movement and equipment which

TABLE IV

Learning Theories Based on Experimentation with Individual Subjects in more Open-ended Situations with a variety of Objects

Exponents	Notable Dates	Typical Material	Representative Phrases
Ehrenfels	1890	Transposed melodies	Gestalt-qualität (form-quality)
Katz	1911	Colours in various combinations	Gestalt or pattern
Bühler	1913	Lines as parts of rectangular figures	Perceptual wholes and constituent parts
Rubin	1915	White figures on black backgrounds	Figure and ground. Figural after-effect
Wertheimer	1912	Visual illusions of movement	Phi-movement (appearance of pure movement). Perceptual pattern, organized in its relationships
Köhler	1913 to 1917	Chimpanzees. Movable boxes and poles. Bananas	Insight. Closure. Prägnanz (tendency to move towards significance)
	1947		Electrical cortical fields. Isomorphic (identical in form) with perceptual configurations
Tolman	1932 1938	Rats Maze-learning	Independent variable (stimulus or observable antecedent condition). Dependent variable (response or observable consequent behaviour). Intervening variable. Purposive behaviour. Choice-point. Sign-significate relations. Cognitive maps

might be used in a variety of fashions in problem-solving experiments. To a greater degree than was realized in the height of their controversy both were the heirs of the psycho-physical tradition of the nineteenth century. They worked with animals at different levels in the phylogenetic scale, and they used material of differing degrees of complexity; but they accepted a clearly defined distinction between stimulation and response, environment and organism, and they both encountered the dilemma consequent on the employment of such terms. The Gestalt psychologists rejected the basic distinction between sensation and perception (and the bundling together of sensations in the forming of a percept); but they continued to search for a means of co-ordinating perceptual experiences to variables in the physical world. They would probably have agreed that one sees with one's eyes and one hears with one's ears although they were prepared to maintain the immediacy of appearances which were in known contradiction to the external stimulations impinging on the organs of sense (in 'illusions' of pattern, transpositions of melodies or blendings of colour). Through their recognition of the significance of objects in relation to other objects the Gestalt psychologists did, however, prepare the way for a concern with animals or human beings in relation to other animals or human beings; and this was followed by experimental studies of learning whose content was more directly relevant to the teaching situation.

REFERENCES

1. For surveys of the field of learning theory see:
   MCCONNELL, T. R., *et al.*, *The Psychology of Learning*. The 41st *Yearbook* of the National Society for the Study of Education. Part II. 1942.
   MCGEOCH, J. A., *The Psychology of Human Learning*. N.Y.: Longmans. 1942.
   HILGARD, E. R., *Theories of Learning*. N.Y.: Appleton. 1948.
   POFFENBERGER, A. T., *Modern Learning Theory. A Critical Analysis of Five Examples*. N.Y.: Appleton. 1954.
   THORPE, L. P., and SCHMULLER, A. M., *Contemporary Theories of Learning with Applications to Education and Psychology*. N.Y.: Ronald Press. 1954.
   A more general discussion of similar material is given in SMITH, F. V., *The Explanation of Human Behaviour*. Lond.: Constable. 1960.
2. For extracts from many of these early studies see:
   DENNIS, W., *Readings in the History of Psychology*. N.Y.: Appleton. 1948.

For extracts from more recent work see also: STOLUROW, L. M., *Readings in Learning*. N.Y.: Prentice-Hall. 1953.

3. SMITH, S., and GUTHRIE, E. R., *General Psychology in Terms of Behavior*. N.Y.: Appleton. 1921.

HILGARD, E. R., loc. cit. [1]. Ch. 3. 1948.

MUELLER, C. G., JR., and SCHOENFELD, W. N., in POFFENBERGER, A. T., loc. cit. [1].

GUTHRIE, E. R., in MCCONNELL, T. R., loc. cit. [1]. 1942.

ROBINSON, E. S., *Association Theory Today*. N.Y.: Century Co. 1932.

See also: HILGARD, E. R., loc. cit. [1]. Ch. 6. 1948.

4. SKINNER, B. F., *The Behavior of Organisms*. N.Y.: Appleton. 1938.

HILGARD, E. R., loc. cit. [1]. Ch. 5. 1948.

VERPLANCK, W. S., in POFFENBERGER, A. T., loc. cit. [1]. 1954.

SKINNER, B. F., *Science and Human Behavior*. N.Y.: Macmillan. 1953.

5. On Gestalt Psychology see: HARTMANN, G. W., *Gestalt Psychology*. N.Y.: Ronald Press. 1935.

KATZ, D., *Gestalt Psychology*. London: Methuen. 1951.

KOFFKA, K., *The Growth of the Mind*. Lond.: Kegan Paul. 1924.

KÖHLER, W., *Gestalt Psychology*. N.Y.: Liveright. 1929.

KOFFKA, K., *Principles of Gestalt Psychology*. N.Y.: Harcourt Brace. 1935.

HILGARD, E. R., loc. cit. [1]. Ch. 7. 1948.

See also: ALLPORT, F. H., *Theories of Perception and the Concept of Structure*. N.Y.: John Wiley. Ch. 5. 1955.

WERTHEIMER, M., Experimentelle Studien über das sehen von Bewegung. *Zeitschrift für Psychol. und Physiol. der Sinnesorgane*. **61**. 161–265. 1912.

6. HULL, C. L., et al., *Mathematico – Deductive Theory of Rote Learning*. Yale U.P. 1940.

HULL, C. L., *Principles of Behavior*. N.Y.: Appleton. 1943.

HULL, C. L., *Essentials of Behavior*. Yale U.P. 1951.

HULL, C. L., *A Behavior System*. Yale U.P. 1952.

HULL, C. L., in MCCONNELL, T. R., loc. cit. [1]. 1942.

HULL, C. L., *Psychol. Rev.* **45**. 3. 271–99. 1938.

MILLER, N. E., and DOLLARD, J., *Social Learning and Imitation*. Yale U.P. 1941.

See also: HILGARD, E. R., loc. cit. [1]. Ch. 4.

KOCH, S., in POFFENBERGER, A. T., loc. cit. [1].

SMITH, F. V., loc. cit. [1]. 1960.

SMITH, F. V., *Brit. J. Psychol.* XLV. 2. 77–81. 1954.

See also: LOGAN, F. A., et al., *Behavior Theory and Social Science*. Yale U.P. 1955.

7. HOBHOUSE, L. T., *Mind in Evolution*. Lond.: Macmillan. 1901.

See also: YERKES, R. M., The Mind of a Gorilla. *Genet. Psychol. Monogr.* **2**. 1. 1–193. 1927.

Cf. KÖHLER, W., *Gestalt Psychology*. N.Y.: Liveright. 1947.

ZANGWILL, O. L., *An Introduction to Modern Psychology*. Lond.: Methuen. 1950.

GIBSON, J. J., in DENNIS, W., *Current Trends in Psychological Theory*. 85–110. Univ. of Pittsburgh Press. 1951.

See also: ADRIAN, E. D., *The Physical Background of Perception*. Oxford: Clarendon Press. 1947.

LASHLEY, K. S., CHOW, K. L., and SEMMES, J., *Psychol. Rev.* **58**. 2. 123–36. 1951.

WILKIE, J. S., *The Science of Mind and Brain*. Lond.: Hutchinson. 1953.

CALVIN, A. D., *et al.*, *Psychology*. N.Y.: Prentice Hall. 1961.

HILL, W. F., *Learning*. N.Y.: Chandler. 1963. Lond.: Methuen. 1964.

VI

EXPERIMENTS IN LEARNING: SOCIAL AND PERSONAL DETERMINANTS

OBSERVATION OF SINGLE subjects in relation to narrowly defined situations had led easily to a variety of interpretations which laid stress on the individual, the structural, and contemporary.[1] When, however, attention was directed to the total setting, and the same subject was seen to react differently to identical stimuli on different occasions, or to respond in fashions which varied according to the presence or absence of an experimenter or of other subjects, and when, further, different subjects responded in differing fashions to the same stimuli on the same occasion, fuller attention had to be given to the possible greater complexity of the 'variable' intervening between situation and response.[2] Attention was thus deflected from 'mere' repetition in the learning of skills; and experimental support was lent to the probability that cognitive structuring as well as sensory stimulation may play a part in learning and that personal relationships as well as primary reinforcement through a physical satisfaction may make some contribution to the fixing of a habit.

Illustrative of this in the field of animal studies were certain of the later experiments reported by Katz into the effect of differences in quantity, in size, and in arrangement of supplies on the feeding of hens of known states of lack of food. Their reactions were largely independent of their physical condition. The amount eaten increased with the amount of grain presented. It increased also with an increase in the size of the grain used and it varied with the number and the social relationships (pecking order, etc.) between groups of hens allowed to feed together.[3]

Social influences upon learning

Comparable conclusions of a not dissimilar kind were meanwhile being formulated within the tradition of the work with human subjects which had been fostered by Ebbinghaus at the turn of the century.

As early as 1913, Bartlett had noted, at the opening of Myers' experimental psychology laboratory in Cambridge, that visitors showed a wide variety of reactions to the exhibits.[4] From this observation he was led to an interest in differences in the field of memory – not only in their relation to differences in time, in frequency and distribution of repetition, and in character of exercise (to use the classification offered by Ebbinghaus), but in the nature of memory traces and their dependence upon understanding. Successive reproductions of schematized drawings passed from one person to another and stories told over long intervals showed tendencies towards organizing the reproductions into drawings much nearer to real life than the originals and towards the structuring of a story into a neater and more compactly significant whole. Bartlett interpreted this by saying that human cognitive reactions can be understood as efforts after meaning, and that learning is a meaningful form of response to a situation which is recognized as leading forward to the solution of a problem. This is very far from the version offered at about the same date by Robinson, Hull, Guthrie or even by Thorndike in his later writings. It has, however, a recognizable affinity to Tolman's contemporary suggestions that the organism is not so much pushed or pulled along by external or internal stimuli as following a path to a goal, looking for signs, building a 'cognitive map' or learning 'sign-significate' relations.[5]

It is to be noted that Tolman's choice of phrases is not based on a revival of introspection as a preferred procedure. Tolman was still writing from the standpoint of a behaviourist, and offered interpretations of behaviour as an outsider might observe it. He was, however, concerned with what has been called its 'molar' aspects -- not the 'molecular' processes (neural, muscular or glandular) which may underlie it; and his references to the possibility of some sort of cognitive structure have been contributory (along with the Gestalt emphasis on the interdependence of the total perceptual structure) to a series of fresh interpretations which are now transforming the theory not only of learning but of the whole field of human mental development.

Awareness of such issues was not a discovery of the 1930s; and their discussion is a re-formulation of much which had been implicit in earlier philosophic references to apperceptive masses, preperception, expectancies, predisposing sets and intentions, the psychology of testimony, and the like.[6] As revived in recent studies of perception this is, however, approached not by way of argument in nineteenth-century fashion but with the support of the techniques evolved in quantitative studies in the fields of psycho-physics and psycho-physiology. It carries with it also a deliberate collocation of the words learning and perception which is in itself indicative of a change in viewpoint (see Table V). Philosophers down the ages attached a clear distinctiveness to the experiences they described as sensation, perception, cognition, affection or emotion, conation or will; and they attributed independent action to mental faculties such as memory, imagination, attention, judgement or reasoning. One of the consequences of the lively experimental investigations of workers trained in the methods of the physical sciences has been the recognition that such distinctions are not only difficult to draw but may not be of primary importance.[7]

Perception, learning, and purposive action

The progression to this position may be traced over the same decades which saw changes from an individualistic to a social interpretation in the case of the intentions, urges or purposes to which appeal was made in the attempt to describe the reasons for human beings behaving as they do (see Chapters II to IV above).

It may be considered from a variety of angles. In those aspects of human functioning which are traditionally described as motivated there was a movement from an over-emphasis on reason through a concern with biological structure to an awareness of patterns in group membership and a sensitivity to the perpetual interweaving of concepts involving self-reference. In the field of learning a quite comparable shifting of emphasis came through patient experimenting and the recording of observations on animal or human subjects in learning situations of differing levels of complexity. Closely interwoven with this was the transition in the study of sensation and perception from a concentration on the physical or the physiological to a recognition of the part played by the perceiver and the relation of perception to the total or molar aspects of human behaving. When these steps had been taken it became necessary to make mention of perception in discussion of motivation. It became reasonable to search for dynamics or purposiveness in the learning process; and it

TABLE V

Learning Theories Based on Experimentation with Subjects in Relation to other Subjects

Exponents	Notable Dates	Typical Material	Representative Phrases
Katz	1930	Hens. Piles of grain	Configurational and social influences
Bartlett	1932	Reproduction stories, etc.	Schemata. Active organization of past reactions and past experience
Lewin	1926 1942	Changes in human habits	Field forces. Action-wholes. Topological psychology. Barriers. Life-space. Level of aspiration
Sherif	1935 1947	Point of light in a dark room	Autokinesis. Frame of reference. Ego-involvement
	1951 1956	Groups of boys in camp	Properties of group-situations. Group-pressures on perception
Murphy	1942 1947 1956	Human subjects	Personal values as directive factors. Perception bi-polar
Bruner and Postman	1947 1951	Human subjects	Central directive states. Value-resonance of perception. Defensiveness and vigilance of organism. Confirming or infirming of hypotheses. Stimulus information. Sensory-input. Expectancy-patterns

became impossible to describe perceiving without reference both to variations in its content and to its social and personal or attitudinal determinants. The various psychological processes – memory, imagination, perception, learning, motivation, and the like – thus came to be seen as specialized ways in which an organism reacts to a situation. For this reason (as will have been noted in earlier chapters) their relevance to the work of a teacher cannot usefully be considered in isolation but reference has to be made to researches in each field at those points at which their contribution seems most significant.[8]

Perception as an approach to social psychology

Mention has for this reason already been made of Sherif's demonstration that perception (as for example of a stationary point of light in a dark room) is the product of the internal and the external factors operating at any given time – the totality of these constituting the frame of reference whose nature determines both action and judgement. From this it was a short step to the later realization of the extent to which perception is patterned by both personal experience and socio-cultural pressures; and on this in turn it has proved possible to build what has been described as a phenomenological approach to social psychology.[9] This in less technical terms means the relevance of things as they appear (as actually apprehended by the behaving individuals) not only to the growth of personality but to the development of harmony or tensions within groups and between groups. Perceptual activity or the self-involvement of attitudes is thus seen to be relevant to the whole issue of social maturing in wholesome or unwholesome fashions.

Illustrative of this are certain experimental and observational studies of groups by Sherif in the field of social psychology and by Redl and Bettelheim in the attempted treatment of delinquency. The latter, though formulated in terms which carry echoes of psychoanalytic stereotypes, are important as detailed recordings of the sayings and doings of small groups of difficult boys brought together in Pioneer Camps and a residential home.[10] The boys were cared for by adults who were prepared not only to work towards rehabilitation but to collect and to publish data on things done and words spoken. The task of the counsellors was that of remodelling the perceptual frame of children whose earlier experiences had taught them to hate and to defy. Their records show sensitivity both to the processes by which deliberate group-pressures determine the activities of group-members and to the more subtle means by which the contagion of an unpremeditated individual action can transform a situation which to an outsider may appear to contain no element of risk. On this account they make an important contribution to the general study of social behaviour and their findings have an affinity with those of writers such as Rogers, Axline, Snygg, and Combs whose intellectual predilections are more clearly phenomenological and self-referent. Someone threw a plate. The refectory became a shambles. Under happier circumstances it might have been: Someone threw a pillow. The dormitory had a pillow fight. The issue in either case is quite relevant to the topic of the fostering of desired patterns of living.

In contrast to this 'operational' research (with its record of a human situation in progress) is the controlled 'action' research of Sherif in which he applied experimental design to the study of a change deliberately produced in matched groups of boys in a holiday camp in an area from which extraneous influences had been excluded.[11] The eighteen days of camping were divided into two periods in the first of which informal intercourse permitted the development of friendships and the emergence of norms of behaviour and observable standards and values in the ordinary interactions within and between groups. Sociometric tests were then applied; and the boys were separated into two teams comparable in other respects but so arranged as to split the budding friendships through putting each into the team which contained the fewest of his choices. The study of spontaneously harmonious groups was thus deliberately supplemented by the observation of the development of new groups and the study of mounting tension between these new groups. The tension was increased not only by the personal removal of boys from the first groups to which they had come to relate themselves (their 'reference' groups) but by the encouragement of competition between the two new 'membership' groups which had been deliberately formed. The camping quarters were separated. The teams used provocative names (the Bull Dogs and the Red Devils). They were invited to excel in games and other camping activities and the losing group was further frustrated by destructive behaviour which seemed to have originated with the more successful team. The tension so produced culminated in a fight so fierce that the councillors had to intervene and the concluding days of camp were spent in an effort to restore some cordiality to inter-group relations.

The actions of the boys appeared to depend not only on their observed individual characteristics prior to camping but also on the structural properties of the group situation and their place in it. This in turn while more or less stable was not immutable. It varied with

82

changes in the experiences and the purposes of the groups and these were influenced by the discriminative judgements or perceptual distortions which followed on the delineation of an 'in-group' from an 'out-group' with a self-justifying and self-righteous attitude towards the in-group and a graduation from friendly to hostile attitude towards members of the out-group. The boys' ways of viewing their companions altered when the deliberately structured membership group became in turn the 'reference' group whose efforts and goals were then accepted as intensely personal. This took place at first in fun, with many backward glances at the friendships formed in the early days of more informal intercourse. It later crystallized into generalized attitudes which were quite tenaciously held. 'He's a Bull Dog. He's a cheat.' 'He's a Red Devil. What else could you expect?' The boys' judgements were not merely cognitive in character (with their meaning and organization immediately given in perception). Still less were they based on the binding together of sensation-like elements in the fashion assumed in traditional psychophysics. Their perceptions were modified along with their conscious motives, feelings, thoughts, and reasoning concomitantly with changes in the meaning of the total group-situation and this in spite of the fact that there could still be noted some reflection of the individual differences in social reactions which had been discernible both to adult leaders and to fellow-members in the days when a measure of friendliness was being established among boys previously unacquainted.[12]

This record is an important complement to Lewin's earlier studies on the patterning of attitudes towards leaders and towards work through changes in the quality of the social climate produced by adults whose attitudes were dictatorial, *laissez faire* or democratic. It carries further the investigations initiated by Moreno into the emotional interactions of group members with one another and, like Redl's observational records of delinquent defences, it is contributory to an understanding of what is perhaps the key to the whole educational situation – the problem as to how social stimulation leads to acquired attitudes (or enduring dispositions) and how these in turn affect behaviour.

Other studies of perception

More directly related to the laboratory study of perception were certain other developments inspired by the work of Murphy in New

York; and in the early 1940s a series of articles published by him and his associates staked the claim of perception to an ever widening territory. These reports were concerned less with the effects of group pressures upon perceptual judgements than with the complementary inquiry into the influence of personal values upon perception itself. Earlier work in this field had formed part of the first experimental studies in social psychology (see Chapter III above), and the step was a relatively easy one from awareness of the attitudinal control of suggestion and learning [13] to concern with topics such as those indicated in the following titles:[14]

Levine, R., Chein, J., and Murphy, G., The Relation of the Intensity of a Need to the Amount of Perceptual Distortion. (*J. Psychol.* **13.** 283–293. 1942.) Proshansky, H., and Murphy, G., The Effects of Reward and Punishment on Perception. (*J. Psychol.* **13.** 295–305. 1942.) Levine, J. M., and Murphy, G., The Learning and Forgetting of Controversial Material. (*J. Abn. Soc. Psychol.* **38.** 507–17. 1943.) Shafer, R., and Murphy, G., The Role of Autism* in a Visual Figure-Ground Relationship. (*J. Exper. Psychol.* **32.** 335–43. 1943.) Postman, L., and Murphy, G., The Factor of Attitude in Associative Memory. (*J. Exper. Psychol.* **33.** 228–38. 1943.)

Learning is bi-polar. It is related both to the instruction given (its quality and its situational setting or social climate) and to the abilities and social attitudes of the learners. Social attitudes are a function of the self-referent fashions in which individuals perceive their world; and perception in turn is bi-polar and affected not only by the external situation but by internal states.[15] There is thus a place for values in a world of facts – to paraphrase a phrase in which Köhler allowed for the study of what has since been called social perception – and in perceiving, as in learning, the human being is not passive but active, bringing all past images, memories, emotions, and needs as non-sensory or directive factors to the organization of a present cognitive or perceptive structure.[16]

Inspired by such findings there was in the late 1940s and early 1950s a significant series of symposia on the relevance of perceptual organization to the theory and the problems of social psychology (Krech and Crutchfield, 1948), to current trends in social psychology

* The organizing of cognitive processes in the direction of satisfaction of the self.

(Dennis, 1948), to personality (Bruner and Krech, 1949, and Blake and Ramsey, 1951) and (perhaps most significant of all) to social psychology at the crossroads between the blind alleys of either an individualistic or a socio-cultural approach (Rohrer and Sherif, 1951).

Out of these there has come an even clearer formulation of the effect upon learning of this 'central directive state'. This is exemplified by the work of Bruner and Postman on the selectivity of perception (the compromise between what is given and what the organism is set to see or wishes to see or wishes to avoid), the value resonance of perception (the organism's preference for objects, words or concepts which it values or needs), and the organism's defensiveness or vigilance (by which it appears to exclude from perception that which is irrelevant or dangerous to prevailing motives, attitudes, and personality structure).[17]

In sequel to this (and also in further continuation of the work of Bartlett, Tolman, and Woodworth) there has followed from Postman an expansion of the phrase 'trial and check' which was used by Woodworth in a short discussion of the re-enforcement of perception.[18] The whole process of perceiving, thinking, and recalling is one of 'confirming' or 'infirming' a hypothesis or expectancy set up by the organism and tried and checked, accepted or rejected, until the hypothesis and incoming 'stimulus information' match sufficiently to give rise to a stable perceptual organization.

This is a somewhat unusual use of the word hypothesis; but it serves as an effective means of describing the complexity of the process of perceiving – its dependence on both internal and external factors – while admitting that much of this process is so far in the background that it is largely unconscious. The perceptual 'hypothesis' includes all predispositions or sets with which the organism approaches a new situation. Its strength is related to the frequency of past confirmations of a congruent type, to the number of somewhat similar alternative expectancies, to its motivational support or instrumental significance (through, any associated emotional disturbance, positive or negative), to the cognitive support given by similar predispositions, and to the social support afforded by group expectancies of similar pattern. The stronger the hypothesis the greater the likelihood of its arousal and the less the stimulus-information which is required to confirm it. The weaker it is the larger the amount of appropriate stimulation which will be required. The strength of the hypothesis can be assessed through observation of the relative amount of stimulation needed in respect of an observable response; and its content can be inferred from the ways in which it selects, organizes, and transforms the 'information' or 'sensory input' which reaches it from the environment. When, through successive trial-and-check, the hypothesis is confirmed, the 'answer' which fits into the expectancy pattern comes into consciousness as a percept, an image, an idea or a memory.

All this is illustrated by Postman and Bruner from experimental work with human subjects – much of it in the field of visual perception – under controlled conditions in a laboratory. With very short exposures of somewhat ambiguous stimuli it can be shown that the more frequently a geometric form has been seen in the past the more readily is it recognized; the smaller the number of types of stimulus expected the more rapid the recognition of the sort of word or letter specified; the higher the probability of either reward or punishment the clearer the perception of relevant stimuli (cooking utensils, food, valued objects or occasions for fear). The more firmly an expectancy or hypothesis is rooted in a larger cognitive organization the more unlikely is it to weaken or 'infirm' and the stronger the rejection of incongruent 'stimulus-information' (letters in reverse, playing cards, and objects in unusual colours). The smaller the amount of appropriate stimulus-information the greater the sensitivity of an observer to the judgements of others is likely to be (movement of spot of light in a dark room).

Many of these experiments are quite similar in design to earlier studies in the field of perception. Their importance lies not in the novelty of their details but in the emphasis they put on the congruence of motivational, cognitive, and social support with what had been observed earlier as to frequency of presentation, length of exposure, intensity, and the like. Through their direction of attention to perception in its total setting these twentieth-century psychologists are not only narrowing the gap between theories of perception and theories of learning but they are establishing the relevance of such laboratory researches both to the building up of attitudes and to the modification of relationships within groups and between groups – in classrooms and in the wider field of inter-racial contacts.[19]

Physiological psychologists

In protest against such attention to the cognitive and selective aspects of perception there comes at intervals a reminder of what has been called the structural, autochthonous or formal side of this perceptual process – in contrast to its more functional, instrumental, and goal-directed aspects.

Notable among such challenges has been the re-emphasis put by workers like Hebb on the physiological basis of the perceptual process.[20] Hebb's arguments were illustrated from studies with chimpanzees reared in darkness and congenitally blind human beings seeing for the first time after the removal of cataract. Perception of the identity of an object appeared to come slowly after what seemed to be a process of attentiveness to separate details (in the differentiation, for example, of a square from a triangle, the naming of an object presented in a new setting or the recognition of a word). To account for this Hebb postulated the organization of sensory and motor neural elements associated in cortical cell-assemblies and reverberating circuits through which the momentary perception of a whole alternated with the perception of its parts (phase sequence); and with illustrations from the observation of children, he endeavoured to elucidate the physiological concomitants of these piecemeal and summative fixations which he believed to be contributory to the recognition of objects or forms. This was in its way a contribution to the thesis that perception is learned; but its stress was on the repetitive excitation of particular cells in the central nervous system in contradistinction to the more molar aspects of expectancy, set, schema or hypothesis.

In slightly different fashion Werner laid stress on the motor as well as the sensory components of perception – the state of the organism, changes of muscular tension and movement, and the part played by physical individual differences.[21] His experiments involved electrical stimulation, tilting of the body, and other modifications of equilibrium (such as the sounding of a tone in one of the ears), and, using these as illustrative of the effects of extraneous stimulation (in addition to sensory processes involving receptors in the cortex), he spoke of sensory-tonic events involving the entire organism.

Further awareness of the complex processes involved in the act of perceiving was indicated in Freeman's concern with what he described as backlash excitations from reflex motor adjustments interacting in the brain with exteroceptive stimulations.[22]

In the description of much of this work there has in recent years appeared a new series of metaphors taken from modern automata with their mechanisms for intercommunication, regulation, and control. This language of 'cybernetics' supplements earlier references to resistances and synapses, electro-chemical fields, and isomorphic correspondences; and its reverberating circuits, scanning mechanisms, input, output, storage, feedbacks, and relays add a certain crispness and modernity to the language in which those of physiological inclination now describe the variables intervening between the initiation and the completion of the activities of learning or perceiving.[23] To no greater extent than is the case of their simpler predecessors of sensori-motor arcs or cortical configurations has it however proved possible to uncover neurological analogues to the complex processes to which they point. The fuller elucidation of these remains still a problem to tantalize the neuro-physiologists of the future.

Summary

The inner and the outer, the central and the peripheral – muscle-tension patterns, tonic states, the residue of past reactions, expect-ancies, sets, and hypotheses as well a present sensory excitations – all these require some consideration in an interpretation of perceptual or learning processes; and in the fashions indicated they are receiving attention in the researches of contemporary workers. Mention has been made of only a small number out of many thousands of studies; but enough has been said to illustrate the extent of the development from the relatively simple designs offered by the physiological psychologists of the nineteenth century to the highly elaborated hypothetical constructs of the learning theorists of the twentieth. Physiological processes and the quality of the organism undoubtedly have a part to play; but more directly relevant to the work of a teacher is the continuing experimentation in the tradition of Lewin and Sherif which, with its emphasis on the complexities of group relation-ships, now links perceptual or phenomenological studies with the use in group situations of techniques comparable to those postulated by Moreno in his therapies of psychodrama or sociodrama.[24]

In some situations physical states or physiological conditions seem direct determinants of action.

On some occasions cognitive processes appear to predominate.

In other circumstances needs, motives, fantasies or imagination may seem most significant.

At other times social pressures, role behaving, or expectations of role behaviour may offer the most useful key.

All are contributory in turn to the understanding of that human being who is both individual and social, a person and a member of a group, observable from the outside and comprehensible and consistent from within – mysteriously complicated and always a product of those interdependent survivals of the past remembered or forgotten no one of which can be isolated from the other elements in the dynamic system that constitutes the human organism.[25]

REFERENCES

1. HILGARD, E. R., *Theories of Learning*. N.Y.: Appleton. 1948.
   HILL, W. F., *Learning*. N.Y.: Chandler. 1963. Lond.: Methuen. 1964.
2. MACLEOD, R. B., in ROHRER, J. H., and SHERIF, M., *Social Psychology at the Cross-roads*. 215–41. N.Y.: Harper. 1951.
   VERPLANCK, W. S., *Psychol. Rev.* 62. 2. 139–44. 1955.
3. KATZ, D., *Gestalt Psychology*. N.Y.: Ronald Press. 1950. Methuen. 1951.
   See also: HARLOW, H. F., in ROHRER, J. H., and SHERIF, M., loc. cit. [2]. 121–41. 1951.
4. BARTLETT, F. C., *Remembering*. Cambridge: C.U.P. 1932. With this may be compared: VERNON, M. D., *A Further Study of Visual Perception*. Cambridge: C.U.P. 1952.
5. TOLMAN, E. C., *Purposive Behavior in Animals and Men*. N.Y.: Century Co. 1932.
   HILGARD, E. R., loc. cit. [1]. Ch. 10. 1948.
   SMITH, F. V., *The Explanation of Human Behaviour*. Lond.: Constable. 1951 and 1960.
   MacCORQUODALE, K., and MEEHL, P. E., in POFFENBERGER, A. T., *Modern Learning Theory*. N.Y.: Appleton. 1954.
   See also: TOLMAN, E. C., *Proc. Fourteenth Internat. Congress Psychol.* 1955.
6. See BRETT, G. S., *A History of Psychology*. Lond.: Allen & Unwin. 1921.
   BRUNER, J. S., and POSTMAN, L., in DENNIS, W., *Current Trends in Social Psychology*. Pittsburgh: Univ. of Pittsburgh Press. 71–118. 1948.
7. Cf. MACLEOD, R. B., loc. cit. [2]. 1951.
   KLEINMUTZ, B. (ed.), *Concepts and the Structure of Memory*. N.Y.: John Wiley. 1967.
8. For fuller discussion of details see: ALLPORT, F. H., *Theories of Perception and the Concept of Structure*. N.Y.: John Wiley. 1955.
9. Progressive stages in this interpretation may be noted in:
   SHERIF, M., *Arch. Psychol.* 187. 1935.
   SHERIF, M., *The Psychology of Social Norms*. N.Y.: Harper. 1936.
   SHERIF, M., and CANTRIL, H., *The Psychology of Ego-Involvements*. N.Y.: John Wiley. 1947.

SHERIF, M., *An Outline of Social Psychology*. N.Y.: Harper. 1948. (Revised ed. 1956.)

SHERIF, M., in ROHRER, J. H., and SHERIF, M., loc. cit. [2]. 388–424. 1951.

SHERIF, M., and SHERIF, C. W., *Groups in Harmony and Tension*. N.Y.: Harper. 1953.

10. REDL, F., *Human Relations*. I. 3. 307–13. 1948.

REDL, F., in EISSLER, K. R. (ed.), *Searchlights on Delinquency*. Lond.: Imago Publishing Co. 315–28. 1949.

POLANSKY, N., LIPPITT, R., and REDL, F., *Human Relations*. III. 4. 319–48. 1950.

BETTELHEIM, B., *Love is Not Enough*. Glencoe: Free Press. 1950.

REDL, F., and WINEMAN, D., *Children Who Hate*. Glencoe: Free Press. 1951.

REDL, F., and WINEMAN, D., *Controls from Within*. Glencoe: Free Press. 1952.

11. SHERIF, M., loc. cit. [9]. 1951.

SHERIF, M., and SHERIF, C. W., loc. cit. [9]. 1953.

12. Cf. HALLOWELL, A. I., in ROHRER, J. H., and SHERIF, M., loc. cit. [2]. 164–95. 1951.

And MACLEOD, R. B., loc. cit. [2]. 1951.

13. MURPHY, G., MURPHY, L. B., and NEWCOMB, T. M., *Experimental Social Psychology*. N.Y.: Harper. 1937.

KRECH, D., and CRUTCHFIELD, R. S., *Theory and Problems of Social Psychology*. N.Y.: McGraw-Hill. 1948.

14. To these may be added two earlier articles:
SANFORD, R. N., *J. Psychol.* 2. 129–36. 1936. 3. 145–59. 1937.

See also: MURPHY, G., *Personality*. N.Y.: Harper. 1947.

MURPHY, G., *Psychol. Rev.* 63. 1. 1–15. 1956.

15. See also: HILGARD, E. R., in BLAKE, R. R., and RAMSEY, G. V., *Perception: An Approach to Personality*. 95–120. N.Y.: Ronald Press. 1951.

BRUNER, J. S., and POSTMAN, L., in DENNIS, W., loc. cit. [6]. 1948.

16. KÖHLER, W., *The Place of Value in a World of Facts*. N.Y.: Liveright. 1938.

POSTMAN, L., in ROHRER, J. H., and SHERIF, M., loc. cit. [2]. 242–72. 1951.

HALLOWELL, A. I., loc. cit. [12]. 1951.

17. Representative discussions are to be found in:
BRUNER, J. S., and POSTMAN, L., loc. cit. [6]. 1948.

BRUNER, J. S., and GOODMAN, C. D., *J. Abn. Soc. Psychol.* 42. 33–44. 1947.

BRUNER, J. S., and POSTMAN, L., *J. Personality*. XVI. 69–77. 1947.

POSTMAN, L., *Psychol. Bull.* 44. 6. 489–563. 1947.

BRUNER, J. S., and POSTMAN, L., *J. Soc. Psychol.* 27. 203–8. 1948.

POSTMAN, L., BRUNER, J. S., and MCGINNIES, E., *J. Abn. Soc. Psychol.* 43. 2. 142–54. 1948.

COMBS, A. W., *J. Abn. Soc. Psychol.* 44. 1. 29–35. 1949.

BRUNER, J. S., and POSTMAN, L., *J. Personality.* **XVIII.** 14–31. 1949.

KLEIN, G. S., and SCHLESINGER, H., ibid. **XVIII.** 32–47. 1949.

MCLELLAND, D. C., and LIBERMAN, A. M., ibid. **XVIII.** 236–51. 1949.

BRUNER, J. S., and KRECH, D., *Perception and Personality.* Durham: Duke U.P. 1949.

See also: NEWCOMB, T. M., and HARTLEY, E. L., *Readings in Social Psychology.* N.Y.: Henry Holt. Ch. II. 1947.

HOLLANDER, E. P., *Principles and Methods of Social Psychology.* N.Y.: Oxford Univ. Press. 1967.

18. WOODWORTH, R. S., *Amer. J. Psychol.* **60.** 119–24. 1947.

See also: TOLMAN, E. C., and BRUNSWIK, E., *Psychol. Rev.* **XLII.** 43–77. 1935.

POSTMAN, L., in ROHRER, J. H., and SHERIF, M., loc. cit. [2]. 1951.

BRUNER, J. S., in BLAKE, R. R., and RAMSEY, G. V., loc. cit. [15]. 121–47. 1951.

See also: ALLPORT, F. H., loc. cit. [8]. 1955.

19. Cf. SHERIF, M., in ROHRER, J. H., and SHERIF, M., loc. cit. [2]. 1951.

20. HEBB, D. O., *The Organization of Behavior.* N.Y.: John Wiley. 1949.

21. WERNER, H., and WAPNER, S., *J. Personality.* **XVIII.** 88–107. 1949.

WERNER, H., and WAPNER, S., *Psychol. Rev.* **59.** 4. 324–38. 1952.

See also: ALLPORT, F. H., loc. cit. [8]. Ch. 8.

22. FREEMAN, G. L., *Physiological Psychology.* N.Y.: Van Nostrand. 1948.

FREEMAN, G. L., *The Energetics of Human Behavior.* N.Y.: Cornell U.P. 1948.

See also: ALLPORT, F. H., loc. cit. [8]. Ch. 9.

23. WIENER, N., *Cybernetics, or Control and Communication in the Animal and the Machine.* N.Y.: John Wiley. 1948.

For an accessible discussion of cybernetics see: ALLPORT, F. H., loc. cit. [8]. Ch. 18.

See also: YOUNG, J. Z., *A Model of the Brain.* Lond.: Oxford Univ. Press. 1964.

24. LEWIN, K., in NEWCOMB, T. M., and HARTLEY, E. L., loc. cit. [17]. 1947.

BENNE, K. D., and MUNTYAN, B., *Human Relations in Curriculum Change.* N.Y.: Dryden Press. 1951.

MORENO, J. L., *Who Shall Survive?* N.Y.: Beacon House. 1953.

MORENO, J. L., *Sociometry and the Science of Man.* N.Y.: Beacon House. 1956.

25. For relevant material see also: HARTLEY, E. L., e¹ al., *Outside Readings in Psychology.* N.Y.: Crowell. 1950.

MACRAE, D. G., *Brit. J. Sociol.* **II.** 2. 135–49. 1951.

FARRELL, B. A. (ed.), *Experimental Psychology.* Oxford: Blackwell. 1955.

See also: MOWRER, O. H., *Learning Theory and the Symbolic Processes.* N.Y.: John Wiley. 1960.

BROADBENT, D. E., *Behaviour.* Lond.: Eyre & Spottiswoode. 1961.

FRANDSEN, A. N., *Educational Psychology: The Principles of Learning in Teaching.* N.Y.: McGraw-Hill. 1961.

FOSS, B. M., (ed.) *New Horizons in Psychology.* Lond.: Penguin. 1966.

PART IV

THE TEACHER AS
AN OBSERVER OF GROWTH

VII

GROWTH AND DEVELOPMENT

IN CONSIDERING HUMAN growth a distinction can usefully be drawn between the word growth and the word development. The word growth is applicable to those changes in bodily proportions and physiological functioning which occur in an established sequence from the moment of conception to that of death.[1] From embryo to foetus, from foetus to infant, from infant to child, from child to adult, the relative as well as the absolute size of bones, muscles, and nerves may be observed to change in fashions which seem characteristic of all human animals as they grow. Accompanying this growth there are, however, even on physical levels, variations of strength and vitality. In the description of these the word development is more aptly used. They may differ with differences in the environment to which the organism is exposed. They may vary with the sustenance it receives; and they may be accompanied by other developmental changes in intellectual, emotional, social or spiritual reactions.

This distinction between growth and development is in some respects similar to that between the changes attributed to maturation and those associated with educative influence; and like that distinction it is difficult to maintain in the description of actual human beings. Its survival serves, however, as a reminder of the complexity of human functioning. Many controversies in the field of human development are simplified if it is recognized that the same issues underlie them as those which provoked lively argument in the discussion of human motivation or human learning. Original endowment as against present relationships. Nature in contrast to nurture. The individual alone as opposed to the individual as a member of a group. In each of the three fields the persistence of these dichotomies may be detected; and in each of the three fields a progression may also be discerned from theorizing as to human beings in general (with reliance upon recollection and introspection as the chief instruments of knowledge) to observation of individuals (with the recording of isolated segments of behaviour), and from that to a study of individuals in their groups (with fuller awareness of the inter-relationships of differing aspects of their maturing).

Traditional beliefs

Early views as to human development are implicit in the Socratic dialogues and in the writings of the Sophists. They are more clearly expressed by Aristotle; and they reach full formulation in the educational writings of the sixteenth and seventeenth centuries. By the time of Comenius, for example, their characteristic outline can quite clearly be discerned. 'The child is other than the man.' Growth is thought of as taking place in distinct stages with definite physical and mental signs; and the transition from one stage to the next is believed to occur at a predetermined date. Variations in wording are found. Rousseau adds details not offered by Shakespeare; and Stanley Hall and Sigmund Freud (who in many respects stand at the point of departure from philosophic fiction) offer a more romantically elaborated picture than that conceived by their predecessors.

By the late nineteenth century it had become necessary to take account of psychological research; and analyses of answers to questionnaires issued by workers in the Child Study Movement in Germany, in the United States, and in Great Britain were combined with the results of more exact measurements obtained by psychologists and physiologists in schools and laboratories.[2] These child-study questionnaires were, however, in many cases addressed to adults; and they offered recollections of early childhood and youth attested by men and women who were already familiar with popular conceptions of the gulf set between childhood and adult status. Material of this kind was supplemented by Freud's clinical interpretations of the attitudes of his patients; and findings from both sources lent support to the traditional expectation of sudden changes at specified periods, and the traditional belief in a clear demarcation between stages such as infancy, childhood, and adolescence. Alongside this were set measurements of average height, weight or speed of reaction obtained from groups of children of different ages; and interpretation of these also suggested both regularity and steadiness of group development and clearly defined differences between pupils of one age and pupils of another.

Educational conclusions

The most influential exposition of the educational conclusions to be drawn from such findings was that offered by Stanley Hall in two volumes on Adolescence published in 1904;[3] but it is worthy of note that his viewpoint was in its essentials the same as that accepted by the English inspectorate four decades earlier in their formulation of educational "standards" for pupils of successive ages.

The average (height, weight, performance) of pupils aged ten is so and so.

The average for age eleven or age twelve is something other.

Pupils aged ten are therefore different from pupils aged eleven or twelve.

Distinct educational expectations are to be entertained of them.

They are to be approached by different educational techniques.

They are therefore best educated apart.

Something like these were the steps taken in educational reasoning on many issues. On grounds such as these Stanley Hall and his imitators deprecated the introduction of coeducation; and on grounds like these his writings lent support to educational systems based on the two notions of constancy or consistency of relative status and of a new birth occurring at about the age of entrance to the teens.

It is hardly necessary to remind the reader that the viability of these concepts has been great. They are superficially confirmed by observation of differences in the behaviour of individual members in groups which have been classified in general terms such as age, sex or racial origin. It is quite likely that an individual in one group will differ from an individual in another group; and it is only too easy to generalize to the effect that all members of both groups differ in precisely those fashions. This has happened especially when attention was directed to the reactions of children considered one by one [4] and when comparisons have been made between groups of different children at successive ages.[5] Its characteristic conclusions appear in most discussions of adolescence published prior to 1939;[6] and its more general educational consequences are to be seen in the proposals for educational segregation or grouping by ability adumbrated in the second decade, tried out extensively in the third decade, and abandoned in many places in the fourth and fifth decades.[7] Its findings have been used in support of proposals for rigid and early streaming into homogeneous groups in countries which for reasons of economy find it convenient to offer different types of educational provision in different buildings. Conclusions of similar nature have been drawn for younger children from cross-sectional studies conceived along the lines of those reported by Piaget or by Gesell.[8]

In terms of the evidence available in these early researches in the field of mental measurement, such educational decisions were not so unreasonable as they now appear. A corrective to the facile generalizations which they encouraged came through improvements in statistical methods, fuller recognition of the range of individual differences at every age, and through long-term studies of the same children over many years in place of the measurement of different groups of children at a variety of ages.

Recognition of individual differences

Recognition of individual differences was not a new concept. Lip-service to it can be traced in the writing of philosophers through many ages; but until the late nineteenth century it seems to have had little effect as a determinant of educational policy. The teachers of England took something like thirty years to overturn the proposal that they should be paid by results; and the assumption that inequalities of response by children were the consequence. of the inefficiency of their teachers appeared in learned journals as late as 1915. The findings of early psychometric surveys of arithmetic and of reading were by then beginning to popularize the conclusion that within any age-range there can be discerned not only a character-istic average performance but a wide range of deviations which seem to persist irrespective of educational or nutritional endea-vour [9]

From this the step might readily have been taken to full recogni-tion of the implications of the 'range of individual differences' at any age in its corollary of the 'overlapping of ability' from one age-group to another. In the 1920s and 1930s this seems rarely to have been realized; and interest in the developing science of psychometrics – the measurement of individual differences – deflected teachers' atten-tion from contemporary modifications of classroom methods [10] to a concern with classification into homogeneous groups and the search for a suitable age-placement for the beginnings of reading, arithmetic, spelling, and the like.[11] The assumption behind these inquiries was still that of discontinuity in development; but through them evidence became available from which a fresh interpretation was soon to win support.

Analysis of test results with consideration of differences in means and standard deviations and the calculation of correlations (degrees of correspondence) between different sets of measurements* led very naturally to statistical descriptions of the extent of change from one occasion to another; and a new approach became possible both to the question of the distinctiveness and permanence of differences (constancy of relative status), and of discreteness of stages as between one age and another (discontinuity of development). Both these issues are definitive in the understanding of human growth and development.

Variability of relative status

Discussion of constancy of relative status came first. This is not so often expected in relation to physical development as it has tended to be in the fields of general intelligence, of scholastic attainment or of moral character (see Chapter XII below). It is, for example, not commonly supposed that a child who is puny or sickly at an early age will inevitably mature into an adult of less than average physical health. It is, however, still sometimes taken for granted that a pupil who shows little effective intelligence or a low degree of initial skill in the basic school subjects will later prove incapable of academic success as an adolescent or an adult; and it is also often assumed that a delinquent pupil should be expelled from a 'good' school.

The issue is one of great importance both for parents and for teachers; and it provoked lively debate from the earliest days of individual and group testing. From an educational point of view it is linked with the problem of the relative influence of inheritance and environment; and the most accessible collections of evidence are not unnaturally to be found in two yearbooks of the National Society for the Study of Education – the twenty-seventh which carried the title: 'Nature and Nurture: Their Influence upon Intelligence'; and 'Nature and Nurture: Their Influence upon Achievement' – and the thirty-ninth which was concerned with 'Intelligence: Its Nature and Nurture.'[12] (The controversy was at its keenest in the 1920s. By the late 1930s attention had turned to a study of the processes through

---

* The standard deviation is obtained by finding the deviation of each score from the mean, squaring each deviation and calculating the square root of the average value of such squared deviations.

which modifications are wrought in the effective use of intelligence, and in the conquest of skills and the learning of acceptable behaviour of various sorts.)

Relevant figures were collected first from comparisons of the average performance of groups taking intelligence tests on different occasions. At a later date consideration was given to the degree of significance of such differences (with admission of the importance of the standard deviation) and by 1933 it was possible to summarize the results of some hundreds of studies of inter-correlations between initial and subsequent testings to the effect that both for individual tests and for group tests the figures show correlations of the order of + 0·81 for periods under twenty-four months falling to + 0·61 for intervals of between five to twelve years.[13]

Discussion of the topic is not easy. Evidence has to be interpreted in the light of differences in the size of the sample, the age of the pupils, the nature of the test, the conditions of its administration, the statistics in which its results are expressed, and the length of the interval between test and re-test. It seems reasonable, however, to conclude that the findings do not indicate a high degree of consistency in relative status. They are quite in line with what is now seen to be the meaning of an early statement by Terman: 'speaking roughly, fifty per cent of the I.Q.s found at a later test may be expected to fall within the range between six points up and four points down . . .'[14] and they confirm Burt's early comments on the intrinsic irregularity of mental growth.[15] In spite of such figures, however, Terman's accompanying suggestion that the intelligence quotient is sufficiently constant to make it 'a practical and serviceable basis for mental classification' has passed into popular speech without the qualifying clauses of its first formulation; and 'constancy of I.Q.' has been used in certain administrative circles as an argument in favour of a differentiation of educational treatment and an exaggerated streaming in terms of early ability for which, after the 1920s, there was not support in psychometric researches.

Long-term studies

Meanwhile by the late 1930s there was coming to fruition a series of long-term studies initiated in the 1920s by the annual testing of groups of children in various places in the United States. Of these the most notable are the Harvard Growth Study reported by Dearborn and Rothney in book form in 1941, the Chicago inquiry organized by Freeman and Flory, the Californian Adolescent Study sponsored by Jones, Tryon, and Meek, the Berkeley Growth Study supervised by Bayley, and the Berkeley Guidance Study under the charge of Honzik, Macfarlane, and Allen.[16]

Published results from the first two and the last of these served to show (by careful analysis of changes in relative status) that, both in physique and in intelligence, variability of rate and direction of development is so characteristic of human beings that prediction of subsequent status is hazardous at any age.

While children as they grow tend to remain within the same grouping if the entire population is divided into three or four large groups, their relative position within such groups may vary so much from year to year that forecasting of the future educational performance or the ultimate physical proportions of any one of them is uncertain. Some improve their position in height, in weight or in skill in comparison with their contemporaries. Some fall behind their peers. Others maintain a constant ratio to the performance characteristic of their age. The exact reasons for these fluctuations or this consistency are not fully understood. There are, however, grounds for the belief that they are linked with the total pattern of a child's life in its physical setting and also in its relationship to parents, teachers, and friends (see Chapters III and IV above); and studies in the United States, in England, in Toronto and in Australia are turning in this direction. It seems possible, also, to asseverate with conviction (as a result of the work of the last few decades) that development is variable and disharmonious in the experience of each human being. At the same time, and from the same long-term studies, it has to be remarked that it is continuous and gradual to an extent of which earlier workers seem to have been unaware.

Continuity of development

There is not in the experience of an individual any crossing of a rubicon nor any rebirth in a physiological or an intellectual sense either at the entrance to infancy, to childhood, to adult life or to old age. Changes come little by little and from day to day. Accession and recession arrive by imperceptible gradations. Social recognition of entrance into childhood, adolescence or old age may come suddenly on a specific occasion. The processes of development are themselves unnoticed and no discreteness of stage is in actual life discernible.

On grounds such as these, recent findings in the field of genetic

E

psychology lend no support to proposals for educational segregation whether in homes, in churches or in schools. Separation into groups may be a matter of convenience. It has now to be effected with awareness that within any group, however selected, there will be wide variations of stage in different aspects of human functioning, that there will be marked overlapping from one group to another, and that within any group changes will occur at different rates in different members but with gentle continuity in all.

For reasons of this sort it is now recognized that many inquiries into the vocabulary, the arithmetical concepts, the interests, leisure pursuits, play activities, wishes, hopes or fears of groups of children of specified ages are of local interest only. They are true of particular children, with certain experiences in a certain setting; but from them generalizations cannot be drawn as to the attributes of 'the infant', 'the child', 'the adolescent', 'the delinquent', or 'the backward child'. Still less would it be regarded as reasonable to make pronouncements as to 'the adult' or 'the pensioner' in terms of a composite of traits or attitudes conceived of as applicable to all. Consideration of growth and development is thus both more difficult and more personal than it was in the days when it was assumed that children lived in an unknown world into which no adult could enter and that there was a vast gulf fixed between the mental, social, emotional, and spiritual functioning of groups demarcated in terms of different ages.

This does not mean that no inquiries should be undertaken into abilities and disabilities, skills and interests, preferences (as to books, broadcasts, television, films, and the like), range of vocabulary, manual dexterity, hobbies or athletic prowess.[17] To the understanding of any group all knowledge of this kind is contributory. It does mean, however, that, to a greater extent than was true last century, teachers and parents can recognize the wide range of variation which at any age lies within the limits of the normal – in the sense that it is observable in large numbers of children. Some children aged three can talk with confidence, can appreciate adult jokes and can accept responsibility. Others show personal diffidence and intellectual indifference. 'This three-year-old is quite unlike that three-year-old.' Some children aged eleven have extensive reading interests combined with social immaturity. Others are socially well developed, academically well advanced but physically retarded. 'This eleven-year-old is not at all like that eleven-year-old.' Of none of these can it be said with assurance from observation on any one date that their disharmonies in development are pathological in kind. Of any of them it may be true that transformations are in progress which will be followed by rapid changes in the pattern of their functioning. Recent insight into the irregularities of growth and the variabilities of development thus encourages in the educator a certain wise passiveness reminiscent of those husbandmen who wait upon the slow processes of natural growth in field or garden – while continuing to offer, by every means in their power, all known provision for optimum development in any direction desired.

Much of the evidence contributory to this interpretation of personal and social development has come from the long-term inquiries described as the Californian Adolescent Study and the Berkeley Growth and Guidance Studies.[18] Similar findings are becoming available from studies initiated by the Scottish Council for Research in Education and the University of London and from inquiries sponsored by the Nuffield Trust and the National Foundation for Educational Research in England and Wales.[19]

Experimental confirmation
Similar conclusions have been reached in much smaller researches such as, for example, those organized by Oakes and others in challenge to Piaget's acceptance of the Greek stereotypes of discrete stages and discrete types of mental functioning.[20] Piaget's work was an extension of the individual questioning in structured interviews initiated by Binet to illustrate the range of individual differences and the overlapping between one age-group and another. Piaget, by contrast, recorded answers to questions and solutions to scientific problems without indication of the intellectual level of his subjects and with no extensive use of the same questions at a variety of ages.[21] His critics, after experimentation with human beings in differing circumstances and at ages ranging from early childhood to adult status, have confirmed the continuity of human mental development and have shown that all varieties of response are obtainable at all ages – from kindergarten pupils to adult men and women. The nature of the reaction to a question or to an experiment is a matter of personal idiosyncracy and personal experience rather than of age. Animistic thinking, illogical interpretations, egoistic self-reference are, like 'symbolic and preoperational thought, concrete operations and formal operations', in certain circumstances,

characteristic of all; and a wider or a narrower vocabulary is an acquisition to which all prior experience is contributory.[22]

This is not dissimilar in its implications to one of the most important findings of the whole testing movement – its asseveration of the extent of the similarity of the thinking processes of mentally older and younger subjects. Prior to the development of standardized tests it was possible to believe that the functioning of a genius and a dullard was in all respects dissimilar. Now it has to be admitted that the differences are more quantitative than qualitative.[23] As was pointed out in an early study, the reasoning processes of children by the age of seven differ from those of adults not so much in form as in the content of the experience in terms of which it is possible for them to function.[24]

Social determinants of change

Quite relevant evidence comes also from studies of the differences in reaction which can be observed in pupils of similar age who have experienced different methods of treatment. Early inquiries into the effects of individualized methods directed attention to the measurement of skills in the basic subjects and showed that improvements were associated with certain sorts of diagnostic and remedial treatment.[25] Later studies such as those of Gardner in England and the Eight-Year Study in the United States, were able to demonstrate personal and social as well as intellectual differences between pupils in experimental groups and pupils in matched control groups under more traditional forms of teaching.[26] Comparable findings came from experiments with leadership of differing kinds[27] and from researches into the effects of differing classroom climates even at so early an age as that of the first few weeks at school.[28] Khan, for example, attempting to discover the type of quantitative thinking characteristic of little children, reached the conclusion that the differences between groups receiving different sorts of teaching were so clear that it had to be recognized that differences in arithmetical response were not a function merely of age or of an inevitable mental maturing but were the reactions of pupils with certain prior experiences to teaching of a certain sort.

Development is continuous.
The rate of development is variable.
The direction of development is uncertain.

Mental as well as physical development is related to the type of experience encountered.

Findings such as these have since the early 1940s presented to the teacher as an observer of growth an educational challenge in the light of which much earlier thinking on educational organization is now recognized as without support. They have also made it more possible to understand the variety of human reactions in differing cultural patterns and the still more suprising variations of behaviour in family circles with differing traditions within what is superficially the same culture.[29]

Physical growth

In no sense does this mean a denial of the reality of a personal progression through the physical experiences characteristic of growth.[30] Each human being travels the road from birth to death. Many survive from infancy through maturity to old age and in the process certain quite marked changes in physical structure occur. Their study belongs properly to the sister sciences of physiology, endocrinology, and biochemistry. From the point of view of psychological evidence all such experiences are, however, subsidiary to the total pattern of a human life; and their significance is not biologically predetermined but is a function of those personal attitudes and social relationships which demonstrably contribute so much to the total life-cycle.

Mental development

In similar fashion it is to be noted that recent findings carry no denial of personal increments in knowledge, in general mental ability or in wisdom.[31] Within the experience of each individual there are changes in range of vocabulary, in interests, in skills, and in attitudes. Understanding comes earlier to some than to others; but understanding comes to none except in terms of gradually widening experiences.[32]

What then can be said from the point of view of the approach of an adult to toddlers, to juniors or to adolescents?

Toddlers

Surprising in their conquest of the beginnings of walking and of talking. Still for the most part the centre of attention – as solitary children just leaving babyhood or as little brothers or sisters in whose enlightenment the older boys and girls find pleasure and pride. The years from two to five for many children cover a period of rapid growth – with changes in bodily proportions as well as bodily size. There is an increase in ability to communicate with others accompanied by an accession of personal independence. In terms of averages it has, for example, been reported that tested vocabulary expands from about twenty words at the age of eighteen months to about two thousand words at the age of five;[33] and the baby who was completely dependent upon others is transformed into an individual who can by active interference make his presence felt in many ways unknown before.

During these same years there is also for most children a change in the social climate of the home. Independence on their part is countered by increasing watchfulness on the part of adults. 'What is that dreadful child doing now?' 'Keep your hands off that.' 'Do not touch it.' 'Sit still.' 'Keep quiet.' Such remarks take the place of an earlier attitude: 'Isn't she wonderful.' 'Isn't he sweet.'[34] For fortunate children there is still the satisfaction of the basic need to be beloved and to be allowed to participate in the activities of an intimate circle. For the less wisely handled the seeds of rebellion and anxiety are sown through the knowledge that they are in the way and of no use to anyone.[35]

Much has been made by writers in the Adlerian tradition of the injurious consequences for an older child of the birth of a younger sibling. Similar experiences of rejection and inadequacy come to all boys and girls as they venture into the outer world of Sunday school, nursery school or groups of children playing in streets or gardens. In these contacts they begin the process of social maturing through which they become both acceptant of themselves and aware of themselves in relation to other people. Trauma of a serious kind is discernible only in those cases in which toddlers are genuinely rejected or despised by those adults (whether parents or guardians) who are of most significance in their lives. For the majority there seems merely a clarifying of the self-picture. 'This is me.' 'These are my friends.' 'This is what we do.' 'I am.' 'I can.' 'I should.'

From accumulated recordings of the actions and sayings of little children it is now known that the concept of the self is reaching clear formulation by the time that their infant speech becomes intelligible to others.[36] Prior to that, childish emotions, fantasies, thoughts, and intentions are so much a matter of inference that their interpretation remains at the level of the personal opinion of the observer. Even from that observational level it is, however, possible to say that human babies are never merely toys, possessions to be exhibited, or animals to be trained.[37] Still less are they 'savages' to be civilized (using the word 'savage' in its nineteenth-century sense of a being who is anti-social, cruel, selfish, and aggressive).[38] From the beginning they are co-partners in the activities of a nursing couple; and later they are contributory members of a human home, modifying the behaviour of others and being influenced in turn by the treatment they receive.

At this point a distinction may usefully be drawn between the word 'social' and the word 'sociable'. All human beings have been so made that they are 'social' in nature. Inescapably they are members of groups – reacting to others and acted upon by others. To a greater or lesser extent, however, they may show delight in the visible presence of others; and differences in the degree to which they are thus 'sociably' inclined can be discerned among groups of toddlers as among groups of older children. In this respect also their relative status varies in response to the reactions of others; and toddlers who show dominance in one setting may show indifference or submissiveness in another.[39]

It is for reasons such as these that it has now to be noted that education is not so much a matter of 'socialization' as a process of acculturalization. It consists not in the transforming of a being who is primarily a-social or anti-social but rather in the introducing of a person who is essentially social to the traditions and the attitudes of a particular social group.

The imputed cruelties of little children, like many of their other misdemeanours, can be seen on closer study to be reactions which are exploratory rather than either 'cruel' or 'wicked'. Toddlers who put the kitten in a pail of water, like toddlers who take possession of the toys of others, are making discoveries which are as real as those of any traveller in an unknown land. Something is being found out as to the properties of kittens and of water. Something is also being added to their knowledge of the human beings in their group. 'No. We don't.' 'Bad. You mustn't.' Words, gestures, and convictions reach the toddlers both from remarks directed to themselves and from all that they hear and see and infer as to the meaning of the complicated and interesting world of which they are every day reaching clearer understanding.

In similar fashion the self-centredness or selfishness of toddlers is easily exaggerated. Their range of vision and their insight are both limited by their experience; and they have an objectivity of attitude which contributes to complete concentration upon an activity in hand. This is, however, very different from behaviour in the description of which the word 'selfishness' can properly be used. In similar fashion it is now·recognized that only by an unwarranted extension of the meaning of the word 'aggressive' can that adjective be applied to behaviour which is active, assertive, eager or questing but carries no hint of rebellion or intentional assault.[40]

A turning away from certain human beings, a deliberate intention to hurt, a definite search for personal gratification to the exclusion of what is desired by others, and a clear invasion of the domain of another can, of course, be found on the part of toddlers as of older human beings. In this again there is wide overlapping as between one age-group and another. What is now admitted to be inadequate is the statement that human babies as a group desire to destroy their seniors or their peers, that they bite because of cannibalistic impulses and destroy because their cruelty and aggressiveness are primary qualities which have to be suppressed in the process of socialization.

Many suppositions of this sort have resulted from generalizations based on the childish recollections of neurotic or psychotic patients. With increasing knowledge of the actual behaviour of children as they grow it is now generally admitted that clear indications of kindliness and co-operativeness are shown by little children if in their first five years they have not been taught to hate through being hated but have remained lovable through being beloved.

An attitude of eager adience (of reaching out to people and to things), some sensitiveness to the intention of others, a lively spirit of inquiry which deepens with the first metaphysical questions as to the nature of the universe – all these serve to account for the joy which many adults find in their contacts with little children; and the years from two to five are those in which the foundations are laid for the friendships between the generations which for many parents more than counterbalance the troubles of child-rearing.[41] Through these friendships there comes to parents an increase in maturity and mental health.[42] Through them also the more fortunate toddlers achieve their clearest insight into the masculine and the feminine role. 'I'm a boy.' 'I'm like father.' 'I'm a girl.' 'I'm like mother.'

Through straightforward answers to direct questions they gain the beginnings of that understanding of the origins of life which is later describable as sex education. For most children this also 'trickles through' with observations and reasonings based upon things seen and heard and with experience of the direct personal suggestion and innuendo which (in different forms in different social circles) reaches even the toddlers as they grow. The thoughts of youth are long, long thoughts; and the games as well as the conversation of little children carry a foreshadowing of later insight into their relationships with one another in this as in other fields of human functioning.[43]

Juniors

Businesslike in their absorption in their own affairs. Competent in their management of body and mind. Contributory in many respects in their role of older brothers and sisters. Children from the time of entrance upon formal schooling are ready to take their places as active sharers in the interests of parents, of teachers, and of older boys and girls. The actual age of transition and the nature of their experience (in day-school or residential institution) varies from one country to another and from one type of home to another; but for most toddlers there comes a change from a state in which the whole attention of some adult is focussed on their actions to a state in which they become members of a group of peers receiving, for many hours of the day, only a portion of the attentiveness of a teacher who values them for their accomplishments rather than for themselves.

The expectations entertained of children inevitably vary in different homes and different schools; but in most parts of the world it is now taken for granted that they will quickly acquire the elements of reading, counting, and writing. Early and efficient conquest of these skills is known to lay the cornerstone of mental health [44], and in those countries where expert tuition is available a beginning is made in their deliberate mastery through a variety of methods soon after attendance at school begins.[45]

In these as in other developmental tasks – of social, emotional, and spiritual maturing – there is, however, wide overlapping between groups of children of different ages and much variability in rate and direction of development. Some five-year-olds can read as well as many seven-year-olds. Some six-year-olds can count as accurately as some nine-year-olds. Some children rejoice in reading. Others delight in counting. A few have met defeat in both. For this reason it is now considered necessary to present each subject step by step in the fashion suggested in the analytic approach of Thorndike and of Skinner. At the same time it is important that teachers should resist the temptation to underestimate the energy and competence of their pupils. This is no easy task. Sensitivity to differences in levels of difficulty tends to an acceptance of rigidity in grading which in many cases has lent support to 'streaming' or segregating pupils according to the ability they happen to show at an early date. This in practice has meant a return to nineteenth-century notions of the gulf set between groups of different ages and differing average achievement. Its ill effects can be seen both in the exclusion of junior school children from participation in adult church services and in the limitations of a school curriculum which in many respects deprives them of opportunities of scientific, artistic or literary explorations in which they could quite happily engage.[46]

In attitudes and speech and habitual occupation juniors reflect the pattern of their homes and, to a lesser extent, of their schools;[47] and the level of competence they reach varies with the nature of the opportunities offered. In physique a few reach adult height; and to some there come the physical changes of an early puberty. Imperceptibly they have passed from babyhood to childhood. With similar gradualness they are preparing for the transition from childhood to adolescence.

Adolescence in general terms may be defined as the period of transition between childhood and adult life. For most boys and girls it includes the experiences of physical growth which precede puberty; but both precocious and delayed genital maturing are more common than is often supposed.

Popular theories have been built up to the effect that the period is one of inevitable emotional ferment and mental turmoil. Psychological changes have been supposed to occur to such an extent as to warrant a modification in the educational treatment of boys and girls. It has been suggested that adolescents are suddenly transformed into beings who are strange, incomprehensible to adults, sulky, moody, unstable, rebellious, insolent, suspicious of parents, and apathetic in the face of the efforts of their teachers. It has been supposed that about the time of the onset of puberty there is in all boys and girls an uprising of passionate anxiety accompanied by a sudden emergence of the ability to reason, an intensified awareness of beauty,'and an abrupt change in attitude towards goodness and truth.

Many of these descriptions are now known to have no solid basis in fact. Research findings derived from long-term studies of boys and girls over the ages of six to eighteen have made it clear that reference to a new birth or a crossing of the rubicon is, in the case of social and emotional as well as in intellectual development, an over-simplification of the experiences of young people as they grow There is a wide range of individual differences; but the fact of passing through adolescence is not a reason for supposing that a youngster must necessarily sow wild oats and cannot help behaving unreasonably or thinking negatively. In the years of adolescence, as at any other time, aberrant behaviour is a symptom which challenges investigation. An awareness of this is probably the greatest recent contribution made by psychologists to the understanding of adolescent development.

Adolescents

Infinite in their variety. Challenging in their promise. Appealing in the tenderness of their youth. Three statements about adolescents merit special attention.

They are more like adults than adults have sometimes been led to suppose.

Their growth is more gradual and continuous than has in certain quarters been suggested.

Their experiences as they grow are more related to their personal circumstances than is often believed.

They are, for example, very like their parents and teachers; and they can best be understood in the light of a firm retention of that fact. They are human beings – not creatures from another planet – and like all other human beings they have certain primary needs. They require to be beloved, appreciated, admired, and accepted by their most intimate group of friends, acquaintances or fellow-workers. They need to be allowed to make a contribution to the welfare of their group. They require to know that that contribution is to some extent a successful one and they need some insight into the purposes for which it is made. They mature in a healthy fashion in so far as these needs are satisfied – just as their parents and teachers do. Through receiving acceptance they become acceptable. Through being given responsibility they become responsible. Through acquiring skills and attaining insight they become useful; and through being useful they develop loyalty.

If they behave in surprising fashions the best advice which can be given to their elders is 'Think'. 'Do not panic.' 'Do not be disgusted.' 'Put yourself in their place.' 'What are they really saying by their actions?' 'Which need are you failing to satisfy?' 'If they behave like creatures from another planet you may be the ones who have sent them there.' 'You may have withheld your friendship – possibly at the age of five.' 'You may have got into the way of thinking that they could not share your experiences.' Too young to read that book. Too young to see that film. Too young to be in the family circle at that discussion.

Young people vary in the contribution they can make. They vary in the age at which they mature and they vary in the interpretation they put upon what they see. They do not, however, vary in their need for participation in the activities of a group; and if they are shut out from one group they will find another which seems to give them what they, at the unconscious level, require.

The years of adolescence are interesting because in those years two sorts of transition occur – the physical passage through puberty from childhood to adult maturity and the social change from non-participation in earning to economic independence.[48] Both of these in some family circles are accompanied by distress and turmoil. Neither of these is so accompanied in all circles. What has happened in the cases where such distress has been avoided? What can be done in those cases where there are problems either of sex or of vocation? Both sorts of problems have a certain organic or physiological basis. Both have an intellectual content; and both have a social meaning. And of these the greatest in significance is probably the social meaning.

Human beings differ in their inheritance. All human beings, however, have all human capacities (in greater or lesser amount); and all human beings seek insight into the meaning of their lives. (They may or may not have the vocabulary in which to express this quest in a fashion understandable by others.) No human beings are merely animal or merely impelled by their biological structure. All are pre-eminently social – affected by their membership of groups – and in consequence educability is probably their most characteristically human attribute.

The sexual behaviour of young people and their economic behaving are the product of what they have seen and are seeing – in the present as well as in the remote past. Both vary with the picture the adolescents have built up of their elders – of what 'they' do and of whether they wish to be accounted one of 'them' or whether they prefer to win acceptance in some other group. It is easy for an observer to exaggerate the importance of physical urges, and to overestimate the limitations set by economic status or family history. It is difficult to be aware of the power of chance remarks, casual gestures, and supposedly unseen actions. What adolescents express by their behaviour is much less a matter of blind inherited impulses than adults have been tempted to suppose.

'Attend to me. I am grown up.'
'Give it to me. I am one of you.'
'Let me try it. I know about it too.'
'Let me do it. I also can do that.'

The adolescent is best understood in such terms; and socially unacceptable conduct is a symptom and a protest rather than an inevitable misdemeanour stemming from uncontrollable forces. To adults in perturbation the message of psychology is therefore 'Try again another way. Actions will change when their meaning is changed.' To adolescents who appear to be in revolt the message is 'Don't be out of date. Nowadays nobody expects you to sow wild oats.' 'Other better things await you.' 'This is really much more interesting.' 'Your help is needed here.'

Through joining in the simple tasks of the home, through sharing in the common beliefs of the church, through participating in the routine actions of the workshops, those adolescents who are fortunate have escaped the temptation to seek personal maturing by rebellion; and through contact with the courtesies of an understanding adult even the defiant and the apparently unteachable can be led towards the sun-lit ways of true maturity. The problems raised by delinquents and by backward boys and girls are, however, of such significance that they merit further and separate consideration at this point.

REFERENCES

1. For an accessible survey see: CARMICHAEL, L., in CARMICHAEL, L. (ed.), *Manual of Child Psychology*. 2nd ed. N.Y.: John Wiley. 1954.

See also: PRATT, K. C., in CARMICHAEL, L. (ed.), ibid.

THOMPSON, H., in CARMICHAEL, L. (ed.), ibid.

GESELL, A., in CARMICHAEL, L. (ed.), ibid.

2. HALL, G. S., in DENNIS, W. (ed.), *Readings in the History of Psychology*. N.Y.: Appleton. 1948.

DENNIS, W., *Psychol. Bull.* **46.** 3. 224–35. 1949.

3. HALL, G. S., *Adolescence*. N.Y.: Appleton. 1904.

4. Illustrations of this are: PIAGET, J., *Le Langage et la Pensèe chez L'Enfant*. Neuchâtel: Delachaux et Niestlé. 1923.

PIAGET, J., *et al.*, *La Genèse du Nombre chez l'Enfant*. Neuchâtel: Delachaux et Niestlé. 1941.

PIAGET, J., *Le Développement des Quantités chez l'Enfant*. Neuchâtel: Delachaux et Niestlé. 1941.

PIAGET, J., *La Formation du Symbole chez l'Enfant*. Neuchâtel: Delachaux et Niestlé. 1945.

See also: PIAGET, J., *The Psychology of Intelligence*. Lond.: Routledge. 1950.

PIAGET, J., *The Child's Conception of Number*. Lond.: Routledge. 1952.

INHELDER, B., and PIAGET, J., *The Early Growth of Logic in the Child: Classification and Seriation*. Lond.: Routledge. 1964.

5. GESELL, A., *et al.*, *The Child from Five to Ten*. Lond.: Hamish Hamilton. 1946.

GESELL, A., *et al.*, *Youth: The Years from Ten to Sixteen*. Lond.: Hamish Hamilton. 1956.

6. MENDOUSSE, P., *L'Ame de L'Adolescent*. Paris: Alcan. 1913.

See also: HUBERT, R., *La Croissance Mentale*. Paris: Presses Universitaires. 1949.

7. STARCH, D., *Educational Measurements*. N.Y.: Macmillan. 1916.

COXE, W. W., *et al.*, *The Grouping of Pupils*. 35th *Yearbook* of the National Society for the Study of Education. Part I. 1936.

8. PIAGET, J., in *Publication No. 111*. Paris: U.N.E.S.C.O. 1949.

AEBLI, H., *Didactique Psychologique*. Neuchâtel: Delachaux et Niestlé. 1951.

For relevant criticism see: BOUCHET, H., *L'Individualisation de l'Enseignement*. Paris: Presses Universitaires. 1933 and 1948.

HILL, K. E., *Children's Contributions in Science Discussions*. N.Y.: Teachers' College, Columbia U.P. 1947.

9. WALLON, H., *Les Origines du Caractère chez l'Enfant*. Paris: Presses Universitaires. 1949.

10. PARKHURST, H., *Education on the Dalton Plan*. Lond.: Bell. 1922.

ADAMS, J., *Modern Developments in Educational Practice*. Lond.: Univ. of Lond. Press. 1922.

DEWEY, E., *The Dalton Laboratory Plan*. Lond.: Dent. 1924.

WASHBURNE, C., VOGEL, M., and GRAY, W. S., *Results of Fitting Schools to Individuals*. Bloomington: Public School Publishing Co. 1926.

11. FLEMING, C. M., *Research and the Basic Curriculum*. Lond.: Univ. of Lond. Press. 1946 and 1952.

12. TERMAN, L. M., et al., *Nature and Nurture*. 27th *Yearbook* of the National Society for the Study of Education. 1928.

STODDARD, G. D., et al., *Intelligence*. 39th *Yearbook* of the National Society for the Study of Education. 1940.

13. THORNDIKE, R. L., ibid. XXIV. 7. 543–9. 1933.

See also: CLARKE, A. M., and CLARKE, A. D. B., *Mental Deficiency*, Lond.: Methuen, 1959.

For discussion of educational implications see: FLEMING, C. M., *Adolescence*. Lond.: Routledge. 1948, 1955 and 1963.

FLEMING, C. M., in JEFFERY, G. B., *Transfer from Primary to Secondary Schools*. Lond.: Evans. 1949.

14. TERMAN, L. M., *The Intelligence of School Children*. Lond.: Harrap. 1921.

15. BURT, C., *Mental and Scholastic Tests*. Lond.: P. S. King. 1921.

16. DEARBORN, W. F., ROTHNEY, J. W., et al., *Predicting the Child's Development*. Cambridge, Mass.: Sci-Art Publishers. 1941.

FREEMAN, F. N., and FLORY, C. D., in BARKER, R. G., KOUNIN, J. S., and WRIGHT, H. F., *Child Behavior and Development*. N.Y.: McGraw-Hill. 1943.

JONES, H. E., *Development in Adolescence*. N.Y.: Appleton. 1943.

BAYLEY, N., and ESPENSCHADE, A., *Rev. Educ. Res.* XIV. 5. 1944.

MacFARLANE, J. W., in BARKER, R. G., KOUNIN, J. S., and WRIGHT, H. F., loc. cit. [16].

HONZIK, M. P., MacFARLANE, J. W., and ALLEN, L., *J. Exper. Educ.* XVII. 2. 309–24. 1948.

MacFARLANE, J. W., ALLEN, L., and HONZIK, M. L., *A Developmental Study of the Behavior Problems of Normal Children between 21 months and 14 years*. Berkeley: Univ. of California Press. 1954.

17. For a list of London studies of this kind see: FLEMING, C. M., and LAUWERYS, J. A., in *Studies and Impressions*. Univ. of Lond., Inst. of Educ. 1952.

With this may be compared: NORTHWAY, M. L. (Chairman), *Twenty-Five Years of Child Study*. Inst. of Child Study. Toronto. 1951.

WALL, W. D., *The Adolescent Child*. Lond.: Methuen. 1948. And for very full analyses of American investigations see: COLE, L., *Psychology of Adolescence*. 4th ed. N.Y.: Rinehart. 1954.

CASTLE, E. B., *Growing up in East Africa*, Lond.: Oxford Univ. Press. 1966.

See also: WALL, W. D., *Brit. J. Psychol.* XXXVIII. 4. 191–208. 1948.

BARSCHAK, E., ibid. XLIII. 2. 129–40. 1952.

JEPHCOTT, P., *Some Young People*. Lond.: Allen & Unwin. 1954.

18. For an accessible survey see: FLEMING, C. M., *Adolescence*. loc. cit. [13].

19. MOORE, T., HINDLEY, C. B., et al., *Brit. Med. J.* II. 1132–7. 1954.

MacPHERSON, J. S., *Eleven-year-olds Grow Up*. Lond.: Univ. of Lond. Press. 1958.

MOORE, T. W., Studying the Growth of Personality. *Vita Humana*. 2. 65–87. 1959.

FALKNER, F., (ed.), *Child Development*. Basel: Karger. 1960.

115

DOUGLAS, J. W. B., *The Home and the School*. Lond.: Macgibbon & Kee. 1964.

See also: DAVIS, C., *Room to Grow*. Toronto: Univ. of Toronto Press. 1966.

20. OAKES, M. E., *Science Educ.* **29.** 137–42. 190–201. 1945.

OAKES, M. E., *Children's Explanations of Natural Phenomena*. N.Y.: Teachers' College. 1947.

KING, W. H., *Brit. J. Educ. Psychol.* **XXXI.** 1. 1–20. 1961.

LOVELL, K., *Brit. J. Psychol.* **52.** 143–53. 1961.

WALLACE, J. G., *Concept Growth and the Education of the Child*. Lond.: Nat. Found. Educ. Res. 1965.

Cf. FREYBERG, P. S., *Some Aspects of Intellectual Development in Children Aged Six to Nine Years: A Longitudinal Study*. Ph.D. Thesis. Palmerston North. 1965.

21. PIAGET, J., loc. cit. *passim*. [4] and [8].

22. MCCARTHY, D., in CARMICHAEL, L., loc. cit. [1]. 1946 and 1954.

23. MORRIS, R., *The Quality of Learning*. Lond.: Methuen. 1951.

24. BURT, C., *J. Exper. Ped.* **5.** 68–77 and 121–7. 1919.

MARKSBERG, M. L., *Foundations of Creativity*. N.Y.: Harper. 1963.

25. FLEMING, C. M., *Individual Work in Primary Schools*. Lond.: Harrap. 1934.

26. GARDNER, D. E. M., *Long-Term Results of Infant School Methods*. Lond.: Methuen. 1950.

GARDNER, D. E. M., *Experiment and Tradition in Primary Schools*. Lond.: Methuen. 1966.

AIKIN, W. M., *The Story of the Eight-Year Study*. N.Y.: Harper. 1942.

27. CARTWRIGHT, D., and ZANDER, A. (ed.), *Group Dynamics*. Evanston: Row Peterson. 1953.

HOLLANDER, E. P., *Principles and Methods of Social Psychology*. N.Y.: Oxford Univ. Press. 1967.

SHEARS, L. W., *Brit. J. Psychol.* **XLIV.** 3. 232–42. 1953.

28. KHAN, Q. J. A., *A Study of the Arithmetical Experience of Certain Groups of Children in an Infants' School*. M.A. Thesis. London. 1953.

29. BOSSARD, J. H. S., *Parent and Child*. Philadelphia: Univ. of Pennsylvania Press. 1953.

MEAD, M., and WOLFENSTEIN, M., *Childhood in Contemporary Cultures*. Chicago: Univ. of Chicago Press. 1955.

HSU, F. L. K., *et al.*, *Internat. J. Soc. Psychiat.* **VII.** 1. 33–53. 1960–1.

COLEMAN, J. S., *et al.*, *The Adolescent Society*. Glencoe: Free Press. 1961.

30. CARMICHAEL, L. (ed.), loc. cit. [1]. 1946 and 1954.

KUHLEN, R. G., and THOMPSON, G. G. (ed.), *Psychological Studies of Human Development*. N.Y.: Appleton. 1952.

See also: OLSON, W. C., *Child Development*. Boston: Heath. 1949.

STOLZ, H. R., and STOLZ, L. M., *Somatic Development of Adolescent Boys*. N.Y.: Macmillan. 1951.

DENNIS, W. (ed.), *Readings in Child Psychology*. N.Y.: Prentice-Hall. 1951.

MILLARD, C. V., *Child Growth and Development in the Elementary School Years*. Boston: Heath. 1951.

GARRISON, K. C., *Growth and Development*. N.Y.: Longmans. 1952.

ALMY, M., *Child Development*. N.Y.: Henry Holt. 1955.

31. FLEMING, C. M., *Adolescence*, loc. cit. [13]. Chs. IX and X.

HAMLEY, H. R., *Relational and Functional Thinking in Mathematics*. 9th *Yearbook* of the National Council of Teachers of Mathematics. 1934.

BARKER, R. G., KOUNIN, J. S., and WRIGHT, H. F., *Child Behavior and Development*. N.Y.: McGraw-Hill. 1943.

32. CARMICHAEL, L. (ed.), loc. cit.˙[1]. 1946 and 1954.

HONZIK, M. P., MACFARLANE, J. W., and ALLEN, L., loc. cit. [16].

TYLER, F. T., *J. Educ. Psychol.* XLVI. 285–93. 1955.

For discussion of intelligence-test performance among adults see: NISBET, J. D., *Brit. J. Educ. Psychol.* XXVII. III. 190–8. 1957.

HUNT, J. MC.V., *Intelligence and Experience*. N.Y.: Ronald Press. 1961.

33. MCCARTHY, D., loc. cit.·[22].

THOMPSON, H., in CARMICHAEL, L., loc. cit. [1]. 1946 and 1954.

34. MURPHY, G., MURPHY, L. B., and NEWCOMB, T. M., *Experimental Social Psychology*. N.Y.: Harper. 1937.

35. PLANT, J. S., *Personality and the Cultural Pattern*. N.Y.: Commonwealth Fund. 1937.

See also: MCLEAN, D., *Nature's Second Sun*. Lond.: Heinemann. 1954.

MOUSTAKAS, C. E., *The Teacher and the Child*. N.Y.: McGraw-Hill. 1956.

COLEMAN, J. S., *et al.*, loc. cit. [29]. 1961.

ALLPORT, G. W., *Pattern and Growth in Personality*. N.Y.: Holt, Rinehart and Winston. 1963.

37. SAYLES, M. B., *The Problem Child at Home*. N.Y.: Commonwealth Fund. 1928.

38. See also: FRANK, L. K., in SENN, M. J. E. (ed.), *Problems of Infancy and Childhood*. N.Y.: Josiah Macy Jr. Foundation. 1951.

39. MURPHY, G., *et al.*, loc. cit. [34]. 1937.

BÜHLER, C., in MURCHISON, C. (ed.), *A Handbook of Child Psychology*. Worcester, Mass.: Clark U.P. 1933.

40. On the unwarranted use of the word 'aggression' see survey in: SHERIF, M., and SHERIF, C. W., *Groups in Harmony and Tension*. N.Y.: Harper. 1953.

See also: JACKSON, L., *Aggression and its Interpretation*. Lond.: Methuen. 1954.

41. JERSILD, A. T., *Child Psychology*. 3rd ed. N.Y.: Staples Press. 1947. 4th ed. 1954.

42. WATSON, G. (ed.), *Civilian Morale*. Boston: Houghton Mifflin. 1942.

43. FLEMING, C. M., loc. cit. [13]. 1948, 1955 and 1963.

44. MOODIE, W., *The Doctor and the Difficult Child*. N.Y.: Commonwealth Fund. 1940.

45. FLEMING, C. M., loc. cit. [11]. 1946 and 1952.

46. BOUCHET, H., loc. cit. [8].

117

HILL, K. E., loc. cit. [8].

47. MURPHY, G., *et al.*, loc. cit. [34].

BLAIR, A. W., and BURTON, W. H., *Growth and Development of the Pre-Adolescent*. N.Y.: Appleton 1951.

48. See also: DEBESSE, M., *Comment Étudier les Adolescents*. Paris: Presses Universitaries. 1937. (3rd ed. 1948.)

SHERIF, M., in SHERIF, M., *An Outline of Social Psychology*. N.Y.: Harper. Ch. 13. 1948.

JAMES, H. E. O., and TENEN, C., *Brit. J. Psychol.* **XLI.** 3 and 4. 145–72. 1950.

JAMES, H. E. O., and TENEN, C., *The Teacher was Black*. Lond.: Heinemann. 1953.

WALL, W. D., and SIMSON, W. A., *Brit. J. Educ. Psychol.* **XX.** III. 153–63. 1950; and **XXI.** II. 81–8. 1951.

Typical of many such reports are:

TENEN, C., *Brit. J. Educ. Psychol.* **XVII.** II. 72–82. 1947.

REEVES, J. W., and SLATER, P., *Occup. Psychol.* **XXI.** 3. 111–24. 1947.

MCKELLAR, P., and HARRIS, R., *Brit. J. Educ. Psychol.* **XXII.** II. 101–13. 1952.

PIERCY, E. F., *Brit. J. Delinq.* **II.** 3. 229–37. 1952.

CAMPBELL, W. J., *Brit. J. Educ. Psychol.* **XXII.** II. 89–100. 1952.

EID, N. M., *An Investigation into the Out-of-School Activities of a Group of Adolescents*. M.A. Thesis. London. 1948.

PIERIS, H. E., *A Comparative Study of the Interests of Adolescent Girls in Certain Urban and Rural Areas*. M.A. Thesis. London. 1949.

OPPENHEIM, A. N., *Brit. J. Sociol.* **VI.** 3. 228–45. 1955.

MOUSTAKA, C., *A Study of the Reactions to Beauty of Certain Groups of Adolescent Pupils*. M.A. Thesis. London. 1953.

MacARTHUR, R. S., *Canadian J. Psychol.* **9.** 1. 42–54. 1955.

For a survey see: WATTENBERG, W., *The Adolescent Years*. N.Y.: Harcourt Brace. 1955.

FLEMING, C. M., *et al.*, *Educ. Res.* **II.** 3. 221–4. 1960.

MEYER, G. R., *Austral. J. Educ.* **5.** 1. 27–40. 1961. Ibid., **5.** 2. 105–15. 1961.

MEYER, G. R., and PENFOLD, D. M. E., *Brit. J. Educ. Psychol.* **XXXI.** 1. 33–7. 1961.

HANMER, J., *Girls at Leisure*. Lond.: Union of Youth Clubs. 1964.

SCHOFIELD, M., *et al.*, *The Sexual Behaviour of Young People*. Lond.: Longmans. 1965.

MAYS, J. B., *The Young Pretenders*. Lond.: Michael Joseph. 1965.

For evidence on age of puberty and the complexities of its study see:

FLEMING, C. M., *Adolescence*. Lond.: Routledge. Revised Edition 1963.

POPPLETON, P. K., and BROWN, P. E., *Brit. J. Educ. Psychol.* **XXXVI.** 97–101. 1966.

NISBET, J. D., and ENTWHISTLE, N. J., *Age of Transfer to Secondary Education*. Edinburgh: Scottish C. Res. Educ. 1966.

118

VIII

DELINQUENCY
AND BACKWARDNESS

THE DELINQUENT, the bad boy, the undisciplined girl. Down the ages they have challenged parental authority and disturbed the complacency of their elders. The Spartan thief, the sons of Eli, the youngsters in Sodom and Gomorrah, the worshippers of false gods the 'sons of Belial flown with insolence and wine'. Many have been the interpretations offered and many the remedies proposed.

Over the centuries, however, in this field of misdirected learning and motivation gone awry there may be discerned a progression from less adequate to more adequate understanding that is quite parallel to that traceable in the more general study of human motivation and human learning.[1]

An attitude of fatalism and an ascription of misdemeanours to demonic possession or innate malevolence seem to have characterized the first approach and this won credence for so long that its echoes may still be heard in popular parlance. 'She's bewitched.' 'He's a devil.'

By the nineteenth century interest had turned to the more external signs of an evil inheritance. The lowering brow. The sinister glance. The malformed face or misshapen ear.[2] Criminals were still held to form a group apart; but attention centred on a study of family resemblances and an awakening concern with genetics led to the analysis of the ancestry of present delinquents and the history of descendants of reported criminals.[3] 'He's destined for the gallows. What else can you expect?' 'Some can no more keep out of the hands of the law than they can add one cubit to their stature.'[4] 'Hers is bad seed.'

Within this framework of opinion there was established in Chicago in 1909 a Juvenile Psychopathic Institute, and to it William Healy went as Director.

By this time, it may be remembered, the experimental study of animal learning was well on the way. Thorndike had published his earliest reports.[5] Dewey and Hobhouse had protested against a reflex-arc psychology and against the theory of trial-and-error learning.[6] Freud from a different viewpoint had challenged a mechanistic and physical interpretation of neurotic distress,[7] and Witmer, Sully, Binet, Stern, Claparède, and Decroly had been pleading for an application of the methods of psychological study to the child as a living individual.[8] Experimental education for normal children was already an accepted proposal. Search had lighted a torch in Pueblo. Meumann was reporting inquiries in Leipzig. Dewey had founded a laboratory school at Chicago.[9] The time was ripe for the application of similar methods to the study of delinquency and to the reform of individual delinquents. In its essentials this was the step taken by Healy in Chicago and a few years later by Burt with a control group in London. Attention thus turned to the consideration of the intelligence of deviating children, and to the possible societal determinants of their behaviour – the adults in their family circle, their brothers, their sisters, their friends; and a sociological approach to delinquency superseded pronouncements in Platonic style as to types of men and qualitative differences in inheritance.

Social circumstances

Writers on delinquency began to publish case-histories describing the story behind the crime – the home with its drunken or brutal parents, the poverty, the lack of possessions, and the absence of attractive recreational opportunities.[10] Emphasis was laid on the variety of contributory conditions and the multiplicity of their incidence in each individual case; and remedial treatment of problem children was attempted through visiting teachers and probation officers with an enthusiasm as great as that shown in contemporary endeavours to adjust the school to the child. Much of this was, however, still coupled with more or less explicit reference to the hereditary antecedents of criminal behaviour – the over-endowment with instincts of aggressiveness, acquisitiveness or sex – or to the comparable Freudian theory of libidinal development through satisfactory expression of component instincts associated in turn with erogenous zones such as the mouth, the anus, and the genitalia.[11]

This uneasy partnership of sociological interest and a theory of instincts carried within it an inherent contradiction which reduced its effectiveness as an inspiration to treatment. The adult who desired to secure reform was advised in one breath to limit the expression of undesirable instincts and to refrain from interference with the healthy self-expression of the primitive and the infantile. Civilized living was thought of as a second best. Through repression it socialized the human animal but contributed to his discontent while increasing his neurotic tendencies. The individual and society were conceived of as inevitably in conflict; and it was believed that the balance was precariously maintained between the undue tenderness of social conscience which led to neuroticism and the lack of guilt which resulted in the anti-social actions of delinquents. Character-formation was attributed to the experiences of the first two to five years; and reformation was expected only from a return to childish relationships through the re-education offered in the seclusion of a psycho-analyst's consulting room.[12]

Loving care

Criticism of this interpretation came from two sources – from those who, like Thrasher in Chicago or Moreno in Vienna, worked with groups of young people in areas which to outsiders seemed irretriev-ably delinquent and from those who, like Aichhorn within the school situation, turned from a pre-occupation with the redirection of component instincts through conversation with an impartial analyst to an emphasis on the need for loving adult care which (though expressed in psycho-analytic terms) was reminiscent of the teaching of Christ rather than of that of Freud.[13]

Thrasher and Moreno, with their concern for the gang as a whole or the sociometric group in its inter-relationships, had prepared the way for the more social treatment of delinquency. The concepts of Aichhorn as they infiltrated into psycho-analytic interpretations contributed to the recognition of the ubiquity of the psychological need to be beloved, to experience tenderness, and to receive apprecia-tion or approbation. From this, the step was readily taken to that concern with the mental and emotional consequences of consistent and uninterrupted maternal care in early childhood which has, in certain circles, replaced earlier shibboleths as to physical stigmata, constitutional defects or other hereditary inadequacies of criminal characters.[14]

Participation

Meanwhile from psychological studies of morale in industry or the armed forces, from remedial procedures in educational and Child Guidance Clinics, and from inquiries into the relationships of pupils and teachers at all levels of school life, there had come an admission of the human need to participate in the affairs of some intimate and friendly group.[15] Reactions to unemployment, to overwork, to monotonous tasks or to danger were observably more wholesome in the case of those adults who were aware of their responsibilities both as bread-winners at home and as key-workers in some co-operative endeavour. Neurotic symptoms and behaviour disorders occurred most frequently in those without that background; and destructiveness and quarrelling decreased when opportunities were given for informed and friendly service. Children, in comparable fashion, learned more rapidly in contact with adults who gave them not only insight into their difficulties and not merely the consolation of being beloved but also the chance of engaging in acceptable activities in which they could succeed.[16]

Certain improvements in the treatment of delinquency had followed upon the proposal that an atmosphere of kindly acquiescence should replace the punishment and upbraiding of traditional adult reactions.[17] Further developments came from the admission that both for children and for adults there is value in the adequate playing of a role (making a contribution), as well as in the receiving of appreciation (status), or reward.

Detailed recording of treatment in this field (as in that of clinical psychology) is of relatively recent date. In 1930 it was possible to report that, while much could be said of diagnosis, little was known of the process of therapy.[18] Statistical analyses of the number and the types of recurrent offences had lent impressiveness to figures of the kind offered by the Gluecks and Ackerson (and later by Norwood East, Carr-Saunders and Mannheim, and others) but these observations had remained somewhat externalized and had provided in many respects merely a continuation of earlier sociological studies.[19] Much was said of concomitant conditions, of the multiplicity of possible causes, and the personal uniqueness of each individual delinquent. There was clear recognition of the significance of home life and of the discipline and the attitudes maintained within it. Much information was also available as to the test per-

ice of delinquents of various ages; and something was known
: pattern of sociometric choices of friends in various types of
/ity in specified settings.[20] Personal attributes, relationships
adults, and relationships to peers (companions) were all fully
scussed; but it was not until the 1940s that records began to be
.vailable of the stages through which actual reactions to treatment
passed.[21] Like contemporary interest in the details of psychotherapy, concern with these was consequent on increasing sensitivity
to the extent of self-reference observable in the growth of social
attitudes (see Chapter IV above). *Laissez-faire* procedures in their
simplest forms had provided delinquents with an admirable means
of testing the genuineness of expressed affection or approval. Through
contact with groups in which such experimental reactions were only
too obvious, it began to be apparent that there was often a progression from what appeared to be aimless restlessness and destructiveness or apparently deliberate provocativeness to selective good
behaviour in relation to one or two chosen adults and only later
(or not at all) to a permanent acceptance of social values and an
abandonment of delinquent joys, delinquent methods of self-
defence or delinquent search for substitute satisfactions.[22]

Why shouldn't I?
This will serve them right.
Do they really mean it?
This will make up for what I haven't got.
Will he draw the line at this?
Perhaps he's as bad as the rest.
He's a decent chap.
I'll do it for him.
We'll do it with him.
I'd like to be one of them.
I am one of them.
We do not do such things.

Through many disappointments and many fluctuations between
success and failure, workers in the field of the treatment of delinquency thus passed from a theory of instinctive and hereditary
origins through a study of individual attributes to concern with the
concomitants of delinquency, and from that to inquiries into the
effects of leadership techniques, social climates, and the processes
of interaction in gangs or small groups. The recognition of the

delinquent as a human being with a problem to be solved was followed by the discovery that love alone is not enough, that somehow controls from within must be developed even by children who hate, and that somehow the self-picture of a rebel and an outcast must be transformed into a concept of the self which includes service as well as self-seeking, and participation as well as greed. Delinquents who offend against the canons of their social group do so not because of inborn peculiarities (the nature of their organism), nor because of special circumstances (the nature of their situation), but rather because, being both individual and social, they react in certain fashions to certain experiences and have come to accept a certain status and a certain role – the status of an outcast from the group by which they are branded as delinquents and the role of a rebellious destroyer of its property or its values.

This interpretation strikes a note of optimism – though not of ease. If action is controlled by attitude (if personality is organized and developed through the concepts which one forms about oneself), and if concepts are subject to change with changes in perception and in meaning, then modifications in action may be effected and changes in disposition are not impossible. Civilized behaving can be offered to delinquents, not as something foreign to humanity and imposed by a social contract which is essentially self-centred, but as the more mature and fuller expression of a human nature which is most completely itself when permitted to show that co-operativeness which is as characteristically human as any personal search for appreciation or reward.

Christianity and psychology

Here, as has been suggested above, psychology and Christianity join hands.[23] In earlier decades when, through a misinterpretation of the theory of evolution and of Lloyd Morgan's canon of simplicity, an attempt was made to explain the human in terms of the animal and the mental in terms of the physical, it was not possible to find psychological analogues for that awareness of religious experience whose reality is attested in all ages and in all human societies. With an increase in understanding of the significance of the satisfaction of the human need to give and to receive, to attain insight, and to achieve success it becomes possible to understand the effectiveness of the work which is done among delinquents, among outcasts, drunkards, and criminals by those who approach its difficulties in the full armour of God – in that spirit of faith and prayerfulness which carries within it both the approach of the lover and the attitude of the democratic guide. This has no scorn for the sinner but lends vitality to the belief that change is possible; and behind it lies a conviction of the love of God for all men – the prototype and exemplar of the love of the good teacher for his erring pupils. 'Underneath are the everlasting arms.' 'God so loved the world' – and within that world are included the most rebellious and the most spiteful of the sons of men.

'With men it is impossible, but not with God.'
'Though your sins be as scarlet, they shall be as white as snow.'
'Ye are of more value than many sparrows.'
'We are God's fellow-workers.'

Group values and contagion

Echoes of this therapeutic message of the Bible and of the organized mission of the Christian churches are to be heard in those developments of group therapy which are directed to the consolation and the support of the ailing. Recovery Incorporated or Alcoholics Anonymous offer something akin to the sustenance of shared religious experience.[24] It is to be noted also that they do more than provide friendly reassurance from others who have recovered from mental illness or escaped from defeat by alcoholic cravings. They invite participation by each member in the responsible task of succouring another. The burden is no light one. The difficulties of the reformer are many; but through experiences such as these evidence is accumulating which casts light on the processes by which salvage is being effected in work with delinquent youngsters in remand homes, approved schools, Borstal institutions, and the like.[25] Among these processes, and in fashions which are only now beginning to be realized, members of delinquent groups also reach out to influence one another in those unwitting forms to which the term 'contagion' can usefully be applied. This is distinguishable both from imitation and from the acceptance of direct influence from acknowledged leaders.[26] Within a peer-group it is in some ways the counterpart of the subtleties discernible in the interaction of teachers and taught; and it likewise can be interpreted only in terms of the group status of the initiator, and the values accepted by the group – its immediate wishes and interests, its size, and the nature of its inner relationships.[27]

In the setting of such complexities of behavioural contagion within groups and the subtleties of procedures deliberately directed to the rehabilitation of offenders there comes the reminder that delinquents, like the physically sick, are of many sorts and at many levels of distress. Some delinquent acts are merely experimental. 'What will happen if . . .?' These are not repeated when the experiment proves unacceptable. Some are attributable to social or intellectual immaturity.[28]

'I must do as the others are doing.'

'There is no harm in it.'

From these, most human beings escape with the passing of years. Others are perverted expressions of quite wholesome human needs.[29]

'He will like me if I can give him presents.' (stealing)

'They will praise me if I give the answer they want.' (lying or cheating)

These are almost insensibly abandoned when fuller appreciation and successful participation are offered. Others are the revengeful and desperate acts of children who hate because they believe they have been hated – who distrust all adults because of the cruelty of a few.[30] The reclamation of these can be effected only through the combined agency of group contagion and the personal devotion of dedicated adults. The analogue of such reclamation is on the physical and mental level to be seen in the efforts of Recovery Incorporated and other therapeutic group agencies, and on the spiritual level in the co-operative sharing of experience in a Christian church – with its combination of instruction, reassurance, and dedicated service.

From the point of view of the teacher in the classroom (in this special field as in that of backwardness) what has also to be said is that delinquents and non-delinquents are more alike than teachers have sometimes been tempted to suppose.[31] They share all human longings for appreciation and for chances of participation. They are helped by the diagnostic provision of activities (reading, counting, writing, drawing, games – and their derivatives) at a level in which they can attain the satisfaction of success. They are bound by emotional ties (of friendliness or dislike) to their contemporaries and also to their seniors. They can be arrested by a gesture, diverted by fresh interests or defeated by the recurrence of situations which seem similar to those in which their delinquent reactions have formerly occurred. The strategies which are successful in their reclamation are essentially the same as those employed in daily living by the skilful teachers and parents of those boys and girls whose backslidings (since they are recognized as temporary) have attracted none of that public disgrace which follows upon the labelling of a misdemeanour as a symptom of delinquency. For this reason the careful study of the reported reactions of delinquent children burdened with problems which they have failed to solve is of direct relevance and significance to teachers and parents in whose daily experience such crises may, happily, form a very small part.

Backward boys and girls

Childish misdemeanours are not necessarily followed by offences against the law. Sluggishness in response does not inevitably point to ultimate failure. Both are matters of professional concern to teachers and, in relation to both, classroom reactions have in many places changed over the last forty years.

In the early 1920s representative replies to a questionnaire issued by a Child Guidance Clinic showed that teachers considered the most serious offences to be those which challenged their authority as law-givers, rulers, and classroom potentates. Talkativeness, untruthfulness, truancy, and impertinence caused greater distress than signs of maladjustment, unsociability, suspiciousness, and unhappiness.[32] Fifteen years later the emphasis of a comparable group had shifted to more awareness of the importance of wholesome attitudes;[33] and a recent inquiry shows still greater sensitivity to the significance of personal and social development.[34] In similar fashion in the late 1910s backwardness in learning was almost universally held to be a disgrace; and no hesitation was felt in punishing or expelling pupils who failed to do credit to a school. By the early 1930s teachers had followed workers in Child Guidance Clinics into a concern with mental testing, home background, and socio-economic level; [35] and to these they now add a consideration of the more intimate relationships which contribute to the quality of the social climate of a group.

Little official attention was in the nineteenth century given to the reasons for educational defeat beyond branding teachers as 'inefficient' and pupils as 'lazy' and exhorting both to make better use of their time.

Mention has already been made of the studies which challenged the first assumption; and it is not now so often supposed that failure among pupils is wholly attributable to lack of energy on the part of their teachers. It has taken longer to discredit the belief that certain unsuccessful pupils are 'underfunctioning' or 'retarded' – to use the modern counterparts of the earlier adjective 'lazy'.

Successive stages in the study of the topic may be noted. In the 1910s, when neither of these phrases ('inefficiency' and 'laziness') had yet been countered by formal evidence, many teachers were already co-operating with psychologists in experimentation under classroom conditions; and a tentative beginning had been made with what was later called the psychology of the school subjects. By the late 1920s this had developed into a lively interest in children's difficulties; but both teachers and psychologists were still under the influence of contemporary dichotomies between nature and nurture, inherited tendencies and environmental influences. In spite of evidence as to the inconstancy of performance in intelligence tests it was taken for granted, for example, that such tests measured innate ability apart from acquired attainment; and a clear distinction was drawn between dullness, backwardness, and retardation. These words are still in current use along with the related concepts of 'mental age' and 'intelligence quotient', and the importance of the issues which are involved merits a reminder of the line taken by their early exponents.

Backwardness, dullness, and retardation

A child with a mental age of ten was defined as one who was able to answer questions involving what is commonly called intelligence with the accuracy and speed of rather more than half of a representative sample of ten-year-olds. (The actual percentage varied slightly from one test to another and from individual tests to group tests.) A child was said to have an 'intelligence quotient' of 100 when mental age so calculated coincided with chronological age – when the ratio of standardized test performance to age was as one to one. In similar fashion lower or higher relative status could be expressed as a quotient of chronological age in relation to subject age (in arithmetic, reading, and the like) or of subject age in relation to mental age.[36] Using this convention, a 'backward' child was one who was distinctly below the educational level of the majority of his own age – whose subject age on standardized tests of attainment when divided by chronological age yielded a quotient of less than 0·85. A 'dull' child was one whose performance in tests of intelligence was well below that of most others of his age – whose mental age on standardized intelligence tests divided by chronological age was less than 0·85; while a 'retarded' child was one whose performance on comparable tests of educational attainment and intelligence gave a quotient below 0·85 for subject age divided by mental age. For convenience these quotients were multiplied by 100. Thus a backward child was said to have an educational quotient of less than 85 (subject age divided by chronological age). A dull child had an intelligence quotient below 85, and a retarded child was described as having an achievement quotient of less than 85 (subject age divided by mental age).

This formulation in terms of quotients was used both as a means of identifying varying types of irregular development and as a guide to educational prognosis. It was assumed that there was in the ideal state a complete coincidence of mental age and subject age. A retarded child who was 'not functioning to capacity' was therefore expected to improve to the level indicated by his mental age; but a dull child was thought of as one who could never rise to the level of those of his contemporaries whose intelligence quotients were higher than his own.

The interpretation was, in intention, an admission of the existence of individual differences; and it was at first a necessary protest against the earlier assumption of the equality of all minds and the consequent ascription of 'laziness' or deliberate defaulting to less successful learners. In practice, however, it led to the belief that the backwardness of dull children was irremediable – that they were of differing clay and required a teaching programme in all respects distinct from that of their more successful contemporaries. Teachers were therefore tempted to reduce their efforts to stimulate learning in pupils who had little initial success; and at the same time they were encouraged to put pressure upon those who appeared to be functioning less highly than was warranted by their so-called 'innate ability'. There was, therefore, a continuance of something very like the crude nineteenth-century belief that such pupils 'could do better if they tried', were 'lacking in interest' or 'unwilling to concentrate'.

A challenge to the interpretation which had attributed constancy to intelligence quotients and had presupposed the lack of environmental components in intelligence test scores came, as has been indicated above, through long-term studies which established the intrinsic irregularity of mental growth. The same sort of conclusion followed from inquiries which showed a lack of parallelism in differing aspects of development. The Harvard Growth studies sponsored by Dearborn lent no support to the notion that growth spurts in physique or intellectual ability occurred inevitably at the same time and the Californian studies analysed by Tyler indicated no coincidence of such forms of development as genital maturing and learning to read.

Through these same researches there came also a fuller understanding of the difficulties inherent in the making of comparisons between results obtained from tests of differing origins and constructed along differing lines. Much less use than formerly is therefore now made of the notion of a mental ratio or quotient. It is recognized that the significance of such statistics varies with the extent to which a test tends to scatter the performance of pupils or to confine it within a narrow range. If, for example, the standard deviation of a series of educational quotients in one subject is 15 and that for a series in another subject is 20, it is now known that the quotient of a candidate in the top two per cent of the group will be expressed as 130+ in the one instance and 140+ in the other. Both quotients indicate a score of at least two standard deviations above the mean of 100; but their form of expression obscures the fact that the relative position they describe is the same in both. (To meet this difficulty it is now recommended that norms showing relative status be offered in the form of percentiles, standard scores or standardized scores; and this convention is commonly used in reporting test results both of attainment and of intelligence.)*

For all these reasons the appeal to a hypothetical examinable 'innate' ability has been gradually dropped along with the twin notions of the irretrievable backwardness of the dull child and the reprehensible retardation of those pupils who may do better in a test of general mental ability than in one of scholastic attainment. It has ceased to be supposed that if pupils have been efficiently taught and have worked well, there will inevitably be a close correspondence between their relative status in educational tests and in tests of general mental ability. There is now much evidence in support of the finding that when achievement quotients are calculated from scores obtained in tests standardized on the same population quite large numbers of pupils have quotients both above 100 and below 100.

* For fuller details see Figure III and page 168 in Chapter XI below.

In a study of an entire school conducted by the writer there were, for example, out of 532 pupils, 182 pupils with an A.Q. above 100 (subject age in a standardized silent reading test higher than mental age in a test of general mental ability). Of these 117 had an I.Q. below 100, 3 had an I.Q. of 100, and in 62 cases the I.Q. was above 100. In only 18 instances did the reading age coincide with the mental age (A.Q. 100); and in only 2 of these was the I.Q. 100. (In 9 cases it was above 100 and in 7 it was below 100.) Of the 332 boys and girls whose A.Q.s were below 100, 215 had I.Q.s above 100, 7 had I.Q.s of 100, and 110 had I.Q.s below 100. These figures present an obvious challenge to older beliefs; and, since they represent the performance of pupils of quite equivalent educational history it cannot be claimed that they are explicable in terms of differences in the qualifications of the teachers, the socio-economic level of the children or the equipment of the school. Their chief interest is that they serve to direct attention to the complexity of the conditions which affect progress; but similar findings are available from recent large-scale testing at age eleven in many English counties, and from recorded results of individual tests of intelligence and attainment.

Another way of expressing this is to say that the correlations between results from tests of general mental ability and tests of attainment although positive are not absolute. (They vary from one group of pupils to another; but they are often of the order of $+ 0.6$ and $+ 0.7$ and they rarely approach $+ 1$.) Pupils who are successful in one situation tend on the whole to reach success in others; but there is no reason to suppose that in a school or a class there will be, for example, the same number of pupils above a standardized score of 115 (or below a standardized score of 85) even in abilities so closely comparable as general intelligence, English, and arithmetic. It is therefore not now a matter for astonishment that a pupil's score in a test on any one of these is no pointer to his probable score on any other. A low ratio between age and performance in an attainment test is not, in itself, a justification for criticism of the teacher as inefficient, nor is a low ratio between age and performance in an intelligence test (a low I.Q.) a reason for condemnation of the pupil as unteachable. Still less is there evidence to support the belief that a low ratio between standardized scores in an attainment test and an intelligence test is of itself an indication that a pupil is not 'trying as hard as he might'.

Awareness of this has come slowly down the decades; but through its realization the concept of 'retardation' or 'underfunctioning' has fallen into disuse and is now of academic rather than practical interest. A diagnosis of dullness or backwardness (a low relative status in comparison with one's contemporaries) is also for these reasons now used by discerning teachers as a challenge to hope rather than a pointer to despair. 'What some can do, he may do ... He can at least give it a try.' Wise teachers are in this sense cognisant of the disharmony and variability of growth and they decline to accept as final what so often proves a merely temporary set-back.[37]

Backward children within their groups

Some usefulness is still attached to the convention that a 'backward' child is one whose performance in an accredited test falls at about the fifteenth percentile or is below a standardized score of 85. The statement is, however, used in a descriptive rather than an explanatory or evaluative sense. It is made with the knowledge that there is in all measurable abilities a range of individual differences and that inevitably in any list arranged in order some will do better than many of the group, and some will do worse. Interest has shifted from the assessing of such pupils with a view to prediction of their later performance, to their study as an aid to the understanding of their difficulties. A child who is below the level of most of his companions arrests the attention of his teacher. He may or may not be of low intelligence and his success may vary from one type of learning to another. He may be backward in speech or in physical or social skills. He may be subnormal in emotional maturity or in artistic competence. His development in all areas is now expected to be somewhat disharmonious; and his teachers are not now surprised if his growth is at times observably variable.

As in the comparable field of physical development, the response to tuition is now more clearly seen to be related to the amount and the nature of the nutrition offered; and with the passing of the years there has come a livelier recognition of the complexity of this external stimulation. The methods of the teacher. The adequacy of textbooks. The structure, equipment, and ventilation of buildings. Regularity of schooling. The place in the family. The nature of the home. The education and the attitudes of the parents. Experiences of acceptance or rejection, of successful participation or inadequacy, of bewilderment or insight. All play some part; and, in response to them, children build patterns of friendship or dislike, of indifference or of willingness to co-operate. In reaction to them also they form concepts of themselves which contribute to the consistency of their behaviour – while remaining modifiable by each new experience encountered.

Response to teaching is admittedly also a function of personal differences in reaction; but in this field, as in the field of delinquency, no one developmental inadequacy is now thought of as the chief contributory condition. Backward children, like maladjusted children, delinquent children and those millions who attract no special attention, admittedly function always within the limits set by an inheritance whose effect can not be disentangled from that of their environment—past and present. There is again, as in all learning, an inner and an outer, an organism and a situation; but in relation to backwardness, as to delinquency, the dichotomy between 'nature' and 'nurture' is now seen to present a pseudo-problem whose lack of reality is comparable to the emptiness of theoretical discussions of the 'individual' as opposed to the 'social'.[38] Attention has therefore, in this field also, been deflected to a concern with the ways in which individuals (inescapably members of groups) are both acted upon and react against the environmental pressures to which they are subjected.

For this reason less emphasis than formerly is now put upon specific physical handicaps – sensori-motor defects, laterality, cerebral dominance, congenital word-blindness, eye-voice span, and the like – while at the same time there is less firmness of conviction that any one method of teaching carries the full answer to any one educational problem. Follow-up studies show in general that the flexible and kindly guidance of a democratic classroom results in an increase in examinable competence as well as in wholesome personal maturing; and differences between classes can be related more definitely to differences in method of approach than to differences in initial intellectual ability.[39]

Quite relevant to this are the findings of inquiries into the differences between children in larger and smaller schools in urban and in rural districts. Socio-economic levels are in general paralleled by differences in average performance in tests of intelligence and attainment; but there is wide overlapping on the part of individual schools and individual pupils; and relatively high scores are obtained in small rural schools and large urban schools where teachers' attitudes are good and parental co-operation is effective.[40] There is at the same time some reason to doubt the permanence of the improvement effected by what has been called remedial education, when that is given under special conditions in clinics or remedial centres at a distance from the schools.[41] Among pupils whose hardly-won skills in arithmetic or in reading meet no approval from their reference groups there has, for example, been reported a subsequent decrease in rate of progress quite comparable with that of the back-sliding recorded among delinquents after their return to homes and gangs whose meanings and purposes have not in the meantime been transformed.[42] In another setting somewhat similar lapses into traditional ways have been noted among teachers returning from refresher courses to colleagues who see no reason for sharing their enthusiasms.[43] This does not mean that efforts should not be made to carry further the education of dull or backward pupils, delinquent children or teachers in active service. It does serve as a reminder that learning is not a matter of mechanical responding to impressions received through drill, indoctrination or instruction. What is perceived is selective; and the selective process is sensitized by the whole situation as it appears to the learner. Some part is played by psychological equipment and by the independent variables of external stimulation. Much seems determined also by the subtle interrelationships of expectancy, of level of aspiration, and of a ubiquitous personal longing to see oneself as acceptable, participatory, and a member of the group to which one believes oneself to belong.

REFERENCES

1. For a general discussion see: FLEMING, C. M., *Adolescence*, Ch. XVI. Lond.: Routledge. 1948, 1955 and 1963.
   STRANG, R., *et al.*, *Juvenile Delinquency and the Schools*. 47th *Yearbook* of the National Society for the Study of Education. Pt. I. 1948.
2. For a recent analogy see: SHELDON, W. H., *et al.*, *Varieties of Delinquent Youth*. N.Y.: Harper. 1949.
3. For accessible descriptions see:
   GODDARD, H. H., *Feeble-mindedness*. N.Y.: Macmillan. 1914.
   PINTNER, R., in MURCHISON, C. (ed.), *A Handbook of Child Psychology*. 2nd ed. revised. Worcester, Mass.: Clark U.P. 1933.
4. Cf. MAGUINNESS, O. D., *Environment and Heredity*. Lond.: Nelson. 1940.
5. For an accessible reproduction of this see:
   THORNDIKE, E. L., in DENNIS, W., *Readings in the History of Psychology*. N.Y.: Appleton. 1948.

6. DEWEY, J., in DENNIS, W., ibid.
   HOBHOUSE, L. T., *Mind in Evolution*. Lond.: Macmillan. 1901.
7. FREUD, S., *The Psycho-Pathology of Everyday Life* (1901). Lond.: Penguin Books. 1938.
8. SULLY, J., *Studies of Childhood*. Lond.: Longmans. 1895.
   BINET, A., *Les Idèes Modernes sur les Enfants*. Paris. 1910.
   STERN, W., *Die Differentielle Psychologie in ihren Methodischen Grundlagen*. Leipzig: Barth. 1911.
   CLAPARÈDE, E., *Psychologie de l'Enfant et Pedagogie Expérimentale*. Genève: Le Signal. 1905.
   DECROLY, O., *Le Programme d'Une Ecole dans la Vie*. 1908, in BOON, G., *Initiation Générale aux Idèes Decrolyennes*. Bruxelles: Collection Ivoire. 1937.
9. SEARCH, P. W., *An Ideal School*. N.Y.: Appleton. 1901.
   MEUMANN, E., *Vorlesungen zur Einfuhrung in die experimentelle Pädagogik und ihre psychologischen Grundlagen*. Leipzig: Engelmann. 1907.
   DEWEY, J., *The School and Society*. Chicago: Univ. of Chicago Press. 1899.
10. HEALY, W., and BRONNER, A. F., *New Light on Delinquency and its Treatment*. New Haven: Yale U.P. 1936.
    BURT, C., *The Young Delinquent*. London: Univ. of London Press. 1925.
    SHAW, C. R., *The Jack-Roller*. Chicago: Univ. of Chicago Press. 1930.
    SHAW, C. R., et al., *Delinquency Areas*. Chicago: Univ. of Chicago Press. 1931.
    SHAW, C. R., and MCKAY, H. D., *Juvenile Delinquency and Urban Areas*. Chicago: Univ. of Chicago Press. 1942.
11. BLANCHARD, P., in MURCHISON, C. (ed.), loc. cit. [3]. 1933.
    POWDERMAKER, F., LEVIS, H. T., and TOURAINE, G., *Amer. J. Orthopsychiat*. XII. 58–71. 1937.
12. See, for example, FRIEDLANDER, K., *The Psycho-Analytical Approach to Juvenile Delinquency*. Lond.: Kegan Paul. 1947.
13. THRASHER, F. M., *The Gang*. Chicago: Univ. of Chicago Press. 1927.
    MORENO, J. L., *Who Shall Survive?* Washington: Nervous and Mental Disease Publishing Co. 1934.
    AICHHORN, A., *Verwahrloste Jugend*. 1925. Translated as *Wayward Youth*. Lond.: Putnam. 1936.
    PFISTER, O., in EISSLER, K. R., *Searchlights on Delinquency*. Lond.: Imago Publishing Co. 35–49. 1949.
14. BOWLBY, J., *Forty-four Juvenile Thieves*. Lond.: Baillière, Tindall & Cox. 1946.
15. See Ch. III above.
16. FLEMING, C. M., *Individual Work in Primary Schools*. Lond.: Harrap. 1934.
    WASHBURNE, C., et al., *Results of Fitting Schools to Individuals*. Bloomington, Illinois: Public School Publishing Co. 1926.
    STRANG, R., et al., loc. cit. [1]. 1948.

17. AICHHORN, A., loç. cit. [13].

HEALY, W., and ALPER, B. S., *Criminal Youth and the Borstal System.* N.Y.: Commonwealth Fund. 1941.

SLAVSON, S. R., *An Introduction to Group Therapy.* N.Y.: Commonwealth Fund. 1941.

WILLS, W. D., *Throw Away thy Rod.* Lond.: Gollancz. 1960.

EISSLER, K. R., *Searchlights on Delinquency.* Lond.: Imago Publishing Co. 1949.

BETTELHEIM, B., *Love is Not Enough.* Glencoe: Free Press. 1950.

18. TULCHIN, S. H., *Amer. J. Orthopsychiat.* **I.** 3–60. 1930.

ANDERSON, H. H., and ANDERSON, G. L., in CARMICHAEL, L., *Manual of Child Psychology.* N.Y.: John Wiley. 1954.

See also: GLUECK, S. and E., *Later Criminal Careers.* N.Y.: Commonwealth Fund. 1937.

ROGERS, C. R., *The Clinical Treatment of the Problem Child.* Boston: Houghton Mifflin. 1939.

19. ACKERSON, L., *Children's Behavior Problems.* I. Chicago: Univ. of Chicago Press. 1931.

GLUECK, S., and GLUECK, E. T., *One Thousand Juvenile Delinquents.* Cambridge, Mass.: Harvard U.P. 1934.

ACKERSON, L., *Children's Behavior Problems.* II. Chicago: Univ. of Chicago Press. 1942.

CARR-SAUNDERS, A. M., *Young Offenders.* Cambridge: C.U.P. 1942.

NORWOOD EAST, W., et al., *The Adolescent Criminal.* Lond.: Churchill. 1942.

BAGOT, J. H., *Punitive Detention.* Lond.: Cape. 1944.

MANNHEIM, H., *Juvenile Delinquency in an English Middletown.* Lond.: Routledge. 1948.

NEUMEYER, M. H., *Juvenile Delinquency in Modern Society.* N.Y.: van Nostrand. 1949.

TAPPAN, P. W., *Juvenile Delinquency.* N.Y.: McGraw-Hill. 1949.

TEETERS, N. K., and REINEMANN, J. O., *The Challenge of Delinquency.* N.Y.: Prentice-Hall. 1950.

See also:

MANNHEIM, H., and WILKINS, L. T., *Prediction Methods in Relation to Borstal Training.* Lond.: H.M.S.O. 1955.

20. BURT, C., loc. cit. [10]. 1925.

HEALY, W., and BRONNER, A. F., loc. cit. [10]. 1936.

BRYAN, H. S., *The Troublesome Boy.* Lond.: Pearson. 1936.

HUGHES, E. W., *Brit. J. Educ. Psychol.* **XIII.** III. 113–25. 1943.

DAWSON, W. M., *Occup. Psychol.* **XVIII.** 1. 41–51. 1944.

BANISTER, H., and RAVDEN, M., *Brit. J. Psychol.* **XXXIV.** 2. 60–5. 1944.

BANISTER, H., and RAVDEN, M., ibid. **XXXV.** 3. 82–7. 1945.

KVARACEUS, W. C., *Juvenile Delinquency and the School.* N.Y.: World Book Co. 1945.

MORENO, J. L., loc. cit. [13]. 1934.

See also DÜNSDON, M. I., *Brit. J. Psychol.* **XXXVIII.** 2. 62–5. 1947.

PEARCE, J. D. W., *Juvenile Delinquency*. Lond.: Cassell. 1952.
21. ROGERS, C. R., KELL, B. L., and MCNEIL, H., *J. Consult. Psychol.* **XII**. 3. 175–86. 1948.
22. REDL, F., *Human Relations* **I**. 3. 307–13. 1948.
    BETTELHEIM, B., loc. cit. [17]. 1950.
    REDL, F., and WINEMAN, D., *Controls from Within*. Glencoe: Free Press. 1952.
23. POWERS, E., and WITMER, H., *An Experiment in the Prevention of Delinquency*. N.Y.: Columbia U.P. 1951.
    On the signficance of religious experiences see: PINTO-JAYAWARDANA, W. D., *A Comparative Study of Certain Selected Groups of Delinquent Boys*. M.A. Thesis. London. 1957.
    BRADBURN, E., *The Teacher's Role in the Moral Development of Children*. Ph.D. Thesis. Liverpool. 1964.
24. LOW, A. A., in MORENO, J. L. (ed.), *Group Psychotherapy*. N.Y.: Beacon House. 1945.
25. ROGERS, C. R., loc. cit. [18]. 1939.
    PLANT, J. S., *Personality and the Cultural Pattern*. N.Y.: Commonwealth Fund. 1937.
    See also: SCOTT, P., *Brit. J. Deling.* **II**. 1. 5–24. 1951.
    EISENSTADT, S. N., ibid. **II**. 1. 34–45. 1951.
    MACKWOOD, J. C., *Brit. J. Psychol.* **XL**. 1. 5–22. 1949.
    SOHN, L., *Brit. J. Delinq.* **III**. 1. 20–33. 1952.
    MAYS, J. B., ibid. **III**. 1.5–19. 1952.
    SPENCER, J. C., ibid. **I**. 2. 113–24. 1950.
    MABERLEY, A., ibid. **I**. 2. 125–8. 1950.
    GLUECK, E. T., ibid. **II**. 4. 275–86. 1952.
    GITTINS, J., *Approved School Boys*. Lond.: H.M.S.O. 1952.
    ANDRY, R. G., *Delinquency and Parental Pathology*. Lond.: Methuen. 1960.
    MAYS, J. B., *Growing up in the City*. Liverpool: University Press. 1954 and 1964.
26. REDL, F., in EISSLER, K. R. (ed.), loc. cit. [17]. 315–28. 1949.
    POLANSKY, N., LIPPITT, R., and REDL, F., *Human Relations*. **III**. 4. 319–48. 1950.
    GROSSER, D., POLANSKY, N., and LIPPITT, R., ibid. **IV**. 2. 115–42. 1951.
    REDL, F., and WINEMAN, D., *Controls from Within*. Glencoe: Free Press. 1952.
27 CARTWRIGHT, D., *Human Relations*. **IV**. 4. 381–92. 1951.
    CARTWRIGHT, D., and ZANDER, A. (ed.), *Group Dynamics*. N.Y.: Row, Peterson. 1953.
    HOLLANDER, E. P., *Principles and Methods of Social Psychology*. N.Y.: Oxford Univ. Press. 1967.
28. GLUECK, S., and GLUECK, E. T., *Juvenile Delinquents Grown Up*. N.Y.: Commonwealth Fund. 1942.
    See also: NORWOOD EAST, W., loc. cit. [19]. 1942.

GLUECK, S. and E., *Criminal Careers in Retrospect*. N.Y.: Commonwealth Fund. 1943.

GLUECK, S. and E., *Unraveling Juvenile Delinquency*. N.Y.: Commonwealth Fund. 1950.

GLUECK, S., and GLUECK, E., *Family Environment and Delinquency*. Lond.: Routledge. 1962.

QUAY, H. C., (ed.), *Juvenile Delinquency: Research and Theory*. Princeton: Van Nostrand. 1965.

29. BRILL, J. G., and PAYNE, E. G., *The Adolescent Court and Crime Prevention*. N.Y.: Pitman Publishing Corporation. 1938.

See also: FLEMING, C. M., loc. cit. [1]. 1948, 1955 and 1963.

COHEN, A. K., *Delinquent Boys*. Lond.: Routledge. 1956.

30. STOTT, D. H., *Delinquency and Human Nature*. Dunfermline: Carnegie United Kingdom Trust. 1950.

BETTELHEIM, B., loc. cit. [17]. 1950.

REDL, F., and WINEMAN, D., loc. cit. [22]. 1952.

STOTT, D. H., *Saving Children from Delinquency*. Lond.: Univ. of London Press Ltd. 1952.

See also: Ibid., *Brit. J. Soc. Clin. Psychol.* I. 182–91. 1962.

31. HEALY, W., and BRONNER, A. F., loc. cit. [10]. 1936.

GLUECK, S., and E., loc. cit. [28]. 1950.

POWERS, E., and WITMER, H., loc. cit. [23]. 1951.

32. WICKMAN, E. K., *Children's Behavior and Teachers' Attitudes*. N.Y.: Commonwealth Fund. 1928.

LAYCOCK, S. R., *Brit. J. Educ. Psychol.* IV. 1. 11–29. 1934.

33. MITCHELL, J. C., *J. Educ. Res.* XXXVI. 292–307. 1943.

34. SCHRUPP, M. H., and GJERDE, C. M., *J. Educ. Psychol.* XLIV. 4. 203–214. 1953.

35. SCHONELL, F. J., *Backwardness in the Basic Subjects*. Edinburgh: Oliver & Boyd. 1942.

36. HAMLEY, H. R., *The Education of Backward Children*. Lond.: Evans. 1936.

HIGHFIELD, M. E., *The Education of Backward Children*. Lond.: Harrap. 1939.

37. For sympathetic discussion of the difficulties of such children see: SEGAL, C., *Backward Children in the Making*. Lond.: Muller. 1949.

LLOYD, F., *Educating the Subnormal Child*. Lond.: Methuen. 1953.

See also: MADDOX, H., *Austral. J. Psychol.* 2. 1. 1–18. 1950.

CRUICKSHANK, W. (ed.), *Psychology of Exceptional Children and Youth*. N.Y.: Prentice-Hall. 1955.

EVANS, D., *An Experimental Study of a Group of Seriously Maladjusted Educationally Subnormal Children*. M.A. Thesis. Birmingham. 1956.

ROWE, A. W., *The Education of the Ordinary Child*. Lond.: Harrap. 1959.

HAWKRIDGE, D. G., *A Study of Less Successful Pupils in selected Secondary Schools*. Ph.D. Thesis. University of London. 1963.

HAWKRIDGE, D. G., Univ. Coll. Rhodesia. *Occas. Paper*. I. 1963.

38. WATERHOUSE, J. A. W., in *Yearbook of Education*. Lond.: Evans. 90–116. 1950.

ASHLEY MONTAGU, M. F., in SENN, M. J. E. (ed.), *Symposium on the Healthy Personality*. N.Y.: Josiah Macy Jr. Foundation. 1950.

DAVID, P. R., and SNYDER, L. H., in ROHRER, J. H., and SHERIF, M., *Social Psychology at the Crossroads*. 53–82. N.Y.: Harper. 1951.

39. HUSÉN, T. (ed.) *International Study of Achievement in Mathematics*. Stockholm: Almqvist & Wiksell. N.Y.: John Wiley. 1967.

40. FLEMING, C. M., *Brit. J. Educ. Psychol.* **XIII**. II. 74–82. 1943.

MOWAT, A. S., *City and Rural Schools*. Scottish Council for Research in Education. XI. 1938.

GREENHALGH, A. J., Talent Erosion. *Austral. J. Psychol.* **1**. 1. 11–25. 1949.

SEMPLE, S., *A Comparative Study of the Influences which affect the Education of Children in Urban and Rural Schools*. Ph.D. Thesis. London. 1954.

SCOTT, P., The Geographical Distribution of Intelligence. *Austral. J. Psychol.* **9**. 1. 41–6. 1957.

See also: GOODACRE, E. J., *Reading in Infant Classes*. London: Nat. Found. Educ. Res. 1967.

GOODACRE, E. J., *Teachers and their Pupils' Home Background*. Lond.: Nat. Found. Educ. Res. 1967.

41. VALENTINE, H. B., *Brit. J. Educ. Psychol.* **XXI**. II. 145–9. 1951.

CHILD, H. A. T., in *Studies in Education*, 7. Univ. of Lond. Inst. of Educ. 1955.

CURR, W., and GOURLAY, M., *Brit. J. Educ. Psychol.* **XXIII**. I. 45–55. 1953.

COLLINS, J. E., *The Effects of Remedial Education*. Ph.D. Thesis. Birmingham. 1956.

In contrast, see HENRY, G. B., *A Study of the Short-term and of the Long-term Results of Remedial Teaching in Reading*. M.A. Thesis. Birmingham. 1963.

42. THRASHER, F. M., *The Gang*. Chicago: Univ. of Chicago Press. 1927.

ROGERS, C. R., *The Clinical Treatment of the Problem Child*. Boston: Houghton Mifflin. 1939.

43. BENNE, K. D., and MUNTYAN, B., *Human Relations in Curriculum Change*. N.Y.: Dryden Press. 1951.

SHARP, G., *Curriculum Development as Re-education of the Teacher*. N.Y.: Teachers' College, Columbia U.P. 1951.

See also: CLEUGH, M. F., *Educating Older People*. Lond.: Tavistock Publications. 1962.

IX

THE PUPIL IN THE
CLASSROOM SITUATION

FROM CONSIDERATION OF research into motivation, learning, and growth a return may now be made to the classroom with its assembling of prospective learners face-to-face with a teacher. This collocation of teacher and pupils is the classroom's most characteristic pattern and it may usefully be examined from without (from the point of view of the teacher who enters) as well as from within – in the light of what is known as to its meaning for pupils and teachers.

Much heterogeneity

What is the essence of the situation as seen from without? In the first place – and irrespective of any prior efforts at classification – it is now known to be characterized by an almost infinite variety of attitudes, expectations, and frames of reference established by the total prior experience of each pupil, related to their past and their present, and changing from day to day with their physical health, their interests, their beliefs as to their own competence, and the effect upon them of their relationship to parents, to siblings, to peers, and to acquaintances.

For this reason the task of the teacher is never one of mere routine; and teachers can not predict the exact effect which a day's teaching will produce in any one of their pupils.

Some homogeneity

At the same time, in most parts of the world, there is a considerable measure of homogeneity. There may be a certain sameness of age, of years, months or days of attendance at school, and of legalized expectations as to the amount and the duration of schooling. There may be uniformity of sex, of language, of geographical background, and of religious affiliation. There may be similarity of socio-economic level; and in some schools, in some districts, and in some countries, there may have been classifying or 'streaming' according to ability on a specified earlier date.

Complex network of inter-relationships

Cutting across all this, there is a complicated network of personal relationships – the pupils in relation to their teachers as followers in association with a leader or as a reference group in opposition to an outsider,[1] the children in relation to their peers as co-members of reference groups, of out-groups and in-groups, as rivals or as co-operating teams, the children in relation to their parents with their knowledge of what some adults outside think of schooling in general and of this topic and this teacher in particular.

Overriding these is the common humanity of teachers and pupils with their personal needs for appreciation, participation, and insight; and their persisting concern with the building of a self-picture.

What do they think I am like?
What am I like?
What would I like to be like?

At the same time, both teachers and pupils are changing from day to day in fashions which are both gradual in nature and disharmonious or a-rhythmic in direction. What seems an impossible situation today may thus be transformed by tomorrow. A superficially small alteration in its patterning may be followed by a re-alignment of victors or vanquished, of co-workers or opponents, of in-groups and out-groups.

Supported by this knowledge, the task of the teacher is more challenging as well as more stimulating than it was in the nineteenth century or in the earlier decades of the twentieth century, when the interpretations of Bain and the associationists were still supported by the learning theories of Thorndike and the Behaviourists and had not yet been fully challenged by the contributions which had been made either by Pavlov (with his admission of the possible interference of distracting sights or sounds or relationships to an experimenter) or by the earlier Gestalt psychologists who, with Wertheimer, may have admitted that past experience was a Gestalt factor but still tended to neglect the variety and the variability of the contribution made by perceivers in the process of perceiving.[2]

141

Inadequate interpretations

When tempted to say 'I have told you', it is therefore important to remember that learning is not a mere matter of repetition or practice – that it is not a blind response to a an oft-repeated stimulus. The inattentive singing of the words of a hymn, the chanting of multiplication tables, the conjugation of irregular verbs, the transcribing of errors in spelling, the copying of correct forms of sentence structure. None of these can be expected of themselves to result in improved procedures. Learning is now quite commonly recognized as more than a mere training of faculties or disciplining of wills. It is not so often remembered that it is also more than the mere fixing of a habit through either the recency or the frequency of an external presentation.

Learners are not passive but active; and only those repetitions or exercises which are instrumental to their purposes are effective. In more technical terms, only the 'information' which confirms an existing hypothesis (expectancy or set) is 'perceived'; and only that which is so perceived is learned. The process is not one of conditioning through contiguity (Guthrie) nor reinforcement by simultaneity (Pavlov). The careful stimulation of a well-planned blackboard often carries no 'meaning' to its viewers; and the competent summarizing of a teacher or a fellow-pupil can pass without notice. Only those experiences which fit into an existing pattern of relationships are cognized (Tolman); and the fitting into such cognitive matrices or maps is also facilitated by a social consensus acceptable to the learner (Postman).

The reaction of the perceiver is always to the physical and social world as that is personally apprehended. It is not an automatic sequel to the expert organizing of external conditions. One cannot take a horse to the water and make him drink (Skinner) – or take a child to school and make him learn – except in so far as the necessary prearranging of conditions is held to include the personal involvement of the child or the horse and the relation of the horse or the child to the 'teacher'.

Pupils study teachers

Boys and girls are in all these respects more like their teachers than their teachers have often been led to suppose. From the moment of first encounter teachers are aware that they should somehow study their pupils; and in a fashion less deliberate but quite as real most pupils in turn concentrate on the understanding of their teachers.

Does this one mean what she says?
Does he know what he is talking about?
Am I going to like this one?
Does this one know what he is expected to do?

In intent silence (which the teacher-novice may attribute to appreciation of his skill) the class makes its careful assessments.

He looks as if he could take a joke.
She seems to see me.
I like the sound of his voice.
I don't like that pointing finger.
He can't write on the blackboard.
She doesn't know where the chalk is kept.
He forgets what he has just said.

After a period of avid collection of details, the pupils, with a degree of deliberation which varies with the traditions of the school, proceed to further investigations supported by experiment.

What will happen if . . . ?
Will she draw the line at . . . ?
Does he see what is happening here?

The situation as seen from within

There is some relevance to this in pupils' answers to the question as to what they like best in teachers and in studies of the relationship between the relative popularity of a school subject and the degree of friendliness felt by pupils towards a teacher. There is, on the whole, a preference for the subjects taught by the more popular teachers; but the 'popularity' of a teacher in this sense seems related to competence as estimated by the pupils – a finding confirmed in Birchmore's record that specialist teachers made less appeal when teaching a second subject not their own. It is related also to the satisfaction by the teachers of the pupils' need for personal appreciation and a chance to participate (expressed in the comments 'has not got favourites' and 'has patience'). What is desired is not so much a generalized 'loving' or a sentimentalized encouragement. (Personal praise and blame are characteristic of the authoritarian rather than the democratic atmosphere.) There is a certain cool assessment on the part of pupils as of teachers and an alertness of discrimination on both sides as to the significance of things said and done. At the same time the relationship between each teacher and each pupil is unique. Pupils are rarely rated in the same fashion by all their teachers; and the same teachers are rated differently by different pupils (Birchmore).

The issue is further complicated by the fact that pupils do not necessarily agree with adult views as to the meaning of certain teaching procedures. The words used by a dictator may differ only very slightly from those used by a democratically-minded guide (Anderson); and some dictators appear to be accepted while others are resented (Lewin). Not irrelevant to this was an inquiry with an older group of students carried out by Arbuckle at the University of Boston. Three types of relationship were studied: student-centred, instructor-centred, and a third in which the tutor played the part of a consultant. Groups experienced all three types of treatment without interpretation of their intention; but at the end of the experiment, all three groups believed that the predominating relationship had been 'student-centred'. None was aware that it had experienced an equivalent amount of direct lecturing and instruction as well as treatment intended to take special account of the students' willingness to work independently. The reactions of each group had been to their assessment of the genuine kindliness and friendliness of the tutors – regardless of the words used or the procedures followed. 'How can I hear what you are saying when what you are is thundering in my ears?' In some such fashion pupils at every age look through the externals of the situation and make their decisions accordingly.[3]

Individual differences

At the same time it may be remembered that pupils differ in rate and intensity of reaction and in capacity to achieve clarity of apprehension. Even in the first weeks of life there are observable differences in the responses made by infants to their mothers under what appear to be comparable conditions.[4] The world seems to impinge in differing fashions on different babies; and an asseveration of the possibility of somewhat similar organic variations is implicit in the continuing quest of physiologists and physicists for a verifiable hypothetical construct between stimulation and response either on a neurological model (Zangwill, Freeman, Hebb) or a cybernetic pattern (Wiener).[5]

Pupils differ also from time to time in their immediate reaction to differing types of social climates. This is not because of any static attributes of 'personality' in the teacher or the child but again seems related rather to the 'hypotheses' or 'sets' with which they approach a special situation. The transition from the dictatorship of one teacher to the friendly guidance of another has its special problems (Lewin). It requires some weeks to 'take one's bearings' with a new teacher; and pupils, for reasons which may be quite temporary, find satisfaction sometimes in direct prescriptions and the solving of their perplexities by another – although on other occasions, and at other levels of difficulty, they may appreciate independent inquiry and discussion with their peers.[6] Perception of what is superficially the same situation thus varies according to the practices to which children have been subjected (Orlansky), to the prior attitudes of parents and friends (Murphy), to things heard and overheard (Plant), to group-membership position as leaders or followers (Sherif), to level of aspiration (Lewin), or to expectations of success or defeat (Moodie), as well as in terms of organic qualities of sensitivity of reaction.[7]

These differences may be found in relation to the school as an institution, to teachers as a group, and to lessons in general as well as to the perhaps contradictory frames of references held in relation to a specific classroom, teacher or task. Friend or foe, comforter or tyrant, the one to be followed or the one who is an outsider. The connotation of the word 'teacher' in the eyes of a class carries no constant meaning. It brings echoes of all earlier relationships; but it is perennially new and modifiable in the light of each day's exploratory behaviour (Sherif). The teacher and the task may, so far as intentions go, remain the same; but the pupils' understanding of purposes and intentions may at any time expand or contract. The introduction of a new method or the more sympathetic analysis of immediate objectives can for this reason transform the attitudes of troublesome pupils who have, until their introduction, seen schools as places where teachers set impossible tasks. When pupils reach insight (see what it is all about) they attain a measure of success unknown before; and material which seemed incomprehensible when presented too rapidly and in unanalysed fashion may, by a quite simple rearrangement into graded steps, become attractive and pleasantly contributory to the growth of the self-confidence which waits upon success.

Such classroom experiences react in turn upon the learner's self-picture or concept of the self. Motivational support is gained not merely through the avoidance of annoyance and the experiencing of satisfiers (Thorndike in succession to Bain) but through the translation of these into more personal terms.

They like me. This of mine is approved.
I am of sufficient interest to be noticed (reproved).

In some such fashion the improved responses which occur in favourable social climates follow upon increases in the clarity of the self-picture and its modification in the direction of more confident co-operation in the outcomes desired by the educator.[8] The task of the teacher is not the making of case-studies of each individual pupil in order to attach a label to each. It is rather the assisting of each child to discover his own educational status and requirements – thinking with him rather than viewing him as an object, and recognizing (in the fashion of the non-directive therapists) that he is engaged always in the organizing of his own perceptual field.[9]

At the same time it is reassuring for teachers to note that the expectancies, sets or hypotheses of each group of pupils are a function of the experiences in which they have shared as well as of the characteristic ways in which they regard themselves. While each pupil is more than an automaton at the mercy of environmental forces and while each responds in slightly different fashion to the same leadership, there has been a coincidence of past presentation or 'information' which makes communication possible. This contributes to a considerable congruence of intention as between pupils and teachers. Pupils are in fact aware that there is much that they do not know.[10] They would prefer success rather than failure; and the expectations of their reference groups of parents and friends are in many cases in line with the official intentions of the schools.[11] While learning is not a mere response to externally organized promptings (Thorndike or Skinner) nor a simple sequel to reinforcement through the primary drives of physical threats or rewards (Hull), there is a certain communality in the cognitive maps of children and adults which makes co-operative action a possibility.

What was formerly described as attention or attentiveness is for such reasons now recognized as an issue of extreme complexity. Though there is both an outer and an inner – a stimulation through eye, ear, and other sensory receptors as well as an organism responding in a characteristic fashion – a pupil's reactions in the learning situation are now seen as exploratory rather than random. There is not something which can be vaguely described as a passing 'from the known to the unknown' but rather an enlargement of the known by fuller recognition of its relationships.[12] Conquest of the basic number combinations comes by way of deeper understanding of their meaning coupled with a picture of oneself as one who can both learn to react rapidly and who wishes so to react. Among children as among animals there is also a direct delight in the acquisition of knowledge and manipulative competence;[13] and, through the satisfactions given by such accretions of skill, children can be seen to learn and to pass by a process of reassurance, support, and enlightenment to some measure of acceptability, participation, and insight.

It was an over-simplification on the part of certain exponents of Progressive Education which led in the 1930s to the advice that drill should be forgotten, that atmosphere is more important than textbooks, that one should, for example, not try to teach arithmetic but 'teach discovery, life, and nature through arithmetic'. This had its value as a protest against an exaggerated emphasis on the forming of bonds and as an asseveration (in the language of that time) of the fact that learning is 'subordinate to the growth and the demands of the personality-as-a-whole'. Even in a rat viewed externally at a choice-point in a maze there is reason to assume some complex process of perceptual organization – a cognitive map (Tolman), or a fractional anticipatory reaction to the goal (Hull) – and the learning of human beings whether dull or bright, young or old, is admittedly not a matter of the mechanical forming of associations or the fumblings of blind trial and error.[14] It is, however, now known with greater definiteness than was possible in the 1930s that, while there is a patterning of perception by past individual history, personal endowment, and present social pressures, there are also differences which are related to the quality and the character of the stimulus which is presented.[15] Group influences are most powerful in relation to relatively unstructured phenomena (lines or words of similar length, patterns of vague form, and the like); and the search for honesty of interpretation at quite an early age shows itself in a careful assessment of probabilities (trials and check) which may, on occasion, place the prestige of fellow-pupils higher than that of their teacher in the case of sensory information which is ambiguous in any respect.[16] Children, like all perceivers, select and accentuate and organize; and for this reason also where the directives given by an adult are uncertain they are

147

particularly likely not to 'believe' all that they are told or 'remember' all that they see. In the light of current knowledge as to differences in reaction to differing degrees of stimulation, it is, therefore, important that they receive suitable and skilful tuition – that the phenomena presented to them be adequately structured with sufficient repetition and sufficient clarity of 'information' to support the perceptual 'hypotheses' which the teacher, for any reason, desires to 'confirm'.

The teacher's task

The task of the teacher is thus not merely that of an enthusiastic guide – directing the perceptions of pupils through satisfying their psychological needs and changing the patterns of their self-picture or the degree of their self-involvement. Teachers are also concerned with the quality of the stimulation they offer. They are responsible for analyses of the content and the materials of instruction in the subjects which they teach and they must make decisions as to their methods of presentation (the Teacher as Craftsman). They are also expected to undertake an assessment of the success or the failure of their educational endeavours (the Teacher as Technician); and they must face the issues involved in the educating of human beings who are characterized both by a wide range of individual differences and by the basic similarities of their common humanity (the Teacher as Administrator).

From consideration of these, a return may later be made to the teacher as therapist – as leader in the inter-personal relationships through which children in their groups contribute to the education of one another, or as producer in the presentation of the drama whose ultimate authorship must be accredited to the child.[17]

REFERENCES

1. BERENDA, R. W., *The Influence of the Group on the Judgments of Children*. N.Y.: King's Crown Press. 1950.
   HOLLANDER, E. P., *Principles and Methods of Social Psychology*. N.Y.: Oxford Univ. Press. 1967.
2. BRUNER, J. S., and POSTMAN, L., in DENNIS, W., *Current Trends in Social Psychology*. Pittsburgh: Univ. of Pittsburgh Press. 71–118. 1948.
   VERNON, M. D., *A Further Study of Visual Perception*. Cambridge. C.U.P. 1952.
3. BERENDA, R. W., loc. cit. [1].

4. ESCALONA, S., in CARMICHAEL, L. (ed.), *Manual of Child Psychology.* 971–83. 1954.

5. Cf. MACKAY, D. M., *Brit. J. Psychol.* **XLVII.** 1. 30–43. 1956.
KLEINMUTZ, B. (ed.), *Concepts and the Structure of Memory.* N.Y.: John Wiley. 1967.

6. WISPE, L. G., *Amer. Psychologist.* **8.** 4. 147–50. 1953.

7. LEWIN, K., DEMBO, T., FESTINGER, L., and SEARS, P. S., in HUNT, J. MC. V., *Personality and the Behavior Disorders.* N.Y.: Ronald Press. 333–78. 1944.
ORLANSKY, H., *Psychol. Bull.* **46.** 1. 1–48. 1949.

8. JERSILD, A. T., *Child Psychology.* 4th ed. N.Y.: Prentice-Hall. 1954.

9. ROGERS, C. R., *Amer. Psychologist.* **2.** 9. 358–68. 1947.

10. DANG, S. D., *A Study of Co-operation in Certain Secondary Schools.* M.A. Thesis. London. 1949.

11. GARSIDE, A., *A Study of the Wishes as to Their Children's Development Expressed by a Group of Parents of Primary School Children.* M.A. Thesis. London. 1956.
COLEMAN, J. S., *et al.*, *The Adolescent Society.* Glencoe: Free Press. 1961.
MUSSEN, P. H., *et al.*, *Child Development and Personality.* N.Y.: Harper. 1956 and 1963.
MUSGROVE, F., *The Family, Education and Society.* Lond.: Routledge. 1966.
DAVIS, C., *Room to Grow.* Toronto: Univ. of Toronto Press. 1966.

12. STERN, H. H., *Case Conference.* **2.** 2. 4–14. 1955.
HARLOW, H. F., *Psychol. Rev.* **56.** 51–65. 1949.
HEBB, D. O., *The Organization of Behavior.* N.Y.: John Wiley. 1949.

13. HARLOW, H. F., in ROHRER, J. H., and SHERIF, M., *Social Psychology at the Cross-roads.* N.Y.: Harper. 1951.
From a very different point of view see also: BÜHLER, C., *et al.*, *Childhood Problems and the Teacher.* Routledge. 1953.

14. MORRIS, R., *The Quality of Learning.* Lond.: Methuen. 1951.

15. POSTMAN, L., *Psychol. Monographs.* **68.** 3. 1954.
See also: KATONA, G., *Organising and Memorising.* N.Y.: Columbia U.P. 1940.

16. BERENDA, R. W., loc. cit. [1].

17. RASKIN, N. J., *J. Consult. Psychol.* **XIII.** 2. 92–110. 1948.

PART V

THE TEACHER AS
CRAFTSMAN AND TECHNICIAN

X

CRAFTSMANSHIP IN TEACHING

TEACHERS CAN BE described in many ways. They have been likened to artists, to gardeners, or, more recently, to social engineers; and each phrase conveys some inkling of their power. Each metaphor may, however, also over-emphasize what is merely one aspect. The 'artists' tend towards neglect of what is useful and humdrum. The 'gardeners' may too fiercely discard the weeds and segregate their flowers into the conformities of neat groups. The 'engineers' may lay undue stress upon the study of efficiencies in the control of men.

Better tribute may therefore perhaps be paid to both wisdom and experience by using the more humble word 'craftsman' in designation of a teacher's skill. Teachers are craftsmen in their concern with the material under their hand. They are cognizant of the variety and the uniqueness of their charges and aware of the personal and social processes by which modifications can be wrought. They are craftsmen also in their interest in the stimulation they offer – its content in terms of activity and knowledge, and the materials of instruction through which it can take perceptible shape. They strive also to be experts in the selection of methods through which its conquest can be commended to their pupils. To some consideration of this content and these methods attention may now be given.

In respect of their pupils the consensus of current evidence might be summed up by saying to teachers:

Observe them.
Believe in them.

They are worthy of study. Their behaviour is understandable. They are modifiable; and they are in fact perennially in the process of change.[1]

In respect of the subject-matter of schooling the parallel comments are:

Analyse it.
Organize it.

Discover its content. Observe the relationships of its difficulties; and present it in a setting in which insight is invited and understanding becomes possible.

The contribution of educational research

A transition to this viewpoint was, in brief, the course taken by educational research over the decades since 'experimental education' brought research workers into the schools. The earliest contributions were made by psychologists like Thorndike who, watching a solitary cat in a puzzle-box or a chicken in a maze, came to think in terms of stimulus-response, habit formation, exercise and the effect of success. Through such studies they became convinced that in human learning also one could secure correct responses by applying appropriate stimuli. If learning is largely a matter of the association of experiences – of establishing bonds or connections – then it is necessary to make careful analyses to discover the essentials of each subject – step by step – as a preliminary to the provision of adequate drill in that subject. This led teachers to an emphasis on definiteness of stimulation (one step at a time) regular repetition (drill) and careful assessment of degree of success (testing).

Some thirty years later, Skinner, working with electronically patterned machines, reached similar conclusions from the analysis of billions of cumulative records of the reactions of rats or pigeons to the instantaneous rewarding of desired behaviour. Applying his results to human beings he proposed that the total 'programme' of a subject should be very fully analysed and presented in short statements with questions and the immediate 'reinforcement' of knowledge of successful answering.

It had been suggested in 1926 that questions could be asked and answers could be checked by a machine; and in the 1950s electrical appliances were so far developed that a straightforward (linear) series of questions and their answers could be presented in such a way that pupils could not go on to a second question until they had given a correct answer to the first.[2]

This analytic approach can be criticized from the point of view

154

of over-emphasis on the mechanics of learning. In the 1920s it led to undue concentration upon drill and attention to immediate utility (a search for the most frequent words and the like). It also tempted teachers to underestimate the activity of the learner – the part played by personal responsibility – and purposive behaviour. Some recognition of this appears to have been behind the Dalton Plan with its 'assignments' (later called 'work-cards') and the Project Method with its emphasis on studies which were obviously related to adult life. To these the Winnetka Technique added awareness that both pupils and teachers could become interested in 'diagnostic' testing to locate the exact nature of their difficulties.[3] Provision of such tests made it possible to foster individual effort by permitting pupils to move steadily at their own rate through self-instructive, self-corrective textbooks – conquering each step as they went and revising where diagnosis showed that revision was necessary. (See Chapter XI below.)

In somewhat similar fashion 'linear' programmes were later supplemented by 'branching' programmes which directed pupils to supplementary exercises which could develop fuller understanding and lead to insight through guided discovery.

Provision for such programmed learning is available for many subjects and in many forms – in sheets and textbooks as well as in programmes ('frames' or 'units') designed for 'teaching-machines'. Its significance, like that of any form of analytic material, lies less in its details than in the claim that the direction of learning can be controlled. Its weakness is its under-emphasis on human ability to generalize. This was, in effect, the challenge presented by Katona, Wertheimer and their successors when they drew attention to the significance of insight and recognition of relationships in the conquest of mathematics or science,[4] to the part played by thinking in the process of learning to read,[5] and to the relevance of social maturity in the understanding of history or literature.[6]

A slightly different development was supported by those students of learning who laid stress on the contribution of past experience to present perception. This had its affinities with the work of clinical psychologists and of social psychologists as indicated in Chapters IV and VI above. Its contribution to the teachers' craft lies in its emphasis on the significance of attitude and level of aspiration, on the satisfaction of personal needs and the building of an acceptable self-picture.

Through these three lines of influence the work of psychologists has in the last few decades contributed to a silent educational revolution in the schools of most countries. A fuller understanding of what is to be taught – the analytic approach. A clearer appreciation of the activity of the learner through personal insight – the gestaltists' approach. A deeper awareness of the complexities of interrelationships in the act of perception as well as in the contacts of a classroom group – the perceptual and social approach. Recognition of the significance of these three and a firm retention of the benefits conferred by each is a task worthy of the highest endeavours of the craftsmen who will be teachers in the schools of the future.

Fuller consideration will be given in later chapters to the relevance of these to measurement and to other administrative problems. Here attention is directed rather to representative issues in the presentation of certain subjects chosen in terms of the volume of psychological research which has been devoted to their study. No attempt is made to cover the whole field of the psychology of each school subject.[7] It may, however, be noted that in each field and at every level it is well that analysis be adequate and that opportunities be given for the participation of each pupil and the co-operative support of each group. Beyond this there are certain similarities of structure and procedure which render many possible inquiries both unnecessary and unduly repetitive.

Learning to read

The first formal endeavour of the infant school is directed to the teaching of reading; and success in this comes through the discovery by pupils that communication of meaning is possible through certain symbols on blackboard or paper. This discovery is prepared for by experiences and conversations which encourage children in their belief that the world is interesting and full of new things to do and fresh things to learn.

Boys and girls on entry to school know that they are growing up. Babyhood is left behind. They have come out to 'work'; and the wise teacher neither despises nor neglects their aspirations after the purposeful and the mature. The first steps in learning to read are, however, quite informal. The teacher has a 'book' out of which she 'reads' stories which are a delight. The teacher has a blackboard on which she draws patterns to convey special messages to the class. 'GOOD

MORNING.' 'TIME FOR MILK.' 'STAND UP.' 'SIT DOWN.' The patterns are always the same; and almost unawares the pupils come to distinguish one from another. Meanwhile many other activities prepare the way for further attention to small differences in shape and direction. The pupils match or classify pictures, toys, counters, shells or beads. They draw and paint. They dance to music. They sing. They tell of their adventures and listen to those of others. In the course of these experiences the perceptual processes relevant to reading are quite unwittingly being used. They are 'learning' to differentiate. (This was the point made by Hebb in the elaborate organization of cell-assemblies and phase sequences which he postulated to account for differences in the recognition of details on the part of animals with and without earlier perceptual stimulation. It was explicit also in the stress laid by Bartlett and by Vernon on the contribution of established schemata to present perceiving; and it is expressed in a slightly different fashion by Harlow's reminder that in a very real sense there is a 'learning to learn'.)[8]

The next step is taken when the pupils' record of their thinking is transferred from large surfaces such as pavements, blackboards or poster-sheets to small pieces of paper on which to begin their own first 'book'. This may be, as at Winnetka, an illustration of something which the teacher has read to them at an earlier stage. It may be a story of their own inventing.[9] For a title to each picture the teacher can then supply appropriate words: 'This is Tom. He is coming to play.'; and praise may be given for the accurate 'reading' of each line.

In some such fashion recognition of the shape of words begins for those who are reared in an environment in which words and books are part of the accepted pattern of living. In some such fashion at a much earlier age the first steps were taken in the understanding and the imitation of speech; and in some such fashion also the expert teacher of a foreign tongue later establishes the first contacts of pupils with the rhythms and the patterns of a second language.[10]

From this 'sentence-method' of introducing the process of reading, progress is next made to the division of a sentence into words. This is done, if possible, by the pupil's own use of scissors and paper. The words can then be matched with the sentence from which they came; and games can be played to encourage rapid recognition of each. When knowledge of a few dozen words has been established, a printed book can be introduced in which the same words are to be found – at

157

first in the order familiar to the pupils and later in mixed order leading to the 'discovery' of a new story.[11]

This, in essence, is the content of the initial stages sometimes described as the 'sentence-method' or the 'look and say' approach to reading. They are in direct challenge to the older 'associative' procedure in which a beginning was made with the naming of the letters of the alphabet – A, B, C (the alphabetic approach), with the sound of the vowels and the consonants (the phonic approach) or with phonetic symbols for each sound (the phonetic approach). They make possible the personal activity of pupils through recognition of the meaning of what is seen and through the provision of sets of 'key' pictures and sentences with which any word can be 'matched' if there is uncertainty as to its significance.

No one method

These methods do not begin by drawing attention to the analysis of words nor confuse children by an emphasis on similarities and differences within them. They are not, however, procedures which cover all that has to be learned; and they were not intended by their originators to be the only line of approach. At an early stage the step must be taken to the making of discoveries about words – 'word-making and word-taking', word-matching, word-rhyming, and guessing games involving the recognition that certain words sound alike and, later, that certain words begin with the same sound. 'I am thinking of something. It begins with a b . . .' (If the pupils say 'house' or 'waistcoat' it is probable that they are not yet ready for the phonic analysis of printed material.)

In protest against unduly prolonged emphasis on mere 'looking' and 'guessing' and unwise postponement of any attempt at phonic analysis it has been proposed that some books should be constructed in a fashion which conforms to the simplest rules of direct linkage of sound and spelling.[12] This is a reminder that a contribution is made by hearing as well as by seeing; and it is useful through its provision of alternative material which may be tried with a pupil who has missed the way with other methods.

Many of the successes of remedial treatment are attributable to the fresh hope supplied by a teacher who forgets past failure and permits a backward child to try again in another way. The presentation of the case for phonic analysis is quite in line with the belief in educability which inspires such efforts; and it is thus in direct contradiction to the supposition that a child who fails to learn to read is a child without the organic capacity for reading or one whose 'organismic age' is such that he has not reached the stage at which the learning of reading can most suitably be placed.[13]

Somewhat similar in intention are the variants which employ phonetic material. These offer special symbols for selected sounds as in Pitman's 'initial teaching alphabet' (an off-shoot of the simplified spelling movement). Their weakness appears to lie in the time spent in the learning of symbols which will later have to be forgotten; and research findings do not show that any form of phonetic script is consistently more effective as a teaching aid for beginners than the printed matter which even 'babies' see on every hoarding.[14]

Age-placement

Little emphasis is now put on the topic of 'age-placement' in reading or in other subjects. With fuller understanding of the complexity of each process it is not now said, for example, that reading cannot begin until a mental age of six and a half years, that an interest in spelling does not appear till a mental age of nine or conceptual thinking until thirteen, The contribution made by differences of approach and of attitude on the part of both teacher and learner is now more fully glimpsed; and interest has turned to the need for continued diagnosis and suitable stimulation through primary school and secondary school as well as at the tertiary stages of education in University or College.[15]

Contributory to this also is the recognition that for some pupils, with a certain history of earlier hopes and fears, the method of choice may be one which makes use of muscular skills – a kinaesthetic approach which permits tracing or copying or feeling the outline of raised letters or even the building up of words with the use of a typewriter. Through these a measure of success may be attained which seemed impossible in the light of other past defeats and much earlier experience of inadequacy.[16]

Discovering arithmetic

A similar variety in approach and a similar emphasis on the significance of meaning now characterize the encouragement of quantitative thinking through which boys and girls take their first steps in the discovery of arithmetic.[17]

Much relevant experience comes in the first place through the informal sorting and counting which were contributory to the perceptual skills which prepared the way for reading.[18] Certain number concepts are included in the thinking of many pupils before they come to school.[19] Taller, shorter, many, few, wide, narrow, one, two (three, four, five), more, less – such words may be freely used and their meaning may be understood with greater or lesser clarity. The first more formal steps can be planned with the knowledge that mathematical thinking is concerned with classifying, (the cardinal numbers and the number system in terms of tens) with setting concepts in order (the ordinals and comparisons of size) and with awareness of relationships (the basic number facts $0+0$, $0—0$, 0×0, $0 \div 1$ and their successors in the 390 combinations which form the substructure of arithmetic). These can be approached by the three stages of discovery, recognition, and use.

Discovery comes through counting, comparing, and building up new groups or new models from their contributory parts. How many pupils are ready? How many little tables do we need to make a big one? How many shells are in that box? How many steps are in the big stair? Suitable material in differing colours and geometric shapes has been popularized in Tillich's blocks, in Montessori's modifications of Seguin's apparatus; and, more recently, in the equipment suggested by Stern, Cuisenaire and Dienes.[21] Such blocks are useful as aids to the discovery of the meaning of numbers and as guides in the exploration of their relationships. They are props to be discarded when progression, at any level, is made to the next stages of recognition and of use. An undue enthusiasm for classroom 'activity' has, however, sometimes tempted teachers to linger too long in the rather aimless encouragement of undirected manipulation of miscellaneous objects. The progression to 'arithmetic' is more joyfully accepted by pupils when counting and sorting are early accompanied by the more 'grown-up' undertaking of 'keeping a note'. 'This is how we write the story.' 'Here is what the number looks like.' 'You may write it down.' The picture of the two cows has on it a 'drawing' of the digit 2. The box with eight counters may have in it a card showing eight counters and the digit 8; and the pupils may be supplied with blackboards and with paper on which they may record their own discoveries after they have made them. No emphasis need be put on perfection of shape; and marked variations may be anticipated in the rate of transition from 'sorting' by colour, size or shape to 'counting' the groups produced, and thence to the 'recording' of what has been found out.

How many are there?
I don't know.
Count to find out.
There is no hurry.

This is the first stage of discovery. The transition to recognition comes quite simply.

How many are there?
I think I know.
Write it down.
Count to find if you are right.
There is plenty of time.

This step is assisted by question-answer cards with pictures or digits on one side (the question), and digits and pictures on the other (the question and the answer). 'What is the question? Is the answer right? . . . Turn the card over and find out.' Immediacy of correction discourages the recollection of wrong solutions; and individual and group games can foster speed of reaction.

How many does that make?
I know.
How fast can I give the answer?

From this the transition to the third stage of use may readily be made – through oral stories and problems, through projects in which work is done as a means to an end, and through the intrinsic satisfyness of success and the joy of achievement which can come from progression through wisely graded text-books which provide for preparatory discovery of the meaning of each new step and offer material suited to the diagnosis and remedial treatment of each personal difficulty encountered.[22]

The learning of a language

Quite similar stages are discernible in modern approaches to the study of language.[23] These no longer begin by the deductive or definitory emphasis long favoured by the grammarians: 'The nouns of the first declension are . . .' 'The following prepositions govern the accusative . . .' Discovery of differences in intonation and pronunciation are now made through direct auditory encounter with speech in another tongue. This may take place in a classroom with group use of recorded speech or in a special 'language laboratory' with individual earphones and tape recordings. In either situation, recognition of meaning is effected through interpretation of situations which accompany sounds which were at first unintelligible. Later imitative use of the same patterns is then checked against and rewarded by the comprehension of an audience to whom the remarks are directed.

Gradual differentiation thus follows upon more extensive practice; and usage, at first oral and then written, may later be paralleled by the introduction of material on question-answer cards in association with pictures or designs. Such a direct method of approach to foreign tongues is (like the 'sentence-method' in the introduction of reading and the active exploration of quantitative relationships in arithmetic) in line with the contribution made by insight and by the 'expectation' of meaning in the interpretation of perceptual patterns of more formal style (see Chapter VI above).

The conquest of a skill

In not dissimilar fashion approaches are now made to the conquest of a new skill. In an atmosphere of hope and trust – 'of course you can' – the teacher, with full awareness of individual differences, plans to ensure thorough mastery by careful analysis of content and by preliminary introduction of relevant contributory movements of the larger or smaller muscles in eye or ear or limb. Through orderly arrangement of tasks an attempt is made to avoid unnecessary defeat; and by balanced practice each success is consolidated into a more confident ultimate performance. From the pupil's point of view, a general awareness of the total pattern is followed by insight into and appreciation of its meaning. This comes both through perceptual recognition of its content and through confident use of each contributory skill. The pupil who learns to ski, to skate, to dance, to paint, or to sing can thus be set on the road which leads to success. The teacher who is a craftsman has helped to place him there. The distance he will travel depends on his own attitude, expectancy or set, and also on the social consensus of his group in its effect upon his willingness to persevere with the later experiences which alone will bring his skill to its perfection.

A somewhat similar placing in the total setting of the pupil's development is discernible in modern approaches to the study of certain content subjects. Of these history is an example.

The study of history

The choice of historical topics for history courses in schools has, like the order of their presentation, been influenced by successive interpretations in the fields of philosophy, psychology, and education. It was at one time proposed that they be determined by the supposition that children recapitulate a racial progression from primitive man through agriculturalist to industrialist or technician.[24] It was later suggested that Jung's archetypes should be reflected in the grouping of topics round notions such as mother-father, the hero, the shadow, the wise old man, and the wise old woman,[25] or that historical surveys might be arranged according to centres of interest starting with the familiar things of everyday life and tracing these backwards in time and outwards in space.[26] It has also been claimed that a beginning should be made with stories of romantic adventure followed by treatment of the same episodes in tales reflecting the usefulness of expanding commerce and, later, by an argumentative interpretation of their political relevance. Cutting across all these has been the recurrent proposal that what is necessary is a time-chart showing the events of today, fifty years ago, one hundred years ago, and so on down the ages.[27]

In what is probably the most thorough analysis accessible to English readers, Abouzied makes a survey of these approaches and points through them to the significance of the continuity and the change which are now known to characterize human development.[28] Boys and girls pass from a search for 'truth' and small beginnings of interest in others to a degree of social maturity sufficient to permit their sympathetic reconstruction of the story of the past in terms of some understanding of the motives of other people. The historian is concerned with persons, events in time and place, their interrelations, and the interpretation of these in the light of his own developing vocabulary and his own increasing experience. The pupil studying history makes what is essentially the same pilgrimage. He can only be obstructed by a mistaken condescension which underestimates his human longing for insight and drives him back to a mere memorizing of the details reported by others, without exercise of discriminatory judgment and with no encouragement of a continuous interpreting which goes always as far as it can.

Some inkling of this may be detected in Piaget's anecdotal records of the growth of vocabulary in the fields of causation, quantity, time or space. What Piaget offers can most fully be appreciated when it is placed in this context of the process of learning as it occurs at any age through the exploratory and discriminatory contacts of ordinary living.[29] In the field of history, as in the initial steps in reading, counting, and the like, children are all the time 'learning to learn'; and through the invitation to interpret and to carry out personal investigations in 'source-books' and primary records, the craftsmen among the history-teachers of today are maintaining interest and enthusiasm in groups of pupils who formerly, under less skilful procedures, showed what was taken to be both 'inevitable unwillingness' and 'biological unreadiness' to learn.

In fashions such as these attention is turning in different fields to the organizing and reorganizing of material and the guiding of pupils towards insight and co-operative activity. It is thus no longer suggested that the teacher's responsibility lies mainly in the provision of drill whether on sounds and letters, on tables, on words or on dates; and in these, as in other subject fields, both teachers and pupils are reaching fuller understanding of the complexities and the delights of the learning situation.

REFERENCES

1. On this see also: PRESCOTT, D. A., *et al., Helping Teachers Understand Children.* Washington: American Council on Education, 1945.
2. SKINNER, B. F., *Cumulative Record.* N.Y.: Appleton-Century-Crofts. 1959 and 1961.
   GOLDSMITH, M. (ed.) *Mechanisation in the Classroom.* Lond.: Souvenir Press. 1963.
   MARKLE, S. M., *Good Frames and Bad.* N.Y.: John Wiley. 1964.
   PRESSEY, S. L., Auto-Instruction in Hilgard, E. R. (ed.) Theories of Learning and Instruction. *63rd Yearbook Nat. Soc. for the Study of Educ.* Part I. 1964.
   RICHMOND, W. K., *Teachers and Machines.* Lond.: Collins. 1965.
   HAWKRIDGE, D. G., *J. of Assoc. for Programmed Learning.* Feb. 1966.
   UNWIN, D., *Educ. Rev.* **18.** 2. 136–46. 1966.
   ROUCEK, J. S., *Programmed Learning.* Lond.: Peter Owen. 1966.
3. For an accessible summary see: FLEMING, C. M., *Individual Work in Primary Schools.* Lond.: Harrap. 1934.
   HAWKRIDGE, D. G., Univ. Coll. Rhodesia. *Occasional Paper I.* 1963.
4. KATONA, G., *Organising and Memorising.* N.Y.: Columbia U.P. 1940.
   BROWNELL, W. A., *Arithmetic in Grades I and II.* Durham: Duke Univ. Press. 1941.
5. RUSSELL, D. H., *Children Learn to Read.* Boston: Ginn. 1949.

WERTHEIMER, M., *Productive Thinking*. N.Y.: Harper. 1945.

STERN, C., *Children Discover Arithmetic*. N.Y.: Harper. 1949.

PEEL, E. A., *Brit. J. Educ. Psychol.* XXV. III. 135–44. 1955.

LEE, D. M., ibid. XXV. III. 178–89. 1955.

See also relevant chapters in: GATES, A. I. (Chairman), *Reading in the Elementary School*. 48th *Yearbook* of the National Society for the Study of Education. Pt. II. 1949.

STRANG, R., MCCULLOUGH, C. M., and TRAXLER, A. E., *Problems in the Improvement of Reading*. N.Y.: McGraw-Hill. 1946 and 1955.

BIRCH, L. B., *Brit. J. Educ. Psychol.* XX. II. 73–6. 1950.

6. ABOUZIED, H., *An Enquiry into the Learning of History by Adolescent Pupils between the ages of Sixteen and Nineteen*. Ph.D. Thesis. London. 1955.

7. For relevant summaries see: FLEMING, C. M., *Research and the Basic Curriculum*. Lond.: Univ. of London Press, 1946 and 1952.

See also recurrent summaries in the *Review of Educational Research*, and reports in the *British Journal of Educational Psychology*, the publications of the Scottish Council for Research in Education and the corresponding bodies in Australia, New Zealand, England and Wales, etc., the Bureau of Education, Teachers' College, Columbia University, New York, *The Journal of Educational Psychology*, *The Journal of Educational Research*, *The Journal of Experimental Education*, *The Elementary School Journal*, the *Mathematical Gazette*, the *Mathematics Teacher*, the *Yearbooks* of the National Council of Teachers of English, of Mathematics, of the Social Studies, etc.

8. See, for example, VERNON, M. D., *A Further Study of Visual Perception*. Cambridge: C.U.P. 1952.

GIBSON, E. J., *Psychol. Bull.* 50. 401–31. 1953.

9. FLEMING, C. M., loc. cit. [3]. 1934.

RUSSELL, D. H., and KARP, E. E., *Reading Aids through the Grades*. N.Y.: Teachers' College, Columbia U.P. 1938 and 1951.

10. HODGSON, F. M., *Learning Modern Languages*. Lond.: Routledge. 1955.

11. For a description of the Winnetka material see also: WASHBURNE, C., *Adjusting the School to the Child*. N.Y.: World Book Co. 1932.

12. DANIELS, J. C., and DIACK, H., *Learning to Read*. Lond.: Chatto & Windus. 1954.

FLESCH, R., *Why Johnny can't Read*. N.Y.: Harper. 1955.

DANIELS, J. C., and DIACK, H., *Progress in Reading*. Univ. of Nottingham, Inst. of Educ. 1956.

DIACK, H., *Reading and the Psychology of Perception*. Nottingham: Ray Palmer. 1961.

With these may be compared:

GAGG, J. C. and M. E., *Teaching Children to Read*. Lond.: Newnes Educational Publishing. 1955.

HESTER, K. B., *Teaching Every Child to Read*. N.Y.: Harper. 1948 and 1955.

GRAY, W. S., *The Teaching of Reading and Writing*. U.N.E.S.C.O. 1956.

HARRIS, A. J., *How to Incrase Reading Ability*. N.Y.: Longmans. 1940 and 1956.

MORRIS, J. M., *Standards and Progress in Reading*. Lond.: Nat. F. Educ. Res. 1966.

13. See also: TYLER, F. T., *J. Educ. Psychol.* **XLVI**. 2. 85–93. 1955.

14. SOUTHGATE, V., *Educ. Res.* **VII**. 2. 83–96. 1965.

DIACK, H., *In Spite of the Alphabet*. Lond.: Chatto and Windus. 1965.

DOWNING, J., and JONES, B., *Educ. Res.* **VIII**. 2. 100–14. 1966.

i.t.a. SYMPOSIUM. Lond.: Nat. Foundation Educ. Res. 1966.

15. FLEMING, C. M., loc. cit. [7]. 1946 and 1952.

GRAY, W. S. (Chairman), *Reading in the High School and College*. 47th *Yearbook* Nat. Soc. Study of Educ. Pt. II. 1948.

BAKER, W. D., *Reading Skills*. New Jersey: Prentice-Hall. 1953.

BLACK, E. L., *Brit. J. Educ. Psychol.* **XXIV**. 1. 17–31. 1954.

CLIFT, D. H. (Chairman), *Adult Reading*. 35th *Yearbook* of the National Society for the Study of Education. Pt. II. 1936.

16. FLEMING, C. M., loc. cit. [7]. 1946 and 1952; and FLEMING, C. M., loc. cit. [3]. 1934.

See also records of the efficacy of a non-directive therapeutic approach:

BILLS, R. E., *J. Consult. Psychol.* **XIV**. 2. 140–9. 1950.

BILLS, R. E., ibid. **XIV**. 4. 246–9. 1950.

POTTER, M., ibid. **XIV**. 4. 250–5. 1950.

SEEMAN, J., et al., ibid. **XVII**. 6. 451–3. 1954.

17. STERN, C., loc. cit. [4]. 1949.

KHAN, Q. J. A., *A Study of the Arithmetical Experience of Certain Groups of Children in an Infant School*. M.A. Thesis. London. 1953.

18. For general discussions see: RUXTON, I. M., *The Pathway Plan*. Lond.: Univ. of London Press. 1938 and 1951 (revised).

MELLOR, E., *Education through Experience in the Infant School Years*. Oxford: Basil Blackwell. 1950.

SERJEANT, F. IRENE, *From Day to Day in the Infant School*. Lond.: Blackie. 1952.

19. A summary is given in:

MARTIN, W. E., *Genet. Psychol. Monographs*. **44**. 147–219. 1951.

20. See Buswell's work as reflected in published text-books and in BUSWELL, G. T. (Chairman), *The Teaching of Arithmetic*. 50th *Yearbook* of the Nat. Soc. Study of Educ. Pt. II. 1951.

See also: FLEMING, C. M., *Teaching the Elements of Mathematics*. Lond.: Ginn. 1961.

21. On Tillich (1780–1807) see: PUNNETT, M., *The Groundwork of Arithmetic*. Lond.: Longmans, Green. 1914.

MONTESSORI, M., *The Advanced Montessori Method*. Lond.: Heinemann. 1918.

DRUMMOND, M., *Learning Arithmetic by the Montessori Method*. Lond.: Harrap. [n.d.].

STERN, C., loc. cit. [4]. 1949.

CUISENAIRE, G., and GATTEGNO, C., *Numbers in Colour*. Lond.: Heinemann. 1954.

MACFARLANE SMITH, I., *Education Papers*. Newcastle upon Tyne: King's College Education Society. **VIII.** 3. 14–25. 1956.

DIENES, Z. P., *Building up Mathematics*. Lond.: Hutchinson. 1960.

BRUNER, J. S., *Toward a Theory of Instruction*. N.Y.: Harvard Univ. Press. Lond.: Oxford Univ. Press. 1966.

22. See, for example: FLEMING, C. M., *Beacon Number Books*. Lond.: Ginn. 1948.

FLEMING, C. M., *The Beacon Arithmetic*, Lond.: Ginn. 1948 and 1961.

23. HODGSON, F. M., loc. cit. [10]. 1955.

24. HALL, G. S., *Educational Problems*. N.Y.: Appleton. 1911.

Cf. WILSHERE, P. N., *An Attempt to Consider a Syllabus in World History Suitable for a Year's Course in a 'Senior' School*. M.A. Thesis. London. 1931.

25. HENDERSON, J. L., *The New Era in Home and School*. **37.** 1. 1965.

26. JEFFREYS, M. V. C., *History in Schools*. Lond.: Pitman. 1939.

HEMMING, J., *The Teaching of Social Studies in Secondary Schools*. Lond.: Longmann. 1949.

27. BURSTON, W. H., *Educ. Rev.* **III.** 2. 100–8. 1951.

28. ABOUZIED, H., loc. cit. [6]. 1955.

See also: BASSETT, G. W., *An Experimental Study of Mental Processes Involved in the Comprehension of Historical Narrative*. Ph.D. Thesis. London. 1940.

BRADLEY, N. C., *Brit. J. Psychol.* **XXXVIII.** 2. 67–78. 1947.

29. VAN HIELE, P. M., *Development and Learning Process*. Groningen: J. B. Wolters. 1959.

XI

THE MEASUREMENT OF
ATTAINMENT

THE MEASURING OF attainment is not an activity of recent date. It has always, in one form or another, been a part of the teaching-learning situation.

Teachers desire to know the effectiveness of their tuition. They wish to discover the main difficulties encountered by their pupils. Have I succeeded in teaching what I intended to teach? What part of the work requires to be repeated?

Teachers are also interested in the relative success of individual pupils (ranking them in order of achievement) and they are concerned with the specific mistakes and weaknesses of the groups with which they are immediately concerned. Which pupil is in most need of attention? What exact help is particularly required?

In questions such as these the science of examining had its origin. It was an extension of the ordinary give-and-take, question-and-answer of the classroom; and in its essentials it took two forms – the examining or testing designed for a general survey of the field (survey testing) and the testing planned to permit diagnosis of individual difficulties (diagnostic testing). Of these, survey tests were developed first and their consideration may take precedence over the more specialized topic of diagnosis.[1]

Survey tests

Survey tests in a very direct sense have their prototypes in the routine class examinations which are conducted in written or oral form by teachers in their own classrooms or within the limits of their own schools. These examinations are devised for a known group of pupils and cover the tasks prescribed in a specified period – a week, a month, a term or a year. They are intended for use with one group only. They are of no predetermined length or content. Their wording is based on the classroom pattern of more or less generalized instructions: 'Write an essay on . . . Give an account of . . . Find the answer to . . . Solve the following problem . . .' They provide clues to the amount of learning which is occurring and to the nature of the difficulties experienced by a class as a whole. They permit active participation on the part of pupils. They stimulate revision. They encourage the extension of interpretations to new fields and they foster the acquisition of new skills.

So long as a contribution of this sort within the limits of one classroom was all that was required, there was no serious challenge to what have been called old-type (or essay-type) examinations. When, however, through the pressures of an enlarging school population in the schools of Europe and North America at the end of the nineteenth century studies began to be made which needed an order of merit within a larger group and questions were asked which required a knowledge of the exact nature of a scholastic difficulty, it had to be admitted that old-type examinations must be supplemented by instruments of a more discriminating kind.

The attack on the traditional type of examining came from two quarters:

(a) from those who criticized the subjectivity of its marking (the idiosyncrasies of examiners and the limitations in their power to appreciate degrees of merit in a complex performance); and
(b) from those who challenged the narrowness of the sample of ability which it assessed.

The first was among the earliest fruits of the movement for the scientific study of education. The second was stimulated at a slightly later date by the analysis of the content of school subjects undertaken under the influence of the theories of learning developed by Thorndike and his followers.

Criticism of subjectivity of marking

In London in the 1880s Edgeworth, with illustrations provided by Bryant from the marking of a variety of subjects, discussed the element of chance in teachers' marks.[2] Twenty years later similar findings were turned to practical use by Dearborn and Rice in criticisms of school procedures and in suggestions for the reorganizing of educational activities.[3] Since then many other research workers have offered relevant evidence based upon different types of inquiry in relation to different numbers of pupils and different age-groups. [4] These studies may be classified according to differences in design and differences in the statistical treatment of results. Most of them fall into one or more of the following patterns:

1. the marking of old-type papers in school subjects such as Mathematics, Classics, Physics or English by a number of markers – Edgeworth 1888, 1890, Starch and Elliott 1912, 1913, Hartog and Rhodes 1935, 1936;

2. the marking of a small number of essays by a large number of markers – Starch 1916, Boyd 1924, French inquiry cited in Hartog and Rhodes 1935;

3. the marking of a considerable number of essays by a small number of markers – Edgeworth 1890, Hudelson 1923, Thomson and Bailes 1926, Hartog *et al.* 1935, 1936, 1941, Cast 1939, Morrison and Vernon 1941, French inquiry cited in Hartog and Rhodes 1935, Wiseman 1949, Finlayson 1951, Vernon and Millican 1954, Nisbet 1955, Penfold 1956;

4. the remarking of essays or papers by the same marker after an interval – Edgeworth 1890, Starch 1916, Hudelson 1923, Hartog *et al.* 1935, 1936, 1941, Morrison and Vernon 1941, Wiseman 1949, Finlayson 1951, Nisbet 1955;

5. the marking of more than one essay from the same candidates – Thomson and Bailes 1926 (reported independently), Hartog and Smith 1941 (reported independently), Hudelson 1923, Finlayson 1951, Vernon and Millican 1954;

6. the marking of essays according to differing marking schemes by the same examiners – Hudelson 1923, Hartog and Smith 1941, Cast 1939, 1940, by different examiners, Morrison and Vernon 1941, Nisbet 1955;

7. the marking of essays by teams of examiners – Hudelson 1923, Finlayson 1951 (random selection); Wiseman 1949, Nisbet 1955 (team selected after prior trial);

8. the marking of essays in conjunction with the marking of new type tests worked by the same candidates – Hartog and Smith 1941, Finlayson 1951, Vernon and Millican 1954, Nisbet 1955, Peel and Armstrong 1956, Pidgeon and Yates 1957.

From the point of view of conclusions formulated it can be said that all essential findings as to the elements of chance in subjective marking and the disagreement of examiners are to be found in

Edgeworth 1888 and 1890, Starch 1916, Boyd 1924 and Hartog and Rhodes 1935, 1936. They have been confirmed by correlation techniques by Hudelson 1923, Thomson and Bailes 1926, Hartog *et al.* 1935, 1941, Cast 1940, Morrison and Vernon 1941, Wiseman 1949, Finlayson 1951, Vernon and Millican 1954, Nisbet 1955, Penfold 1956, elaborated by factorial analysis, Cast 1940, Hartog and Smith 1941, Morrison and Vernon 1941, Finlayson 1951, Penfold 1956; and expressed in more exact form by analysis of variance, Cast 1939, Hartog and Smith 1941, Morrison and Vernon 1941, Finlayson 1951, Vernon and Millican 1954, and by analysis of co-variance, Penfold 1956.

All essential findings as to the inconsistencies of examiners from one occasion to another are reported in Edgeworth 1890, Starch 1916, Hartog *et al.* 1935, 1936. They have been elaborated in Hartog and Smith 1941, Morrison and Vernon 1941, Wiseman 1949, Finlayson 1951, Nisbet 1955.

All essential findings as to the disagreements in marking by teams selected at random are included in Hudelson 1923 and confirmed by Finlayson in 1951. The inconsistencies in marking shown even by highly selected teams are exemplified by Wiseman 1949, Finlayson 1951, and Nisbet 1955.

In spite, therefore, of variations in experimental design and in statistical techniques it has to be admitted that no investigation has refuted the general early conclusion:

> that the marking of essays or essay-type questions shows significant inconsistencies as between one marker and another as well as by the same marker from one occasion to another.

Criticism of narrowness of sampling

Discussion of the sampling of ability in traditional examinations took at first the form of inquiries into the consistency of the performance of the same candidates from one occasion to another. Very detailed evidence on this is available in the research reported by Hudelson in the Twenty-Second *Yearbook* of the National Society for the Study of Education (1923) in which four hundred and eighty-one pupils of ages thirteen to eighteen wrote upon thirty-two topics chosen as representative of adolescents' interests and experiences.[5] Consistency in performance was not high. One essay-answer did not evoke the same skills as another essay-answer. No one essay could be regarded as anything like a full sampling of a candidate's ability to write; and the younger the pupils the more unpredictable seemed to be the nature of the assignments that would appeal to them. Similar conclusions have come from more recent studies such as those of Finlayson (1951) and Vernon and Millican (1954).[6] Whatever the data collected and whatever the type of statistical analysis employed it seems necessary to agree that the responses of pupils to material of this kind vary significantly both with differences in subject matter and with topics of similar nature on different occasions.

These findings provided the impetus for the search for more reliable means of sampling pupils' skills and more satisfactory ways of describing their performance.

From essay-type to new-type tests

The essential difference between the old examining and the new lies not in the length of the questions but in their wording and in the definiteness of the thinking which is behind their formulation. New-type tests may be directed to the examining of the same geometrical, historical or linguistic prowess as that tested by old-type papers; but essays and essay-type questions because of the indeterminateness of their wording leave more to the judgement of each examiner. 'What do you understand by the Feudal System?' 'What do you think of the trial scene in *The Merchant of Venice*?' 'Write notes on: specific gravity and specific heat.' 'Indicate the meaning of the following: latitude, longitude, Mediterranean climate, trade winds.' Answers to questions of this kind depend not only on knowledge but on speed of writing and on skill in expressing ideas. The marker has not only to decide whether the candidates have understood the questions but whether they have succeeded in expressing the knowledge which they in fact possess. Marking an essay is, on this account, not unlike interpreting a response to the unstructured material of what have been called projective tests – in which a psychologist presenting ink-blots, vague pictures, incomplete sentences, and the like, seeks information as to the past experiences, personal values, and emotional reactions of his subjects.[7] In somewhat similar fashion teachers using essay-type questions invite their pupils to display their store of knowledge, their attitudes, their sense of values, and their skill in communicating their thoughts. To an assessment of these the teachers bring their own intentions, their expectations, and their personal theories as to appropriate performance. It is little

172

wonder that agreement as to the marking of essays or essay-type questions varies from one assessor to another in a fashion not dissimilar to the perceptual variations recorded in the interpretation of projective test protocols (see Chapter XIII below).

New-type tests directed to the examining of the same mathematical, historical or linguistic skills were, in contrast, so worded that each question covered a clearly delimited portion of the field, that only one reply was correct, and that the time of the candidate was not expended on activities extraneous to the purpose of the question.

Put a circle round the anwers which you believe to be correct. Find the word or set of words which gives the best answer and draw a line under it. Fill the empty space with the number (or word) which you think should be there. Which house was the middle one? Who saved the most in the second week?

The material they offer is thus of known difficulty, of a kind which can be reproduced in tests of equivalent form for use on different occasions; and, if the tests have been standardized, they contain items of known validity arranged in an order of difficulty which has been determined by prior trial with pupils similar to those for whom the test is intended.

The transition from the exclusive use of essay-type examinations to the present co-existence of essay-type questioning and objective standardized tests has come gradually. It is significant that developments in new-type tests have been paralleled by changes in methods of teaching; and those in turn have affected both the content and the form of examining.

New-type tests had their formal origin in the test procedures used in experimental psychology laboratories in the latter part of the nineteenth century.[8] For the measurement of rate and accuracy of perception (in tests of memory and in experiments on attention and distractability) psychologists used the simpler processes of arithmetic, oral reading, and the recollection of sentences seen or heard.

Subtract: 627642936431948457
           185838682725423585
           ─────────────────────

Multiply: 9548249479253341325
                           4
           ─────────────────────

When, in face of evidence as to differences of judgement among markers of traditional lengthy essay-type answers, the same psychologists set themselves the task of improving examinations, they turned experimentally to the use of such material.

In the decades since then the volume of research in the fields of Arithmetic and English has been so great that the development of more modern forms of testing may usefully be illustrated from the changes which have taken place in these two subjects.

In the field of arithmetic

In Arithmetic in the first and second decades the new tests devised by Courtis and by Starch took the form of: (a) a series of problems of increasing difficulty chosen from a larger number after trial with pupils of suitable seniority, and (b) pages of examples of addition (three columns wide and nine rows of figures), subtraction (eight to nine columns), multiplication (four columns of digits multiplied by two digits) and division (five columns of digits divided by two digits).

These tests were used to compare class with class, school with school or city with city in the great educational surveys of the 1900s and the 1910s. 'Measure the efficiency of the entire school, not the individual ability of the few,' said the psychologists; and the possibility of thus examining and comparing the effectiveness of different teachers was one of the arguments used by administrators in support of expenditure on the new 'standard' tests which carried a meaning beyond the limits of one teacher's classroom.[9]

The tests in turn gained widespread support from teachers because they secured evidence of the reality of individual differences and challenged the nineteenth-century supposition that all pupils were capable of equal achievement and that failure to learn was therefore a sign of inefficient teaching.

Changes in text-books and methods of teaching

Meanwhile a nineteenth-century inquiry into the effectiveness of instruction in spelling bore belated fruit in discussions of ways of economizing time in school work. Rice in 1897 had concluded that results from schools giving forty or fifty minutes instruction per day were not better than those from schools devoting only ten or fifteen minutes daily to the subject.[10] By the 1910s many workers were actively engaged in the search for reasons for such individual differences; and in the field of Arithmetic Thorndike made what was in many respects the most significant contribution. His experimental work led him to investigate the content of contemporary text-books; and detailed analysis of several series of these showed that many steps in the process of learning were omitted. Pupils working in the traditional manner for four or five years might, for example, meet only 82 instances of a basic fact such as 9×8 while 668 opportunities of using the combination 2×2 were encountered and many steps in problem-solving did not appear at all. These findings, combined with analysis of pupils' errors in the new standard practice tests, resulted in increased awareness of the complexity of the tasks involved in the learning of Arithmetic.[11] No longer was it sufficient to say that to eliminate variability in marking it was desirable to test by means of a considerable number of one-step exercises, and that examples of approximately equal difficulty could be constructed by following simple patterns such as 'for subtraction . . . three of the figures in the bottom line are greater than the figures above them and two of them come together'.[12]

It became necessary to distinguish many different levels of difficulty; and it became possible to establish an approximate order of difficulty for these. The publications of Osburn, Brueckner, and Schorling revolutionized the teaching of Arithmetic along these lines; and text-books were rewritten so that pupils could no longer work through a whole series without learning certain basic facts and without encountering any instance of certain of the procedures in the four fundamental operations.[13]

By the 1920s the psychologists' enthusiasm for scientifically balanced teaching materials had been welcomed with delight by the heirs of the work of Search in Pueblo and Burk in California.[14] New teaching procedures[15] and new text-books were followed by a new type of standard tests: and it began to be claimed that these, like the text-books, provided more adequate sampling of ability than the traditional class examination with its lengthy exercises and uncritical mixing of processes. The use of the earliest forms of new-type tests had raised questions which led to the analysis of text-books; and the new teaching materials which followed this analysis were in turn influential in moulding both the content and the form of successive series of objective tests. An outline of a test is shown below.[16]

PLAN OF A MODERN TEST IN ARITHMETIC

A. *Basic Facts and Processes* (5 minutes)

On this page you are to add or subtract. Write on the dotted lines the answers which you believe to be correct. You may do any working you wish in the space alongside. Be sure to write each answer in full, especially in the case of measures such as money, weight, length, liquids or time.

On this page you are to multiply or divide, etc., etc.
(10 minutes)

B. *Vocabulary* (5 minutes)

(i) In the next lines write the missing numbers or words.

(ii) Draw a line under the right ending to each sentence below.

C. *Problem Solving* (10 minutes)

Read each question carefully and answer exactly what each asks. You may, of course, do any working you wish.

D. *Interpretation of Graphs and Tables* (5 minutes)

Answer the following questions.

Interpretation of the Meaning of Fractions

In the next lines write the missing numbers or words.

E. *Insight into the Relationship of the Various Processes*
(5 minutes)

In the next four additions some numbers have been left out. Write them in.

(Similarly for subtractions, multiplications, and divisions.)

In the field of English

Similar developments may, in the same decades, be traced both in the teaching and in the examining of English.

Nineteenth-century lessons in the comprehension of English took the form of: (*a*) oral reading with attention to correct enunciation and pronunciation and (*b*) the answering of oral questions as to the meaning of words and sentences 'taking the intelligence of the reading lesson'. Nineteenth-century tuition in English was through the writing of essays (themes or compositions) coupled with early and continuous exercises in grammar. Objective testing both of reading and of written expression at first followed closely on these patterns.

Reading tests

At the opening of the twentieth century Binet in his individual tests provided for the oral reading of a short passage followed by its verbal reproduction. Scoring was by number of errors made and number of ideas correctly reproduced. By the second decade, oral reading was being challenged. 'We use silent rather than oral reading in practical life,' wrote Starch in 1916; and in his tests he asked for silent reading for thirty seconds followed by reproduction in writing immediately after the reading. He used a series of passages which had been 'selected so that the increases in difficulty from one sample to the next represented fairly uniform steps'. Scoring was by noting the number of words read per second and the number of words written which correctly reproduced the thought. (The validity of his tests was defended on the ground that a comparison made in a school of 256 pupils showed a close agreement between the tests and the reading as estimated by the teachers, and the method of scoring was said to be 'fully as accurate as the combined judgement of ten competent' teachers.)

With this test of silent reading Starch combined an English Vocabulary Test with sets of 100 words selected at uniform intervals from Webster's *New International Dictionary*. On these the pupils were to mark the words of whose meaning and use they were sure and to write the meaning after words familiar to them about whose meaning they were not sure.

In the same volume Starch published contemporary tests by E. L. Thorndike and by F. J. Kelly. These are of interest as other samples of what was new in the second decade. In Thorndike's Visual Vocabulary Scale a series of words whose difficulty had been established experimentally was arranged in steps each containing five words; and pupils were asked to carry out eight instructions of the type: 'Look at each word and write the letter F under every word that means a flower.'

His 'scale for the understanding of sentences' consisted of a set of passages after each of which there were questions which could be answered by one or two words. Kelly's Kansas Silent Reading test carried simplicity of scoring one step further in a five minutes exercise to which answers could be given by writing single words or by 'putting a line round' one of a number of possible replies. Half-way through the second decade the style of answering had thus passed from vague reproductions in the fashion of an essay ('Tell me all about it') to single word replies, the writing of simple symbols or the putting of a ring round a response believed to be correct.

Changes in text-books and methods of teaching

With test material of this kind extensive surveys of achievement were carried out in various schools systems, and in Reading, as in Arithmetic, a wide range of individual differences was disclosed in each class along with much overlapping of performance from one class to another. This again was at first attributed to inefficiency of teaching;[17] but it was soon admitted that administrators had been given evidence of a general phenomenon for which some provision must be made. Realization of this was followed by lively discussion as to whether individual differences should be taken into account in the organization of schools. ('Should these pupils be reclassified into higher or lower classes according to their capacities?' asked Starch in 1916.) It also stimulated criticism of existing methods of teaching along with interest both in the processes involved in study-ing and in the relation of silent reading to economy of effort. New reading material (typified by the Courtis Standard Practice Sheets) was produced to meet the inadequacies revealed by the new tests; and by the middle 1920s detailed prescriptions were available as to methods by which skill in silent reading could be developed. These methods in turn were reflected in more analytic reading tests through which it became still more possible to adapt tuition to observable differences. By 1927 it was not uncommon to find clear differentiation between such elements as word-recognition, word-pronunciation, reading to get the general significance of a passage, reading to anticipate the outcome of given events, reading to understand precise directions, and reading to note significant details; and new Reading Books designed for self-aided study were beginning to make it possible to provide for some measure of individual progress in Read-ing as well as in Arithmetic.

Experimentation with new types of tests, in this field also, fostered discussion of classroom purposes and procedures. Concern with variations in the level of pupils' understanding was followed by attention to the processes involved in their learning. This resulted in modifications of methods and alterations in teaching materials; and questions and exercises were constructed in the light of evidence as to the difficulties experienced by pupils both in comprehension of vocabulary and in interpretation of sentence structure. By the middle of the fourth decade the style, the content, and the format of school-books had been changed in the field of English to an extent almost as remarkable as the transformation which had been wrought in the field of Arithmetic. Modern objective tests in reading reflect these changes.[18] Their predecessors – the new-type tests of Courtis, Thorndike, Starch, Ballard, and Burt – had provided the first challenge to nineteenth-century procedures. Present-day tests are now soundly supported by what is routine practice in the schools of today.

Tests of written expression

These also were, at first, in line with the routine teaching procedures of the late nineteenth-century and were concerned solely with the marking of essays, subsidiary arts such as spelling and handwriting, and a knowledge of grammar.

An increase in objectivity in marking was at the turn of the century sought through the use of composition 'scales' consisting of reproductions of representative samples of children's work at different levels. Rice (1903), Hillegas (1912), Ballou (Harvard-Newton) (1914), and Thorndike (1915) had, by 1916, all made contributions to the more accurate and objective rating of composition by the provision of means by which the general merit of each essay might be assessed in direct comparison with others at successive steps in a scale; and various inquiries indicated that through the use of such 'scales', consistency between markers could be increased. In the very process of constructing such scales, however, psychologists had been stimulated to keener discrimination between the content and the structure of an essay; and by 1922 the work of Rice, of Willing, and of Van Wagenen was directing attention to differences in elements such as spelling, punctuation, functioning grammar, sentence sense, vocabulary, and paragraphing – within the broad structure of a composition or a theme.[19]

This differentiation was at first reflected in handwriting scales constructed on the same pattern as the composition scales, in spelling lists (based at first on random selection from a dictionary and later on an analysis of the frequency of use of words in books, in the writing of adults and in the compositions of children of different ages), and in tests for the measuring of grammatical correctness and ability in punctuation.

In his book on Educational Measurements published in 1916 Starch, for example, provided samples of composition scales, writing scales, and spelling lists along with what he called grammar scales and punctuation scales. For the grammar scales he provided a series of sets of four sentences in increasing steps of equal differences of difficulty. In each sentence two words or phrases were inserted in parenthesis as possible ways of filling a gap, and the pupils were asked to indicate which they preferred. For the punctuation scales he gave comparable sets of four sentences and correction of their errors was required. As a further measure of grammatical knowledge he offered tests of three minutes' duration in which pupils were asked: (a) to indicate the parts of speech (by inserting the initial letter of each above each word), (b) to mark the case of each noun or pronoun as: nominative-n, possessive-p, objective-o, and (c) to show the case and mode (mood) of each verb in a set of short sentences.*

With apologies for the limited range of these tests, Starch pointed out that a test on sentence analysis or diagramming ought very likely to have been added. Only with such an addition could the tests have covered what was, in the second decade, routine practice in the schools.

Changes in text-books and methods of teaching

The extent of the transformation wrought by the critical reconsideration of teaching and testing procedures which characterized the next twenty years may be judged by a comparison of these early efforts at educational measurement with the detailed analysis of the content of English learning outlined by Smith in the Thirty-Fourth *Yearbook* published in 1935. Still closer approximation to present practice is observable in the Forty-Third *Yearbook* (1944) in which fuller illustrations are given of the varied procedures by which teachers of English now foster a delight in writing, give opportunities for written and oral expression, and interest their pupils in mutual criticisms and improvement of the form and the content of their written work.

* Standard scores for Grades 7 to University level ranged from 30 to 60 for (a), from 13 to 45 for (b), and from 13 to 45 for (c).

In 1923 the foreshadowing of this was substantially a minority report in the discussion of Hudelson's experimentation on the marking of English essays. By the sixth decade more highly diversified and expert techinques in the fostering of expression through classroom projects and activities of many kinds were reflected in the analytic and functional structure of objective standardized tests of the type outlined below.

PLAN OF A MODERN TEST IN ENGLISH

A. *Comprehension* (15 minutes)

Each part of the story below is followed by questions which can be answered by one of the words, or sets of words, to the right. Find these words and draw a line under each. (The first one has been done for you.)

Originality

xvii. What do you think John said when he looked out from the top of the cliff? Write one sentence giving the exact words he used and also telling how he said them ....

....

B. *Written Expression* (5 minutes)

Word Usage

Below is the next part of the story. From it some of the words have been removed. These words have been placed on the right along with other words that have nothing to do with the story. Find the word in each line that belongs to the story and draw a line under it. (The first one has been done for you.)

They......towards the stream.   go, came, goes, <u>went</u>, come.

Now go back to the beginning of the story and write each word into its proper place in the story.

Paragraph Structure (10 minutes)

1.   Below is another part of the story; but in this part the order of the sentences has been mixed. The sentences are not in the right order. Read the sentences and arrange them in your mind in the right order. Then copy them carefully and fully in that

order below, starting each sentence on a fresh line. (The first one is begun for you.)

Interpretation

2.   Write one sentence giving your reason for thinking that that was the country to which he was going.

Spelling   (10 minutes)

Have you a good memory? In each of the sentences below parts of some of the words have been missed out. Think what each word should be and *write it in full on the dotted line* to the right.

Sentence Structure. Coherence

Below are some sentences. The first line of each set has been underlined. Two of the next five lines give most nearly the meaning of the line underlined. Find these two and draw a line under each.

Sentence Structure. Punctuation and Word Usage.

The next two sentences are taken from a letter John wrote home to his mother. They have some mistakes in them. Read them carefully. Think what the mistakes are and write the two sentences correctly below.

Vocabulary

In each sentence below a word has been underlined. Alongside are five words or sets of words. One of these gives most nearly the meaning of what was underlined. Find this and draw a line under it.

Lively discussion still continues as to the relative efficacy of the marking of essays by what is now called 'general impression' in contrast to a more analytic approach. There have been many modern successors to Boyd's analysis of the qualities of a good essay into:

A. *Mechanical*
   (*a*) neat and legible script,
   (*b*) correct spelling and punctuation,
   (*c*) grammatical accuracy,
   (*d*) fluency.

B. *Aesthetic*

(*a*) good vocabulary,

(*b*) good clause structure,

(*c*) good sentence structure,

(*d*) effective arrangement of material.

It is, however, no longer supposed that the writing of essays and the study of grammar provide all that is necessary in the process of learning to write; and the contents of objective standardized tests reflect what is now current teaching procedure more closely than would a revival of the one-time prescription of:

Write an essay on...

Parse the words underlined...

Analyse the following sentences...

Write nouns corresponding to the following verbs...

Give the plural of...

This does not mean that extensive experience in 'composition' is not required at the primary as well as the secondary stage. Opportunities for creative writing occur at many levels and in connection with many school activities. The presenting of stories and plays in written as well as in oral form, the writing of letters, the keeping of diaries, the summarizing of reading – all such functional uses of language form a sound basis for later delight in the accurate and attractive communication of ideas. The reproduction of stereotyped phrases which in the past accompanied the attempt to prepare junior pupils to write essays under examination conditions is not now asked by skilful teachers; and it is known that an interest in word-usage and the like can be stimulated by methods which are both more diversified and more successful.

Modified content in newer objective tests

It is to be noted that these modern objective tests have in English as in Arithmetic passed beyond the use of the mere crossing out, ticking off or underlining which were characteristic of the earliest forms of new-type material. Responses through the underlining of correct replies are still asked for in sections involving interpretation of consecutive passages of prose or poetry (silent reading or problem-solving), in tests of Arithmetical vocabulary, or of English word-meaning, word-usage, and the like. In all such instances, activities such as handwriting or the construction of sentences are unnecessary

183

skills whose inclusion would detract from the measurement desired. In other cases – such as the testing of ability to present ideas in correct literary form or to perform certain definite operations in Arithmetic – objectivity is now secured by limiting the content of each item. Pupils may be presented with selected ideas (as in the Cotswold Series), asked to arrange them mentally in the correct order and required to copy them with a degree of accuracy dependent on their understanding of accepted conventions of punctuation, capitalization, and the like. They may be invited to find the answer to a series of exercises in Arithmetic in each of which a distinct difficulty is encountered, or required to solve a set of problems to each of which an answer may be given by the writing of a limited number of words or digits. They may be asked (as in certain later Moray House tests) to write in full a series of words whose identity has been indicated by their place in a given sentence and by the printing of their initial and final letters. They may be required to give a corrected version of a sentence or a calculation into which certain mistakes have been inserted (each mistake chosen as one liable to occur in the writings of their peers). All such exercises are 'objective' in the sense that they require prior analysis of subject-matter, that the correctness of their answers has been determined after experiment with pupils of comparable age and experience, that the nature of their wording is such that only a reply of a definite sort is acceptable, and that therefore subjectivity in their marking has been reduced to the point at which the degree of agreement between attentive examiners (the 'reliability of marking') is represented by a correlation coefficient of $+ 0.99$. This is significantly higher than the corresponding figures given in the case of essays marked either by randomly selected and different teams of examiners (Hudelson 1923, Finlayson 1951) or by carefully chosen teams from which inconsistent markers have been eliminated (Wiseman 1949, Finlayson 1951, Nisbet 1955). Adequacy of sampling and consistency of performance as indicated by test-retest, by split-half reliability (odd items as against even items) or by the use of equivalent forms are also of the order of $+ 0.95$ or $+ 0.96$ in contrast to the much lower figures obtained when a comparison is made of different essays by the same candidates.[20]

Changes in the reporting of results of tests of attainment

Changes in methods of describing the performance of pupils in school examinations, like changes in the form of tests, followed upon comparisons between the marks given by one teacher or examiner and those given by another. It was early recognized that teachers differed both in the averages of the marks they gave and in the range of the marks they used; and from this it was a short step to the realization that marks reported either in the form of letter grades (A, B, C), verbal descriptions (Excellent, Good, Fair), numerical assessments with an arbitrary total (out of 20, out of 100, and the like) or numerical orders of merit, carried no meaning beyond the confines of one classroom and permitted no comparisons between one class and another or one school and another.

The first step towards standardization of marking was taken by an emphasis on the concept of the median or the average and by the substitution of phrases such as 'above average', 'average', and 'below average' for the more indeterminate 'excellent', 'good', 'fair'; and early in the inquiries into the marking of essays the idea was mooted that examiners by prior discussion might come to an understanding of what they expected from an average pupil and might agree that a specified mark would be given to an average performance.

A further development was represented by attention to the nature and degree of the deviations from the average; and inquiries were undertaken into the random variations which occur even between examiners who are alike both in average marks and in deviations from the average.

The standardizing of marks was next improved by the proposal that marks should be reported in a form which showed the relation of each to the average mark in terms of multiples of the standard deviation of the set. The average for a class or school might then be described as 0, and a mark one standard deviation above the average could be said to have a standard score of $+1$, while a mark one standard deviation below the average would be described as -1. These 'standard scores' were an improvement on the more ambiguous earlier unstandardized form of reporting. Their use was open to the criticism that they conveyed no information as to the nature of the distribution (widely scattered or narrowly concentrated).

The next step took the form of the suggestion that such 'standard scores' should themselves be 'standardized' by expressing them not as $\pm$ 1, 2, 3, etc. (multiples of the obtained standard deviation above or below the mean) but in terms of a standard deviation of an agreed size – the same for all. The exact figure varied in different contexts; and the full meaning of a 'standardized score' can be known only if the convention accepted for mean and standard deviation is specified. The most widely used forms are the T (ten) scores of certain American tests with mean 50 or 100 and standard deviation 10, and the standardized scores most common in this country with mean 100 and standard deviation 15.

For these there is sometimes substituted the calculation of percentile rank for each pupil. The word percentile can be understood by thinking of a large group of human beings which has been arranged in an order of merit and then divided into one hundred numerically equal sets. Each such set may then be said to have a 'percentile' rank; and a 'percentile score' of 98 is the average score of the set of people holding the 98th 'percentile' rank. The relationship between percentiles, standard scores, and standardized scores is shown below in Figure III. The pupil who scores 122 in a group the standard deviation of whose scores is 16 and the mean of whose scores is 90, can thus be described as having a 'standardized score' (with standard deviation 15) of 130, or an approximate 'percentile' rank of 98.

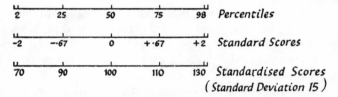

Figure III. Chart showing relationship between percentiles, standard scores and standardized scores.

This new style of reporting is 'standardized' in the sense that it carries a meaning beyond the confines of one classroom and permits comparison of relative status in attainment on different occasions and with different tests.

New-type tests of attainment can thus be analytic in content, objective in form, and standardized in the procedures through which they provide a description of relative success or failure. On grounds such as these their use can now largely supersede the use of old-type tests, especially when surveys of attainment have to be made or definitive distinctions have to be drawn between one pupil and another. Quite similar improvements may be traced in the content of tests designed to uncover the exact requirements of each pupil.

Diagnostic tests

The detailed content needed for the diagnosis of individual difficulties has already been indicated. By the 1930s much was, for example, known as to the learning of the basic number combinations in Arithmetic ($0 + 0$ to $9 + 9$, $0 - 0$ to $18 - 9$, 0×0 to 9×9 and $0 \div 1$ to $81 \div 9$). Much had also been discovered as to the steps involved in the learning of each process, as to the processes in denominate numbers (money, weight, liquids, length, time, capacity), as to the meaning and the use of fractions, and as to the solving of problems. Efforts were made to apply this information to the organizing of individualized instruction in which testing and teaching would go hand-in-hand.

Survey testing had made a broad covering of this field, ranging from very easy examples to quite difficult ones but not professing to include every known difficulty. Diagnostic material had to be so constructed that it contained each recognizable step – its general contribution being to discover the exact stage reached by each pupil and the particular obstacle which was being encountered by each.

The purpose of such tests is not classificatory. They are not intended to permit objective comparisons between pupils in one school and pupils in another. Their function is remedial. It is a temptation to their misuse to publish 'norms' inviting discussion of relative status; and such norms are on this account rarely provided.

Illustrative of the detailed analysis which is required is the following plan of a diagnostic series of tests in subtraction:

16				
2				Answers below 20.

24	367		
1	3		Subtraction in one column only.

37		
22		Subtraction in two columns.

95	83	40	65	
70	43	20	63	Zero difficulties.

42	Units in upper line less than in line below.
7	One figure in subtrabend;

and so on for twelve other varieties.* Similar detailed analysis is now characteristic of units of programmed instruction. Cross-reference to appropriate lessons or 'frames' gives encouragement to each pupil to obtain further practice on the exact portion of work in which difficulty is being experienced; and pupils from an early age can participate in the fostering of their own skills.[21]

The use of diagnostic tests

In consequence of the use of such diagnostic or programmed material teachers have passed beyond their earlier search for correct 'age-placement' of topics to the study of 'readiness' – readiness for number concepts, readiness to begin addition, readiness to pass from elementary arithmetic to more advanced mathematics. The concept of 'age-placement' carried echoes of the assumption that all children of a given chronological or mental age are inevitably ready for the same sort of work. The concept of 'readiness' sets teachers free to adapt tuition to the exact point which has in fact been reached. The opening decades of the century saw the first survey tests, the recognition of widespread individual differences and of the overlapping of performance as between one age-group and another. The third and fourth decades saw the spread of diagnostic testing and remedial teaching. The fifth and sixth decades were characterized by awareness of the variability of growth and the fluctuations concealed by figures representing median scores or average rates of progress. Educational guidance now signifies continuous analysis and sensitivity to the varying requirements of boys and girls as they pass from nursery or infant school to College or University.†

In the field of English this diagnostic testing and concern for personal readiness has attained less prominence than comparable work in Arithmetic; but from experiments in schools attempting individualized instruction there have come 'workbooks' and programmes for use both in learning to read and in acquiring the finer arts of English Composition. A series such as Steel's *Introduction to the King's English* – developed in years of close association with the **Scottish Council for Research in Education** – while it does not profess to incorporate diagnostic tests, is planned on diagnostic lines

* Fleming, C. M., *Teaching the Elements of Mathematics*. p. 218. London: Ginn & Company, Ltd. 1961.

† For detailed examples of tests in various fields see: *STEP* (*Sequential Tests of Educational Progress*). Princeton; Cooperative Test Division. 1957.

and provides for progressive practice in the difficulties of which teachers become aware in their attempts to help pupils both to understand other people and to be understood by them.[22] His table of contents is informative. How words are used. (Difficulties of Vocabulary and English usage.) How sentences are built. How sentences are joined. (Sentence Building. Paragraph Building. The Difficulties of Coherent Expression.) Finding the Best Words. (Fitness. Difficulties of Appropriate Expression.). Ways of Saying the Same Thing. (Flexibility. Difficulties of Readiness or Fluency.) What it Means. (Exercises in Comprehension.) How to Describe a Story. How to do it. How it Works. How to Write a Letter. Dialogue. (Exercise in Composition.)

American studies on reading at the College level carry comparable analyses to older age levels and offer expanding horizons both to the diagnosis of the difficulties of older age groups and to the fostering of higher levels of interest and appreciation.[23]

REFERENCES

1. For discussion see:
   LINDQUIST, E. F. (ed.), *Educational Measurement*. Washington, D.C.: American Council on Education. 1951.
2. JORDAN, A. M., *Measurement in Education*. N.Y.: McGraw-Hill. 1953.
   GREENE, H. A., JORGENSEN, A. N., and GERBERICH, J. R., *Measurement and Evaluation in the Secondary School*. N.Y.: Longmans. 1954.
2. EDGEWORTH, F. V., *J. Royal Statist. Soc.* LI. 599–635. 1888.
   EDGEWORTH, F. V., ibid. LIII. 460–75 and 644–63. 1890.
3. For articles published over about a decade, see:
   RICE, J. M., *Scientific Management in Education*. Philadelphia: Hinds, Noble & Eldredge. 1913.
4. STARCH, D., *Educational Measurements*. N.Y.: Macmillan. 1916.
   STARCH, D., and ELLIOTT, E. C., cited in STARCH, D., ibid.
   HUDELSON, E., *English Composition*. 22nd *Yearbook* of the National Society for the Study of Education. Pt. I. 1923.
   BOYD, W., *Measuring Devices in Composition, Spelling and Arithmetic*. Lond.: G. Harrap. 1924.
   THOMSON, G. H., and BAILES, S. M., *The Forum of Education*. IV. 2. 85–91. 1926.

HARTOG, P., and RHODES, E. C., *An Examination of Examinations*. Lond.: Macmillan. 1935.

HARTOG, P., and RHODES, E. C., with a memorandum by CYRIL BURT. *The Marks of Examiners*. Lond.: Macmillan. 1936.

HARTOG, P., with a statistical Report by C. EBBLEWHITE SMITH. *The Marking of English Essays*. Lond.: Macmillan. 1941.

CAST, B. M. D., *Brit. J. Educ. Psychol.* IX. III. 257–69, 1939, and X. I. 49–60. 1940.

MORRISON, R. L., and VERNON, P. E., ibid. XI. II 109–19. 1941.

WISEMAN, S., ibid. XIX. III. 200–9. 1949.

FINLAYSON, D. S., ibid. XXI. II. 126–34. 1951.

VERNON, P. E., and MILLICAN, G. D., *Brit. J. Statist. Psychol.* VII. II. 65–74. 1954.

NISBET, J. D., *Brit. J. Educ. Psychol.* XXV. I. 51–4. 1955.

PENFOLD, D. M. EDWARDS, *ibid.*, XXVI. II. 128–36. 1956.

PEEL, E. A., and ARMSTRONG, H. G., ibid. XXVI. III. 163–71. 1956.

PIDGEON, D. A., and YATES, A., ibid. XXVII. I. 37–47. 1957.

5. HUDELSON, E., loc. cit. [4]. 1923.

6. FINLAYSON, D. S., loc. cit. [4]. 1951.

VERNON, P. E., and MILLICAN, G. D., loc. cit. [4]. 1954.

7. SIMS, V. M., *Educ. and Psychol. Measurement*. 8. 15–31. 1948.

8. WHIPPLE, G. M., *Manual of Mental and Physical Tests*. Baltimore: Warwick & York. 1910.

9. STARCH, D., loc. cit. [4]. 1916.

10. RICE, J. M., loc. cit. [3]. 1913.

11. THORNDIKE, E. L., *The Psychology of Arithmetic*. N.Y.: Macmillan. 1922.

12. BOYD, W., loc. cit. [4]. 1924.

13. OSBURN, W. J., *Corrective Arithmetic*. Boston: Houghton Mifflin. 1924 and 1929.

BRUECKNER, L. J., *Diagnostic and Remedial Teaching in Arithmetic*. Chs. VII and IX. Chicago: John C. Winston Co. 1930.

SCHORLING, R., and CLARK, J. R., *Mathematics in Life*. N.Y.: World Book Co. 1935.

14. For the earlier variants see: MCLELLAN, JAMES A., and DEWEY, JOHN, *The Psychology of Number*. N.Y. and Lond.: Appleton. 1895.

BOOLE, M. E., *Lectures on the Logic of Arithmetic*. Oxford: Clarendon. 1903.

15. For a survey see: FLEMING, C. M., *Research and the Basic Curriculum*. Lond.: Univ. of London Press. 1946 and 1952.

16. Examples of test material are taken from the Cotswold Series of *Tests of Ability in English and in Arithmetic*. Glasgow: Robert Gibson.

17. WILSON, H. B., *et al.*, *Minimum Essentials in Elementary School Subjects*. Pt. I, *passim*. 14th *Yearbook* of the National Society for the Study of Education. 1915.

18. Information on earlier forms is obtainable for a variety of subjects in: BURT, C., *Mental and Scholastic Tests*. Lond.: King. 1921.

HAWKES, H. E., LINDQUIST, E. F., and MANN, C. R. (ed.), *The Construction and Use of Achievement Examinations.* Boston: Houghton Mifflin. 1936.

RINSLAND, H. D., *Constructing Tests and Grading in Elementary and High School Subjects.* N.Y.: Prentice Hall. 1937.

BROOM, M. E., *Educational Measurements in the Elementary School.* N.Y.: McGraw-Hill. 1939.

For more recent work see: FLEMING, C. M., loc. cit. [15]. 1946 and 1952.

LINDQUIST, E. F. (ed.), loc. cit. [1]. 1951.

JORDAN, A. M., loc. cit. [1]. 1953.

See also the work of TRIGGS, F. C. (Chairman), *Committee on Diagnostic Reading Tests Inc.* N.Y.

19. Cf. HUDELSON, E., loc. cit. [4]. 1923.

20. FERGUSON, G. A., *The Reliability of Mental Tests.* Lond.: Univ. of London Press. 1941.

See also: FLEMING, C. M., *Cotswold Measurement of Ability.* Series I to XII. Glasgow: Robert Gibson. 1947–1961.

BUROS, O. K., *Tests in Print.* New Jersey: Gryphon Press. 1961.

21. *Marking the Beacon Arithmetics.* Lond.: Ginn. [n.d.]

22. STEEL, J. H., *An Introduction to the King's English.* Lond.: James Nisbet. 1932.

23. BELLOWS, C. S., and RUSH, C. H., *J. Appl. Psychol.* 36. I. 1–4. 1952.

XII

THE TESTING OF
INTELLIGENCE

LIKE STANDARDIZED AND objective measures of attainment, modern
tests of intelligence were developed out of traditional procedures by
psychologists familiar with the psycho-physical experiments of the
nineteenth century and interested in the discovery of ways of giving
consistent and unprejudiced descriptions of the ability of pupils who
came from a wide variety of homes.

A good head.
A fine forehead.
A dull face.
Bright eyes!
Sensitive to touch.
As quick as a needle.
An accurate worker.
A good memory.
A wide vocabulary.
Ability to classify.
Can see relationships.
Good at drawing conclusions.

From external appearance and the shape of the head (Gall) to the
expression of the face (Lavater), and thence to the powers of the body
in speed and competence.[1] Such was, in brief, the course taken up
to the days when Binet in Paris, Burt in England, and Dearborn and
Terman in the United States followed the lead given by Galton and
directed attention more specifically to the significance of the powers
of the mind.[2] This was next followed by the elaboration of their
proposals into individual tests of a variety of types and into group
tests containing words, numbers, pictures or diagrams.[3]

Test construction

These tests are objective in the sense that decisions as to their answers are not left to the personal opinion of the marker; and standardized in the sense that both in their construction and in the reporting of their results reference is made to the performance of representative samples of pupils of the age of those for whom the tests are designed.*
Their construction, like that of objective tests of attainment, involves a lengthy process of elimination of ambiguous items through establishing an order of difficulty for pupils of a given age and through finding the validity of each item in terms of its correlation with the whole test or with some other accepted measure of intelligence. The external criterion of validity was at first the opinion of a teacher; but since the 1920s reference is more usually made to other objective tests whose validity is already established.[4]

Definitions of intelligence

In the case of tests of intelligence even more lively debate has been directed to the nature of the ability under examination than in the case of measures of arithmetic, reading or written expression. Much of this discussion is linked with the dichotomy between inheritance and environment whose spurious significance stimulated research in the 1920s; and much of it is presented in somewhat technical surveys of the statistical methods employed.

Various definitions of the word 'intelligence' have been given.[5] Binet conceived of it as a fundamental faculty of the utmost importance for practical life – 'judgement, otherwise called good sense, practical sense, initiative, ... adapting one's self to circumstances. To judge well, to comprehend well, to reason well: these are the essential activities of intelligence.' Stern spoke of it as the ability to adjust oneself to new situations. Terman emphasized the capacity to form concepts and to grasp their significance – the ability for abstract thinking. Thorndike took more account of the quantity of bonds or connexions – 'the intellect capable of the highest reasoning and adaptability differs from the intellect of an imbecile only in the capacity for having more connexions'. Spearman suggested the

* Information as to details of test construction is accessible in the *Bulletins* of the National Foundation for Educational Research in England and Wales. See also the manuals of series such as the Moray House Tests (University of London Press), the Cotswold Series (Gibson, Glasgow), and the School and College Ability Tests (Cooperative Test Division, Princeton).

significance of the ability to observe one's own mental processes, to discover essential relations, and to make further inferences therefrom. In addition, in view of the tendency to positive correlations between success in different types of intellectual activity, he postulated a hypothetical general factor underlying all cognitive performances of any kind. Knight added that 'the man of high intelligence is one who, faced with a problem, can seize upon the significant aspects of the objects or ideas before him, and can bring to mind other ideas that are relevant'. To Hiem it is noteworthy that intelligent behaviour may admit of differences in kind as well as in degree – intelligent activity consisting in grasping the essentials in a given situation and responding appropriately to them. Vernon would agree that intelligence is a very fluid collection of overlapping abilities comprising the whole of mental life.[6] Hunt more definitely conceives intelligence as intellectual capacities based on central processes which develop in the course of a child's interaction with environment; and these, for him, are approximately analogous to the strategies for information-processing and action which are used in electronic computers.[7]

Some of these definitions lay emphasis on biological aspects of mental functioning, others on competence in a variety of fields, and others again on the influence of environment and on adaptation to cultural or social and emotional pressures. Some stress what have been called the 'nominal' elements in the attempt to define.[8] (a) They may bring together in convenient form a consensus of opinion from a reference group whose character is more or less openly admitted (the 'lexical definition' or definition in terms of common usage). (b) They may on the other hand be 'stipulative' in the sense that they express an opinion peculiar to the writer in terms of a special theory or stipulation. Others are more 'real' – formulated from an empirical or operational point of view. What do intelligent people do? What are the differences in reaction between the more and the less intelligent as these are exemplified in a variety of situations?

Such discrepancies in approach go far to account for the differences in wording which lend complexity to discussion of the topic. Divergencies in terminology are also understandable if it is noted that, in this field as in the study of motivation, learning, and perception, there has been a gradual movement towards awareness of the interrelatedness of human functioning. Galton in the 1870s was quite representative of his time when he embarked upon an inquiry into human 'faculties'. Subsequent research has discredited the notion that there are separable entities such as attention, memory, judgement or intelligence; and many psychologists now believe that Binet's concern with good sense in a variety of fields gives a more adequate account of the nature of intelligent behaviour than definitions which assume that it has an 'essence' peculiar to itself and distinct from other aspects of mental activity.[9] Associated with this is the disappearance of a sharp differentiation between tests of intelligence as indicative of what is innate and tests of attainment as measures of what has been acquired. It is now admitted that both are directed to the appraisal of what human beings are able to do – the former from a more general point of view and the latter in the more specific sense of the conquest of samples of those subject-fields in which tuition is commonly offered in schools.

Capacity or ability

Reminiscent of the older viewpoint is the fact that the word 'intelligence' itself is still used by some writers indiscriminantly in the two senses of (a) inherited or innate capacity and (b) actual or present ability. The distinction between capacity and ability was clearly drawn by Dawson in a discussion of the use of tests in vocational guidance in the early 1930s.[10] It was elaborated in the late 1930s by Prescott.[11] It was applied in the field of secondary school selection about a decade later;[12] and given fresh formulation by Hebb in his re-emphasis on the physiological basis of behaving.[13] To these discussions further point was added by Vernon in the 1950s through his supplementing of Hebb's categories of Intelligence A (an innate potential conceived of as a good brain and a good neural metabolism) and Intelligence B (the continuous functioning of a brain in response to environmental stimulation) by a third category Intelligence C – that sampling of Intelligence B which is all that can be attempted in any one test of intelligence on any one occasion of testing.[14] Hebb's formulation was significant in that it brought together the physiological implications of Thorndike's interpretation and the more phenomenological approach which was adumbrated by Bartlett's work on perception and later supported by Bruner, Postman, and others. Vernon's annotation carries with it the reminder that the tests devised for the measuring of intelligence are constructed on empirical lines; and that they have, in fact, always sampled abilities rather than measured potentialities.

Confusion between the two uses of the word underlies many

current arguments as to constancy or inconstancy of intelligence quotients. It seems justifiable to suppose that words such as capability, capacity or potentiality can suitably be applied to those elements of original endowment or physiological quality which form the basis of individual differentiation. It seems also justifiable to consider that these are constant and unmodifiable by personal or social action. Intelligence as capacity in this sense is, however, a hypothetical construct – convenient for the purposes of discussion but not separable from the present abilities through whose sampling its existence may be inferred. The contrast may be expressed in the fashion shown below.

TABLE VI

Capacity	Ability
Native wit	Effective intelligence
Potentiality	Performance
That of which the organism is capable	That which the organism is able to do
A hypothetical construct	An observable reaction
Unmodifiable	Modifiable by experience
Constant	Variable
Incapable of measurement	Susceptible of appraisal

From a theoretical point of view both are components of any intelligent behaviour; and, in paraphrase of Hebb's phrases, it may be remarked that the prime determinants of intellectual growth are a completely necessary innate potential and the opportunity to establish its usefulness in a completely necessary stimulating environment. This is, however, merely to say again in another fashion that there is both an inner and an outer, and that human behaving is the manifestation of a certain sort of organic endowment as it has functioned in the past and functions in the present in response to certain experiences – pre-natal and post-natal. With increasing recognition of the complexity of this functioning it has become less surprising that relative status as expressed in an intelligence quotient (like that expressed in an educational quotient) shows some degree of variability from time to time. It has also become more possible to agree that the ideal intelligence test is neither independent of environmental influences nor a 'pure' estimate of capability in its most general form.

Contributory to this change in viewpoint was the transition, described in Chapter VII above, from cross-sectional researches (involving the re-testing of discrete groups) to long-term studies based on the following-up of the responses of the same pupils to the same tests over a number of years. Conducive also to its formulation was the careful statistical analysis of results obtained from the use of intelligence tests over the same decades.[15]

Statistical analysis

Notable in this connexion are the names of Pearson, Spearman, Burt, Thomson, Kelley, Thurstone, Fisher. The detail of the procedures they used is a matter of greater concern to professional psychometrists than to teachers.* It is, however, relevant to note that through the calculation of correlations it became possible to consider degrees of correspondence between test results obtained on different occasions or from different tests. By the use of regression equations and their derivatives, research workers then became able to separate out the contribution of different elements in a complex battery; and, through the analysis of resemblances and differences in the inter-correlations of results from a variety of tests, they devised ways of classifying responses to different sorts of material and of describing the components (factors) in the pattern discernible. They can now also estimate the degree of significance of the differences obtained; and they can, by analysis of variance and co-variance, advance beyond the somewhat rough comparisons of factorial techniques to the disentangling of the effect of various elements in a complex situation like that involving different markers, different types of test-material, and different candidates.[16]

The theory of these developing procedures belongs properly to the advanced study of Mathematics – enriched by the application of statistical models derived from physics, horticulture, and eugenics.[17] Their contribution to the improvement of tests of intelligence has been in their demonstration of the complexity of intellectual functioning; and their findings have led to greater caution in the interpretation of results obtained through testing. At an early stage Burt estimated the contribution made by education to the scores

* A survey of methods and results is given in Vernon, P. E., *The Measurement of Abilities*. London: University of London Press Ltd. 1940 and 1956. Vernon, P. E., *The Structure of Human Ability*. London: University of London Press Ltd. 1950. Their relevance to secondary education is discussed in Fleming, C. M., *Adolescence*. London: Routledge & Kegan Paul Ltd. 1948, 1955 and 1963.

obtained in intelligence tests.[18] Multi-variate analysis now illustrates the complex pattern of relationships between earlier and later testing or between initial testing and performance in a related activity some years later; and, through study of the contribution made by different combinations of initial and final testing, the artistry of those who undertake vocational or educational guidance is now supported by the subtleties of differential testing of present abilities and interests.[19]

The use of intelligence tests

Teachers, like vocational counsellors, use such tests with the knowledge that through their sampling of intelligent behaviour in a variety of settings they supply information which can be set against more specialized performance in skills which have deliberately been taught. They serve as a general estimate to counterbalance possible irregularities of attendance or exposure to different methods of teaching and on occasions when special advice has to be given (in situations such as allocation to courses of a more advanced kind, at the transition from one school to another or at the stage of passing from school to employment) it has been shown that they make a significant contribution.[20]

Group tests of intelligence, like group tests of attainment, are the transference to pencil and paper of questions and answers not unlike those which can be used in oral questioning or interviewing. Like individual tests, they are essentially 'structured' interviews in which both content and procedure are, by intention, the same for all. It is therefore essential that teachers when administering such tests should follow exactly the instructions supplied as to words to be used and timing to be given in each test. The suitability of both method and time have been determined by prior testing, and the intention is that each candidate should be occupied for a known number of minutes on activities of a selected kind. Any departure from this renders the test invalid for purposes of comparison.

The material used is in the form of pictures, diagrams, words, numbers or three-dimensional objects; and the activities invited are in line with the findings of three decades of research into the inter-relationships of human abilities and the processes involved in relational and functional thinking.[21]

PLAN OF A MODERN TEST OF MENTAL ABILITY*

A. *Classification* (5 minutes)

In each of the following rows of numbers there is one which is most unlike the others. Find this number and draw a line under it.

3   5   8   11   17

Now find the word in each row which is most unlike the others in the same row, and draw a line under it. (The first one has been done for you.)

stool   table   chair   <u>fork</u>   desk

B. *Ordering* (5 minutes)

Each of the sets of words or numbers below can be arranged in order. Think of each set arranged in order and draw a line under the word which then comes in the middle. (The first one has been done for you.)

foot   mile   inch   furlong   <u>yard</u>

C. *Recognition of relationships* (5 minutes)

In each of the rows below, each sentence can be completed by one of the words or numbers shown on the right. Find this word or number and draw a line under it. (The first one has been done for you.)

(*a*) Hen is to chicken as dog is to ...   calf   kitten   mutton
<u>puppy</u>   dog.

In each of the next rows, the sentence on the left can be completed by two of the words on the right. Find these two words and draw a line under them both. (The first one has been done for you.)

(*a*) Wool is to sheep as ... is to ...   cloth   <u>fur</u>   blanket
comb   <u>rabbit</u>

D. *Reconstruction of relationships* (5 minutes)

In each of the lines of numbers or letters below there are two blank spaces showing where some numbers or letters are

* Examples are again chosen from the Cotswold Series of Tests. Glasgow: Robert Gibson & Sons.

missing. Fill in the spaces with the numbers or letters which you think should be there.

Are you a careful worker? In each of the lines below some letters or numbers have been missed out. An asterisk (*) has been put in place of each letter or number which is missing. Read each line carefully. Think what the missing part should have been and write it after the asterisks.

(a) 1   2   3   4   5   *
(b) author   book   poet   ****
(c) pale   pail   tale   ****

E. *Reasoning and the following of directions*   (10 minutes)

There are two months whose names begin with the first letter of the alphabet. What is the third letter of the shorter of these two names?

Mrs Gray, Mr Smith, and Mrs Wright had lunch on the train.

Mr Smith and Mrs Gray took coffee after their lunch.

Mrs Wright and Mr Smith chose fish instead of chicken.

Mrs Gray and Mrs Wright chose cheese and biscuits and Mr Smith had ice cream.

Who had ice cream as well as coffee?
Who had fish but not cheese and biscuits?
Who had chicken and cheese and biscuits?

Criticism of tests of intelligence

Criticism of tests of intelligence, like discussion of its definition, is most usefully considered in the light both of what is known as to mental functioning and in terms of the intentions of those who are essaying through them the impartial sampling of mental ability.

It has been suggested that group tests lay an undesirable emphasis upon speed. It may be noted, however, that most published tests deliberately contain more questions than candidates are expected to answer. One reason for this is quite simply the endeavour to keep all examinees 'working steadily' in a specified fashion for a given time. Another is that, while there are admitted differences in rates of working (a speed 'factor' in test results), there is a positive relationship between power and speed. Where answers are known they can be recorded quite swiftly; and modern tests, in places where they invite mere underlining of one of five responses, are so planned that guessing by itself does not bring a high reward.

It has been protested that intelligence tests contain questions to which distinguished adults do not know the answer. In comment on this, it may be said that every item in a reputable test has been tested on subjects of the age of those for whom the test is intended. Both the past experience and the present attitude (the 'hypotheses' and the 'expectancies') of eleven-year-old candidates may, however, be so different from those of an adult who approaches a test in a spirit of cautious scepticism as to account for any unexpected difficulties which the latter may meet.

It has further been complained that intelligence tests give an undue advantage to children from prosperous homes.[22] This is a survival from earlier discussions of the contribution of inheritance in contrast to environment; and much of it is based on American reports on social groups whose differences may be greater than those in the more stable communities of Western Europe. The formulation of the criticism has, however, served to make more clear the whole trend of modern emphases (both in child psychology and in the theory of perception) on the complexity and the cumulative character of human functioning.[23] Earlier learning, attitudes, sets, and expectancies are now known to determine the character of what is perceived; and they affect responses in situations inviting 'intelligent behaviour' as well as in situations which ask for 'decision' or for 'recollection of learning'. It is an advantage for a rat, a chimpanzee or a child to have experienced stimulating and encouraging treatment in early youth.[24] Children, like animals, learn to learn;[25] and their learning is contributory to the general mental ability which is sampled by tests of intelligence.

It is to be noted, however, that the findings of standardized tests have been contributory also to the recognition that the overlapping between the ability of children from one socio-economic level to another is more definitely established than the significance of the difference between one level and the next. Through the use of intelligence tests in secondary school selection opportunities are known to have been given to children who suffered some handicap in the nature of their schooling; and it is now acknowledged that while relatively more 'intelligent' children come from the most prosperous homes the largest absolute number of intelligent children is to be found at the lower (though not the lowest) socio-economic levels.[26]

On some such lines as these teachers, as technicians, can now reply to the criticisms of parents or employers who challenge their use of tests of intelligence. The appraisal of intelligence through tests of mental ability remains one of the best means available to expert teachers in their study of the development of their pupils. It is, however, not an instrument to be used alone. No standardized score in 'attainment' or in 'intelligence' can tell the whole story. In the light of contemporary awareness of the indivisibility of human functioning, account must also be taken of those relationships and attributes which are, in traditional parlance, described as personality, character or temperament.

REFERENCES

1. WHIPPLE, G. M., *Manual of Mental and Physical Tests*. Baltimore: Warwick & York. 1910.
2. BALLARD, P. B., *Mental Tests*. Lond.: Hodder & Stoughton. 1920.
   BURT, C., *Mental and Scholastic Tests*. Lond.: P. S. King. 1921.
3. TERMAN, L. M., and MERRILL, M. A., *Measuring Intelligence*. Boston: Houghton Mifflin. 1937.
   VALENTINE, C. W., *Intelligence Tests for Children*. Lond.: Methuen. 1945.
   GRIFFITHS, R., *The Abilities of Babies*. Lond.: Univ. of London Press. 1954.
   WECHSLER, D., *The Measurement of Adult Intelligence*. Baltimore: Williams & Wilkins. 1939.
   For surveys of such tests see: VERNON, P. E., *The Measurement of Abilities*. Lond.: Univ. of Lond. Press. 1940 and 1956.
   GOODENOUGH, F. L., *Mental Testing*. N.Y.: Staples Press. 1949.
   FREEMAN, F. S., *Theory and Practice of Psychological Testing*. N.Y.: Henry Holt. 1950.
   ANASTASI, A., *Psychological Testing*. N.Y.: Macmillan. 1954.
4. LINDQUIST, E. F. (ed.), *Educational Measurement*. Washington, D.C.: American Council on Education. 1951.
   THORNDIKE, R. L., and HAGEN, E., *Measurement and Evaluation in Psychology and Education*. N.Y.: John Wiley. 1955.
5. BINET, A., and SIMON, T., *The Development of Intelligence in Children*. Baltimore: Williams & Wilkins. 1916.
   KNIGHT, R., *Intelligence and Intelligence Tests*. Lond.: Methuen. 1933.
   HAMLEY, H. R., *The Testing of Intelligence*. Lond.: Evans. 1935.
   SPIKER, C. C., and MCCANDLESS, B. R., *Psychol. Rev.* **61.** 4. 255–66. 1954.
6. HEIM, A. W., *The Appraisal of Intelligence*. Lond.: Methuen. 1954.
   VERNON, P. E., *Bull. Brit. Psychol. Soc.* **26.** 1–14. 1955.

7. HUNT, J. MC.V., *Intelligence and Experience*. N.Y.: Ronald Press. 1961.
8. ROBINSON, R., *Definition*. Oxford: Clarendon. 1950.
   Cf. MILES, T. R., *Brit. J. Educ. Psychol.* **XXVII**. III. 153–65. 1957.
9. HEIM, A. W., loc. cit. [6].
10. DAWSON, S., *Brit. J. Psychol.* **XXI**. 1. 39–45. 1930.
11. PRESCOTT, D. A., in EURICH, A., *General Education in the American College*. 38th *Yearbook* of the Nat. Soc. Study of Educ. Pt. II. 1939.
12. FLEMING, C. M., *Adolescence*. Routledge. 1948, 1955 and 1963.
13. HEBB, D. O., *The Organization of Behavior*. N.Y.: John Wiley. 1949.
14. VERNON, P. E., in *Studies in Education*. 7. Lond.: Evans. 1955.
15. SPEARMAN, C., *The Nature of Intelligence and the Principles of Cognition*. Lond.: Macmillan. 1927.
    BURT, C., *The Factors of the Mind*. Lond.: Univ. of London Press. 1940.
    THOMSON, G. H., *The Factorial Analysis of Human Ability*. Lond.: Univ. of London Press. 1939 and 1946.
    THOMSON, G. H., *The Geometry of Mental Measurement*. Lond.: Univ. of London Press. 1954.
    THURSTONE, L. L., *Multiple Factor Analysis*. Chicago: Univ. of Chicago Press. 1947.
    FISHER, R. A., *The Design of Experiments*. Edinburgh: Oliver & Boyd. 1935 and 1936.
16. For a simple statement on factorial analysis see: PEEL, E. A., *The Psychological Basis of Education*. Edinburgh: Oliver & Boyd. 1956.
    For a critical appraisal see: CORTER, H. M., *Psychol. Monographs*. **66**. 8. No. 340. 1952.
    PENFOLD, D. M. E., *Brit. J. Educ. Psychol.* **XXVI**. III. 128–36. 1956.
    See also: GUILFORD, J. P., *Fundamental Statistics in Psychology and Education*. N.Y.: McGraw-Hill. 1942 and 1950.
    JOHNSON, P. O., and JACKSON, R. B., *Introduction to Statistical Methods*. N.Y.: Prentice-Hall. 1953.
17. BUSH, R. R., and MOSTELLER, F., *Psychol. Rev.* **58**. 5. 313–23. 1951.
    BURT, C., and FOLEY, E., *Brit. J. Statist. Psychol.* **IX**. 1. 49–62. 1956.
18. BURT, C., *Mental and Scholastic Tests*. Lond.: P. S. King. 1921.
19. FLEMING, C. M., in JEFFERY, G. B. (Chairman), *Transfer from Primary to Secondary Schools*. Lond.: Evans. 1949.
    VERNON, P. E., and PARRY, J. B., *Personnel Selection in the British Forces*. Lond.: Univ. of London Press. 1949.
20. VERNON, P. E. (ed.), *Psychological Aspects of Secondary School Selection*. Lond.: Methuen. 1957.
    YATES, A., and PIDGEON, D. A., *Admission to Grammar Schools*. Lond.: Nat. Found. Educ. Res. 1957.
21. VERNON, P. E., *The Structure of Human Abilities*. Lond.: Methuen. 1950.
    HAMLEY, H. R., *Relational and Functional Thinking in Mathematics*. 9th *Yearbook* of the National Council of Teachers of Mathematics. 1934.

See also: RUSSELL, D. H., *Children's Thinking*. Boston: Ginn. 1956.
22. DAVIS, A., *Social Class Influences upon Learning*. Cambridge: Harvard U.P. 1952.

SIMON, B., *Intelligence Testing and the Comprehensive School*. Lond.: Lawrence & Wishart. 1953.
23. See: ANDERSON, H. L., and ANDERSON, G. L., in CARMICHAEL, L., *Manual of Child Psychology*. N.Y.: John Wiley. 1946 and 1954.

ALLPORT, F. H., *Theories of Perception and the Concept of Structure*. N.Y.: John Wiley. 1955.
24. HEBB, D. O., loc. cit. [13].
25. HARLOW, H. F., *Psychol. Rev.* **56**. 51–65. 1949.

For a relevant long-term study see: SONTAG, L. W., *et al.*, *Mental Growth and Personality Development*. Child Develpm. Publications. **XXIII**. 68. 2. 1958.

See also: FLOUD, J. E., *et al.*, *Social Class and Educational Opportunity*. Lond.: Heinemann. 1957.

RIESSMAN, F., *The Culturally Deprived Child*. N.Y.: Harper. 1962.

DOUGLAS, J. W. B., *The Home and the School*. Lond.: MacGibbon and Kee. 1964.

DALE, R. R., and GRIFFITH, S., *Down Stream: Failure in the Grammar School*. Lond.: Routledge. 1965.

See also: DAVIS, C., *Room to Grow: A Study of Parent–Child Relationships*. Toronto: Univ. of Toronto Press. 1966.
26. FLEMING, C. M., *Brit. J. Educ. Psychol.* **XIII**. II. 74–82. 1943.

See also: WISEMAN, S., *Education and Environment*. Manchester University Press. 1964.

DAVIES, H., *Culture and the Grammar School*. Lond.: Routledge. 1965.

MUSGROVE, F., *The Family, Education and Society*. Lond.: Routledge. 1966.

PIDGEON, D. A. (ed.), *Achievement in Mathematics*. Lond.: Nat. Found. Educ. Res. 1967.

GOODACRE, E. J., *Reading in Infant Classes*. Lond.: Nat. Found. Educ. Res. 1967.

GOODACRE, E. J., *Teachers and their Pupils' Home Background*. ibid. 1967.

XIII

THE ASSESSMENT OF
PERSONALITY AND THE
KEEPING OF RECORDS

IN THE STUDY of personality certain of the same issues are
involved as in the appraisal of intelligence or the estimation of
attainment; and the same variety of types of definition may be
noted. For this reason one may again discriminate among three uses
of the word: Personality A (an innate potential conceived of as a
certain.glandular balance and physiological rhythm), Personality B
(the functioning of that endowment in response to external stimulation), and Personality C (that sampling of Personality B which is
attempted by assessment in any fashion on any occasion). Of these,
Personality A is a hypothetical construct whose exact contribution
(like that of Intelligence A in Hebb's formulation) cannot be discerned apart from its subsuming in Personality B; and many of the
perplexities induced by conflicting interpretations are again attributable to inconsistency in the use of the three connotations.

Definition of personality

The word personality can be distinguished from other words such as
character, disposition, temperament, and intelligence, which are also
applicable to human beings as they function. When speaking of
character, attention is turned to assessment in terms of moral
judgement. Estimation of actions is made in the light of accepted
values – their rightness or wrongness – and the strength or the weakness of the individual in conforming to or disregarding such values.
The word 'disposition' is used with reference to emotional tendencies
of a sort thought to be permanent in a more literal sense than that in
which the permanence of character is conceived; and sweetness or
sourness, kindliness or hardness are thought of as dispositional

205

attributes. More of a physiological origin is attributed to 'temperament'. Its connotation is still linked with that of the bodily humours conceived of as its source in early Greece and its characteristic qualities are lethargy or melancholy, passionateness or liveliness.

In contrast, the word 'personality' is somewhat more comprehensive than any of these. Some reference to Personality A is, for example, implicit in Allport's description of personality as the dynamic organization within the individual of those psychophysical systems that determine his unique adjustment; and among many pregnant suggestions perhaps the most significant is Allport's reminder of the core of continuity behind the 'persona' or 'informative mask' which each human being presents to the world. Something of revelation and concealment is characteristic always of those responses to which the word personality is suitably applied.[1]

Fuller recognition of the social implications of personality is made by saying that Personality B (that which is open to observation) is a pattern of bodily and mental reactions exhibited by a person in response to a social situation. This admits the complexities of what is again an inner and an outer; and it permits the inclusion of all personal qualities and social relationships as inalienable aspects of a whole. It carries with it the implication of membership of a group; but it also subsumes all that is discernible of disposition, character, temperament, and intelligence as these are seen to function by some other individual.

The study of personality

Most of the methods used for the assessment of personality carry within them an admission of this social entanglement.[2] Their historical development may be summarized by saying that there was a progression from the interpretation of external appearance and physical characteristics, through ratings by friends and acquaintances to a study of expressive movements like writing and drawing, and an analysis of the inferences which could be made from the 'projection' of personal differences into the interpretation of pictures, ink-blots, and indeterminate tracings, or the directions taken by personal choices in activities, speech patterns, and the like. All these have to do with the observation of 'behaviour'; and supplementary to them always is the inquiry into the nature of another's 'experience'.[3] This can take various forms. It may be attempted in an oral interview – planned or informal ('structured' or 'unstructured'), or questions may be asked in pencil and paper tests whose intentions are disguised with greater or lesser deliberateness.[4]

Typical of undisguised and unstructured interviews are those in which a reply is made to a request for advice. These range in length from psycho-analytic sessions extending over many months to the brief appraisal of a stranger who may ask the way. In written form they are represented by autobiographical studies: Write an essay on: 'My Earliest Memory'.[5]

More obviously patterned are the interviews designed to discover attitude on a specific issue [6] or the tests of interests, attitude or values in the style set by Thurstone and his successors.[7] These may invite merely agreement or disagreement.

Put a tick opposite each statement with which you agree.

'No one would work with his brain if he could earn as good a living by using his hands,' etc.

They may ask a rating in terms of a five-point scale.

With which of the following statements do you agree? Give four votes to those with which you agree most strongly and 0 to those with which you do not agree at all, etc.

'The boys and girls who can stay on at school are lucky.'

Give four votes to the statements which are most like what you would have said, etc. etc.

'Tom said he played games because his friends did it. Mary said she did it because she liked doing so,' etc.

Information may be sought by asking details of activities during a specified period – a week-end, a fortnight, a month. These questions again may be uncontrolled (What did you do?) or controlled (Which did you do?)

... designed a toy. ... went skating. ... went to a library. ... read a book on sport. ... read a love story.*

Comparable to these are tests in which drawings or pictures are offered as a stimulus to interest in the questions asked. A modern variant is a film-strip produced by Rudd with photographs of two

* These examples are from Fleming, C. M., Cotswold Personality Assessment, P.A. I. Glasgow: Robert Gibson. 1959.

pupils reacting in differing fashions in situations designed to illustrate co-operation, interest in school work, determination, sociability, and the like.[8] In this, while the photograph is being shown, a standard commentary is read and two questions are asked to which the pupils are to reply by writing: always, very often, sometimes, rarely, or never.

Picture 50. Co-operation

Whilst the netball teams were getting ready, Pamela and Mavis were taking turns at seeing how many times they could bounce the ball and catch it. Now the teams are ready; but Pamela still continues her turn at bouncing. Mavis calls to her, telling her to bring the ball so that they can all get on with the game.

- A. Do you like to finish what you are doing before you join in with the others, as Pamela does, even if it means that they have to wait for you?
- B. Are you, like Mavis, anxious to help the others to do what they want to, even if it means giving up what you want to do?

Picture 51. Sociability

The class is being taken out for the afternoon and teacher has been getting the children in pairs. As a result neither Billy nor George can be with his special friend. George prefers to go with John but Billy prefers to remain on his own.

- A. If you cannot be with your special friend, do you prefer to be with somebody else, no matter who, as George does?
- B. If you cannot be with your special friend, do you prefer to remain alone, as Billy does?

A variant of this, but without pictures, is an adaptation of the Guess-Who? technique in which (instead of inserting the names of others) pupils are asked to rate themselves on a disguised five-point scale.[9] Below are some of the things the class said about ANNA, BETTY, CECILIA, DOROTHY, and EVELYN. Write in the blank space provided here, ..., the name of the girl who is most like yourself. You may cross out the ways in which she is not like you:

    EVELYN: Sullen, not at all helpful; never agrees with others; would neither lead nor follow, but would only raise objections; is never able to work smoothly with others.

DOROTHY: Very seldom offers help; does not accept group decisions and, if not allowed to lead, follows with indifference; often comes into conflict when working with others, but if encouraged in a friendly manner, can be made to work with others, etc. etc.

Of like directness are the tests in which an invitation is given to sort statements into piles ranging from 'Most true about myself' to 'least true about myself' (as I am, as other people think I am, as I would like to be).[10] In Staines' application of this to education the list included: good at school-work, able to speak well, clumsy or awkward, better at . . . than at any other subject, top of the class, popular, like to share things with other people, make lots of mistakes, like to see fair play, like reading, want a better job than other people get, finish whatever I start. With this may be compared the more formal method of scoring adapted by Dang in her study of co-operation[11] in which she invited teachers to record for each colleague an index number ranging from $+ 100$ to $- 100$ on a nine-point scale with descriptive keys such as: I am willing to make a *very great sacrifice* for the sake of '. . .'. I don't mind making a *small sacrifice* for the sake of '. . .'. I am willing to make a *considerable sacrifice* to avoid working with or get away from '. . .'. I am willing to a make a *very great sacrifice* to avoid working with or get away from '. . .'.

The helpfulness of this colleague is the *chief reason* for my happiness, in working for the school. This colleague *sometimes increases* my happiness, in working for the school. This colleague has *no effect whatsoever* on my happiness, in working for the school. This colleague *makes it impossible* for me to work happily for the school.

All such questions as to opinions, values, experience, and attitudes are dependent both on the degree of self-awareness and on the ability to differentiate which characterize the children or adults who are being interviewed. They are related also to their willingness to answer with honesty and frankness; and this in turn is a function of their relationship to and their judgement of the interviewer.

In contrast, all disguised inquiries tend to take a somewhat more artificial form. Prominent among them are the studies of perceptual responses to which reference has already been made. These 'projective techniques' are based on the belief that perception is affected by past experiences and personal motivation 'projected' into what is seen or heard, especially in situations in which the stimulating circumstance is of a somewhat unstructured or vague type (see Chapter VI above). Illustrative of this are Rorschach's series of ink-blots, and Murray's set of pictures designed to invite reaction to a theme – in the Thematic Apperception Test (T.A.T.) standardized for adults or the C.A.T. series presented as a Children's Apperceptive Test (C.A.T.). Similar to these are the games with dolls (Doll-play), the making of a 'world' with blocks or toys (Lowenfeld's Mosaics Test and World Test), the planning of an impromptu play – psychodrama or sociodrama – or the filling in of the balloons in a cartoon. 'Look at this (picture) and tell me all about it.' 'What is the 'world' you have made?' 'What scene are you acting?' 'How do you think he would feel?' 'Some people are angry. Who are they?' Questions of this type present situations of an open-ended sort; and provide material from which ratings of a variety of attributes can be made.[12]

Also disguised but more clearly structured are the more impersonal ways of testing interests and attitudes. Notable among these are the tests of interest through information developed by Peel and Lambert for example in inquiries into the relevance of interests to scholastic success.[13] Of similar intention are the attempts to secure controlled conditions on which to base judgements by giving an invitation to complete a particular scene, to play a specified role or to partake in a leaderless group discussion as to a specified task or on a prescribed topic.[14]

From all these approaches, undisguised or disguised, structured or unstructured, much material has been collected in the last few decades. Many such devices were put to severe test in the large-scale assessment of men and women which was part of the contribution made by psychologists in World War II; and to their analysis as to the analysis of intelligence-test results, the highest skills of psychometric technicians were applied.[15]

Use of results of assessment

Mention has already been made of the fact that in the case of tests of intelligence the earliest reaction of those who attempted their interpretation was to the effect that the abilities discerned were the property or inalienable attributes of the individuals under study, and relative intellectual status was therefore believed to have considerable constancy – a misinterpretation later corrected by the substitution of a long term for a cross-sectional approach.

A similar exaggeration of the fixity, independence, and personal attachment of attributes may be discerned in many earlier discussions of the results of the study of personality. The first school assessments of personality were, for example, used as contributory to the thesis that there are distinct types of children for whom different kinds of educational treatment are required. A corrective to this came not so much through long-term studies of the personal development of boys and girls as from an increase in discernment on the part of social psychologists and from a fuller recognition that trait differences within individuals are greater and more varied than had been suspected.[16] Human beings who, on first impression, seem to be at similar positions on a personality dimension such as sociability or dependability may prove, on closer acquaintance, to be very different in respect of caution, persistence, submissiveness or cheerfulness. Human beings are also appraised in different fashions by different judges; and they respond in different fashions to differing sorts of treatment. Not only do the personal ratings given to pupils by teachers in different subject fields show correlations ranging from − 0·15 to + 0·8, but assessments on single traits such as confidence show little consistency from one teacher of the same subject to another, and even larger discrepancies appear between teachers' ratings and the assessments given by pupils to one another [17] (see Chapter III above).

Similar inconsistencies are found in the interpretations given to protocols obtained from reactions to Rorschach ink-blots, T.A.T. pictures, essays, and the like; and experienced clinicians, psychologists and psychiatrists do not agree with one another on general assessments based on structured or on unstructured interviews.[18] With regret, therefore, it has to be admitted that little progress has been made in surmounting the difficulties presented by the assessment of human 'personality'.[19] 'Personality' is itself always a reaction to a social situation; and its 'perceiving' by another is so emotionally and intellectually involved that any personal rating is as much a 'perceptual activity' or a 'mode of regard' on the part of the rater as it is indicative of a 'quality' of the person who is subjected to the rating.[20]

Teachers' estimates and selective interviews

On this account, extreme caution has now to be exercised in respect of the suggestion that the results of an interview or the estimates of teachers should be used as deciding factors in determining the educational future of a child. In situations in which segregation into specialized schools and a limited number of vacancies force the making of a definite allocation to one course of studies or another, there is reason to believe that the least unreliable method of selection is one which permits pupils to 'speak for themselves' through their performance in a well-balanced variety of tests in general mental ability and in subjects such as Arithmetic and English which are representative of their response to the educational stimulation they have so far received and therefore indicative of their present general level of interest and industriousness.[21]

Various proposals have been made as to procedures by which corrections through scaling standardized test results can be applied to teachers' estimates to meet the known facts that teachers' standards vary from school to school, that their 'marks' cannot be interpreted beyond their own classrooms, and that their opinions are inevitably subject to misconceptions of a variety of kinds.[22] No one of these devices can, however, meet the major criticism that the ranking within a school (to the extent that it depends on personal estimates) is subject to the bias known to characterize all personality assessments. The rank-order given by Miss X would not have been that of Mr Y and neither might have been agreed to by Mrs Z. The personal haloes consequent on perceptual hypotheses may operate in favour of one pupil and against another. An awareness of their significance is characteristic of much informed educational thinking today.

The keeping of records

In partial reaction to this difficulty there has come an alternative suggestion – that for each pupil there should be kept a cumulative record* of the independent judgements of different teachers over a number of years. This commonly includes an invitation to make personal ratings as to persistence, concentration or response in class. It may invite comments on special interests and noticeable disabilities which require consideration. It may ask a record of regularity of attendance or the occurrence of ill health. In addition to all this, the details of standardized test scores obtained at different periods commonly provide a valuable corrective to the subjectivity of much of the rest.

* For fuller discussion see: Fleming, C. M., *Cumulative Records*. London: University of London Press. 1945 and 1954.

The keeping of such records carries with it a great reward in the evidence it marshals as to the serial development of each pupil as well as in the stimulus it gives to the teacher's more discerning observation of each child.[23] Teachers who are wise in their collection of anecdotal records from day to day are led both to unexpected discoveries of the interest and the uniqueness of their pupils and to the delights of novel experimentation into means by which the deviating ones may be reached and held. Out of such discoveries have come some of the finest examples of action research within the classroom.

Cumulative records of this sort are thus contributory to the continuing professional growth of teachers; and from careful study of their content (in the light of the interpretation to be attached to the signatures accompanying each rating) a more informed judgement can be reached in answer to appeals for advice (by parents or prospective employers) than is possible through the unaided opinion of one counsellor. They are therefore of great significance in educational guidance within a school. In the objective discrimination required by competitive selection between pupils from different schools they have, however, less to contribute than the evidence as to present competence and clear-headedness which is provided by the applicants themselves in their own answers to selection tests. Where discrepancies are great between present performances and earlier records the question of further and more careful analysis is raised; and in series of tests designed for mental measurement there is often a means of identifying the most discriminative items which may be doubly weighted when a second means of differentiation seems to be desirable.[24] This does not carry the admission that such discriminatory selection is in line with what is known as to the course of human development and the later responses of human beings of similar initial competence. It does mean, however, that the impact of one human being upon another is now recognized as so great that teachers are passing from a hypostasizing of the assessment of individual attributes to a fuller awareness of the connection between their own reactions and the responses of their pupils. Further consideration may, on this account, be given to the processes of interaction within groups and to the teacher's words and gestures as contributory to classroom morale.

213

REFERENCES

1. ALLPORT, G W., *Personality*. N.Y.: Henry Holt. 1937.
   See also: MURPHY, G., *Personality*. N.Y.: Harper. 1947.
   BRUNER, J. S., and KRECH, D., *Perception and Personality*. Durham: Duke U.P. 1949.
   BLAKE, R. R., and RAMSEY, G. V., *Perception: An Approach to Personality*. N.Y.: Ronald Press. 1951.
   MCCLELLAND, D. C., *Personality*. N.Y.: Dryden Press. 1951.
   BRAND, H. (ed.), *The Study of Personality*. A Book of Readings. N.Y.: John Wiley. 1954.
   Cf. HUNT, J. MCV. (ed.), *Personality and the Behavior Disorders*. N.Y.: Ronald Press. 1944.
   See also: MCNEMAR, Q., and MERRILL, M. A. (ed.), *Studies in Personality*. N.Y.: McGraw-Hill. 1942.
   BURT, C., *Brit. J. Educ. Psychol.* **XV.** I. 107–21. 1945.
   MABERLEY, A., ibid. **XVI.** I. 5–12. 1946.
   ALLPORT, G. W., ibid. **XVI.** II. 57–68. 1946.
   THOMSON, G., ibid. **XVI.** III. 105–15. 1946.
   LUCHINS, A. S., *J. Abn. Soc. Psychol.* **43.** 3. 318–25. 1948.
   CRONBACH, L. J., *J. Consult. Psychol.* **XII.** 6. 365–74. 1948.
   MUSSEN, P. H., *et al.*, *Child Development and Personality*. N.Y.: Harper. 1956 and 1963.
   ALLPORT, G. W., *Pattern and Growth in Personality*. N.Y.: Holt, Rinehart and Winston. 1963.
2. On the study of personality see:
   VERNON, P. E., *Personality Assessment*. Lond.: Methuen. 1964.
   See also: HIMMELWEIT, H. T., in MACE, C. A., and VERNON, P. E. (ed.), *Current Trends in British Psychology*. Lond.: Methuen. 1953.
   EYSENCK, H. J., in MACE, C. A., and VERNON, P. E., ibid.
   FRANKS, C. M., in DAVID, H. P., *et al.*, *Perspectives in Personality Theory*. Lond.: Tavistock Publications, 1957.
   SEMEONOFF, B. (ed.), *Personality Assessments: Selected Readings*. Lond.: Penguin. 1966.
3. Cf. PEEL, E. A., *The Psychological Basis of Education*. Edinburgh: Oliver & Boyd. 1956.
4. See also: CAMPBELL, D. T., *Psychol. Bull.* **47.** I. 15–38. 1950.
5. Cf. JERSILD, A. T., *In Search of Self*. N.Y.: Teachers' College, C.U.P. 1952.
   STRANG, R., *J. Educ. Psychol.* **XLVI.** 7. 423–32. 1955.
6. JAMES, H. E. O., and TENEN, C., *Brit. J. Psychol.* **XLI.** 3 & 4. 145–72. 1950.
   Cf. JAMES, H. E. O., and TENEN, C., *The Teacher was Black*. Lond.: Heinemann. 1953.
   BREWSTER SMITH, M., BRUNER, J. S., and WHITE, R. W., *Opinions and Personality*. N.Y.: John Wiley. 1956.

7. For an accessible survey of work on attitude testing see: VERNON, P. E., loc. cit. [2]. 1964.

See also: CATTELL, R. B., et al., Brit. J. Psychol. XL. 2. 81–90. 1949.

BROGDEN, H. E., Psychol. Monographs. 66. 16. 1952.

8. RUDD, W. G. A., The Psychological Effects of Streaming by Attainment. M.A. Thesis. London. 1956.

9. DANG, S. D., A Study of Co-operation in Certain Secondary Schools. M.A. Thesis. London. 1949.

10. STAINES, J. W., A Psychological and Sociological Investigation of the Self as a Significant Factor in Education. Ph.D. Thesis. London. 1954.

BILLS, R., VANCE, E. L., and MCLEAN, O. S., J. Consult. Psychol. XV. 3. 257–61. 1951.

11. DANG, S. D., loc. cit.

See also: REMMERS, H. H., Introduction to Opinion and Attitude Measurement. N. Y.: Harper. 1954.

DUKES, W. F., Psychol. Bull. 52. 1. 24–50. 1955.

TOMAN, W., J. Abn. Soc. Psychol. 51. 2. 163–70. 1955.

12. For a survey of work on projection techniques see:

VERNON, P. E., loc. cit. [2]. 1964.

See also: BELL, J. E., Projective Techniques. N.Y.: Longmans. 1948.

ROHRER, J. H., et al., Psychol. Monographs. 69. 8. 393. 1955.

MURPHY, L. B., J. Consult. Psychol. XII. 1. 16–19. 1948.

HIMMELWEIT, H. T., and PETRIE, A., Brit. J. Educ. Psychol. XXI. 1. 9–29. 1951.

CUMMINGS, J. D., Brit. J. Psychol. XLIII. 1. 53–60. 1952.

JACKSON, L., A Test of Family Attitudes. Lond.: Methuen. 1952.

For a projection test suitable for use with intending teachers see: PHILLIPS, A. S., An Examination of Methods of Selection of Training College Students. M.A. Thesis. London. 1953.

See also: A Teacher's Day in EVANS, K. M., A Study of Teaching Ability at the Training College Stage. Ph.D. Thesis. London. 1952.

BORSTELMANN, L. J., and KLOPFER, W. G., Psychol. Bull. 50. 2. 112–32. 1953.

SMITH, F. V., and MADAN, S. K., Brit. J. Psychol. XLIV. 2. 156–63. 1953.

HOLSOPPLE, J. Q., and MIALE, F. R., Sentence Completion: A Projective Method for the Study of Personality. Springfield: Charles C. Thomas. 1954.

13. On interests, see again: VERNON, P. E., loc. cit. [2]. 1964.

LAMBERT, C. M., A Study of Interest in School Subjects among Secondary School Pupils at Different Ages. M.A. Thesis. London. 1944.

PEEL, E. A., Brit. J. Educ. Psychol. XVIII. 1. 41–7. 1948.

See also: WISEMAN, S., ibid. XXV. II. 92–8. 1955.

FITZPATRICK, T. F., and WISEMAN, S., ibid. XXIV. II. 99–105. 1954.

SEVERN, D. J., J. Consult. Psychol. XIII. 2. 144–5. 1949.

For different procedures see: STRONG, E. K., *Vocational Interests of Men and Women*. California: Stanford U.P. 1943.

CALVIN, A., and ELLIS, J. M., *J. Consult. Psychol.* XVII. 6. 462–4. 1953.

GAGE, N. L., *Psychol. Monographs*. 66. 18. 1952.

FAIRBAIRN, W. R. D., *Brit. J. Med. Psychol.* XXVIII. 2 and 3. 144–56. 1955.

See also: BERLYNE, D. E., *Brit. J. Psychol.* XXXIX. 4. 184–95. 1949.

PEEL, E. A., *Psychometrika*. II. 2. 129–37. 1946.

PEEL, E. A., *Brit. J. Psychol.* XXXV. 1. 61–9. 1945.

Within this compare BARNEY, W. D., *A Study of Perception and its Relation to the Art Expression of a Group of Adolescents*. Ph.D. Thesis. London. 1952.

14. BUTLER, C. D., *The Assessment of Social Attitudes of School Children*. M.A. Thesis. London. 1949.

HIGGINBOTHAM, P. J., *An Investigation into the Use of Leaderless Group Discussions*. M.A. Thesis. London. 1949.

HAYES, M. M., *A Comparative Study of Spontaneity*. M.A. Thesis. London. 1952.

BEVERSTOCK, A. G., *Brit. J. Educ. Psychol.* XIX. II. 112–20. 1949.

Cf. ANSBACHER, H. L., *Psychol. Bull.* 48. 5. 383–91. 1951.

HIGHAM, M. H., *Occup. Psychol.* XXVI. 3. 169–75. 1952.

BASS, B. M., et al., *J. Appl. Psychol.* 37. 1. 26–30. 1953.

See also: TAFT, R., *Psychol. Bull.* 52. 1. 1–23. 1955.

LUCHINS, A. S., *J. Consult. Psychol.* XII. 5. 313–20. 1948.

See also: FLANAGAN, J. C., *Psychol. Bull.* 51. 4. 327–58. 1954.

O.S.S. ASSESSMENT STAFF. *Assessment of Men*. N.Y.: Rinehart. 1948.

HARRIS, H., *The Group Approach to Leadership Testing*. Lond.: Routledge. 1949.

15. VERNON, P. E., and PARRY, J. B., *Personnel Selection in the British Forces*. Lond.: Univ. of London Press. 1949.

STOUFFER, S. A., *The American Soldier*. Princeton: Princeton U.P. 1949.

See also: CATTELL, R. B., *Psychol. Bull.* 42. 3. 129–61. 1945.

CATTELL, R. B., *Description and Measurement of Personality*. Lond.: Harrap. 1946.

EYSENCK, H. J., et al., *Dimensions of Personality*. Lond.: Kegan Paul. 1947.

EYSENCK, H. J., *The Scientific Study of Personality*. Lond.: Routledge. 1952.

EYSENCK, H. J., *The Structure of Human Personality*. Lond.: Methuen. 1953.

GUILFORD, J. P., et al., *Psychol. Monographs*. 68. 4. 1–38. 1954.

16. ANASTASI, A., and FOLEY, J. P., *Differential Psychology*. N.Y.: Macmillan. 1937 and 1949.

LINDQUIST, E. F., *Educational Measurements*. Washington: American Council on Education. 1951.

ANASTASI, A., *Psychological Testing*. N.Y.: Macmillan. 1954.

17. DAVIS, J. A. M., *Childhood and Youth.* **4.** 3. 12–15, 61–3. 1950.

NATH, S., *An Investigation into the Significance of Teachers' Assessments of the Personal Attributes of their Pupils for Secondary School Selection.* M.A. Thesis. London. 1948.

ALEXANDER, D. J., *The Analysis of Teachers' Estimates and Pupils' Performance at the Stage of Entry to Secondary Education.* M.A. Thesis. London. 1947.

RUDD, W. G. A., loc. cit. [8] 1956.

18. BRUNER, J. S., and POSTMAN, L., in DENNIS, W., *Current Trends in Social Psychology.* Pittsburgh: Univ. of Pittsburgh Press. 71–118. 1948.

AINSWORTH, M. D., *Brit. J. Med. Psychol.* **XXIV.** 3. 151–61. 1951.

GRANT, M. Q., *et al., Psychol. Monographs.* **66.** 2. 1952.

SAMUELS, H., ibid. **66.** 5. 1952.

GIBBY, R. G., MILLER, D. R., and WALKER, E. L., *J. Consult. Psychol.* **XVII.** 6. 425–8. 1953.

See also: MERRILL, M. A., ibid. **XV.** 4. 281–9. 1951.

LA FON, F. E., *Psychol. Monographs.* **68.** 10. 1954.

19. VERNON, P. E., loc. cit. [2]. 1964.

20. STEPHENSON, W., *Brit. J. Psychol.* **XLVII.** 1. 5–18. 1956.

21. For a survey on selection see:

FLEMING, C. M., *Adolescence.* Lond.: Routledge. 1948, 1955 and 1963.

FLEMING, C. M., in JEFFERY, G. B. (chairman), *Transfer from Primary to Secondary School.* Lond.: Evans. 1949.

See also: *British Journal of Educational Psychology, passim,* and the publications of the National Foundation for Educational Research in England and Wales.

NISBET, J. D., Follow-up from 11-plus to Graduation. *Bull. Brit. Psychol. Soc.* **32.** 22. 1957.

On the hazards of prediction see also:

TRAVERS, R. M. W., *Educational Measurement.* N.Y.: Macmillan. 1955.

MCINTOSH, D. M., *Educational Guidance and the Pool of Ability.* Lond.: Univ. of Lond. Press. 1959.

22. MCINTOSH, D., *et al., The Scaling of Teachers' Marks and Estimates.* Edinburgh: Oliver & Boyd. 1949.

SANDON, F., *Applied Statistics.* V. 1. 20–31. 1956.

23. ROTHNEY, J. W. M., and ROENS, B. A., *Guidance of American Youth.* Cambridge, Mass.: Harvard U.P. 1950.

See also: STRANG, R., *Every Teacher's Records.* N.Y.: Teachers' College, C.U.P. 1936 and 1947.

24. See FLEMING, C. M., *Cotswold Series of Measurements of Mental Ability.* Glasgow: Robert Gibson. 1949 to 1961.

XIV

SELF-OBSERVATION AND
THE STUDY OF GROUPS

MENTION HAS ALREADY been made of the work of Lewin and of
Anderson in their combining of the anthropological recording of
behaviour with experimental modification of the 'climate' of the
classroom as that is affected by the teacher's 'classroom personality'.
Other developments of this type of recording are exemplified
in Rudd's analytic observation of pupils under categories such as
problem-solving, social contributions, responses to questions, lend-
ing or borrowing equipment, damaging equipment, refusal to conform, and the like.[1]

The interaction process

Considerable interest also attaches to a series of investigations
sponsored by Harvard University Laboratory of Social Relations.[2]
These are not specifically directed to teaching; and, as formulated
by their authors, they include the use of a somewhat elaborate piece
of apparatus. They are, however, valuable as a reminder of the
complexity of the interactions discernible within small groups; and
their categories are suggestive of aspects which might be investigated
by teachers in 'operational' research of a descriptive kind or in
'action' researches involving changes in their own procedures.

The proposals made by Bales and his colleagues amount to the
requirement that the observer is to disregard momentary impressions
of qualitative distinctions in such matters as vigour of reaction,
social status, relationships, or personal motivation, and give full
attention to the actual process of interaction as it affects the recipient.
By this simplification, the number of categories can be reduced to
twelve somewhat general types:

showing antagonism, tension or rejection,

asking for suggestions, opinions, and information,
giving information, evaluation or direction,
showing understanding, satisfaction or solidarity.

Attention is concentrated on the noting of each action as it occurs; and percentage differences in the appearance of each type are later calculated in settings known (on other grounds) to be characterized by qualitative differences in status, in motivation or in temporal sequences such as 'before' or 'after' a specific event.

The notable element in all these studies is that they are concerned with something other than either the ability, the attributes, and the interests of individual children or the teacher's purposes as expressed by a prevalent classroom climate. A means is here being offered for the recording of interaction between teachers and pupils and between one pupil and another in a fashion which permits both later analysis and the comparative study of psychological settings of differing sorts. In the very simplicity of these proposals there is, however, a danger. In spite of the hope they offer of supplementing stenographic or sound-recording and photographic records by symbolic analysis by observers, they are vulnerable to attack on the grounds of superficiality and subjectivity. They obviously represent an improvement on older procedures of teacher-rating;[3] but to an outsider it seems a simple matter to record the words used in a series of lessons [4] or describe the experience offered to pupils in six months or a year of school life.[5] Only through personal participation in such efforts can it be realized that a new instrument for research is in fact being forged; and only through analysis of the findings of such studies can it be seen that sufficient advance has already been made in the techniques of observing and recording to permit acceptance of statements to the effect that proof is now available that not only do pupils respond in differing fashions to different teachers [6] and in differing fashions to the same teachers using different approaches,[7] but that these differences affect attitudes and other observable personal responses as well as any learning measurable by tests of attainment.[8]

Self-observation

Not all teachers have the opportunity of subjecting their classroom procedures to the analytic study of one who is expert in the recording of the 'inter-action process'. All can, however, exercise some measure of self-study through the quite simple device of listening with awakened interest to the actual words which they themselves use.

Words and gestures are the chief instruments of change; and these derive their effectiveness from their weakening or intensifying of the picture each learner is building as to his own relative status and the functions he can perform in the corporate life of the group – in school, at home, in club or camp or workshop. Both fellow-learners and those who teach determine the quality of their own contribution to this picture through the extent to which they give or deny satisfaction to the primary psychological needs. Three dimensions may therefore be noted in this verbalization:

> appreciation – condemnation;
> participation – exclusion;
> interpretation – prescription;

and to these may be added an element of variety or monotony in each.

Appreciation in contrast to condemnation

Words may encourage the expectation of success or promote a fear of failure. 'You got ten correct yesterday.' 'She'll soon put that right.' 'Of course he can.' 'What you have to do is to think.' 'Be careful.' 'Remember what happened last time.'

They may offer appreciation or condemnation. 'Good.' 'You're working hard this afternoon.' 'Yes. You are absolutely right.' 'You could have done better.' 'That's no use.' 'Think for yourself.' 'This is the C stream of course.'

Participation in contrast to exclusion

Words may be indicative of exclusion. 'What's wrong with Catherine?' 'We can't wait for her.' 'He's no good.' 'He's silly.' 'Go on, Jean. Tell her. She doesn't know it.' 'He's done nothing to deserve to get into the team.' 'We'll see if she's right. Shall we? Was she right? She was not.' 'Walter. No work yet. I've been watching you.' 'Just look what Jim has done. Wrong again.' 'Isn't she a stupid girl!'

They may be suggestive of an expectation that of course everyone wishes to share. 'We'll have to see if it works a second time.' 'We'll see if we can't lull these visitors to sleep with our lullaby.' 'Have we finished everything?' 'Are we ready?' 'I think we could make a little play.' 'Frost kills all sorts of things. Doesn't it, Susan?' 'You're good at this sort of work. Tell us what happens here.' 'What's the first thing we do?' 'Ours is a good class. Isn't it?' 'Let's have a look at it together.' 'This is how we do it.' 'Come on. They can do it. We can.'

Interpretation as opposed to dogmatic prescription

Words may also offer an interpretation. 'Exactly. That is just what Tom meant.' 'You'd have to say it flies quickly. Wouldn't you?' 'I know it's your turn; but would you like to let Jim have a turn instead? He's not had one yet.' 'Talking's all right for little people; but I expect bigger boys and girls to behave better.' 'Did you see what Mary did? She moved the beads in a quicker way then the one I asked. She knows that two rows have twenty beads and she took two rows at a time. It takes much longer to count each bead.' 'You can't always have what you want.' 'It's your arithmetic that is keeping you out of the top group.' 'Bob is especially good at acting. Let's make him the hero.'

They may carry the implication that no responsibility or initiative is expected. 'Look what I'm doing.' 'Sit down.' 'Do this.' 'You can't do it unless you watch me.' 'I don't want any talking about it.' 'When you don't know a word look it up. No guessing.' 'Are you listening? I want all of you to listen now.' 'Don't ask me when I'm helping Billy.' 'Put everything down.' 'Ready! Pay attention.' 'You watch me carefully. I'll write it on the board.' 'We are not doing any more today.'

In response to such remarks human beings come to think of themselves as co-operative, successful, industrious, intelligent, or rejected, useless, inadequate, and dull; and as they think – so also they tend to become.

Attempts have sometimes been made to collect statements representative of what one should 'never say to children'. Never say: 'I told you so.' 'I think very little of . . .' 'What a nit-wit you must be.' The issue is a still wider one which is perhaps expressed most simply by saying: 'Never say to any other: Thou fool.' Many, however, are the variants of that statement and extensive are its disguises.

This does not mean that children or adults should not be told when they have failed; but the manner of the telling is both kinder and more wise when it is directed to the incident at issue and does not carry implications of either scorn or rejection of the person who has met defeat. The teacher who is skilful in the art of correction uses phrases which are task-orientated, 'That sum is wrong', 'That is no use', rather than self-involved 'You are wrong', 'You are no use', and leaves self-involvement for occasions when a positive self-picture can be built. In this sense one can agree with Symonds that all learning is through reinforcement or reward;[9] but the most powerful reinforcements come from psychological rather than from physical satisfactions such as those proposed by earlier workers such as Hull (primary drives), Freud (instincts) or even Thorndike (an impersonally satisfying state of affairs). The fostering of a sense of adequacy and the permitting of some measure of insight are of as great significance in the management of men as the giving of approval or affection; and the views held by children as to the attitudes and the attributes of their teachers are as definitive for education as any adult's willingness to teach.[10] All this is written from the viewpoint of the adult who seeks fuller insight into the behaviour of others. When attention is turned within, a lively awareness of the common humanity of teacher and taught serves as a reminder of the teacher's own longing for appreciation and the teacher's own need to make the fullest possible contribution and attain the deepest possible insight into the task in hand. With this there comes the challenge to perseverance in good works. This the wise teacher both accepts as a personal requirement and offers to pupils as the ideal of self-hood with which alone they can be satisfied.

The interpretation in terms of needs is never a soft gospel offered in condonement of backsliding either in conduct or in learning. It has sometimes been suggested that the good teachers are those who come to terms with the immaturity, the anxiety, the loneliness, and the resentment of the 'child' within themselves.[11] More light is cast upon the teaching situation by the comment that they are men and women who have reached awareness of the processes through which fear, indignation, and hostility are born within their pupils and within themselves. Gaining of self-insight brings some benefit to all; and in this sense also each is more like the other than has often been supposed.

In the light of present knowledge there thus comes to each teacher the challenge of the known effect of habitual phrases and of the resistance to change which characterizes a self-picture when it has once been built. 'He says I can; but I can't. I am not that sort of person.' Much of this used to be discussed in more ambiguous fashion in terms of the attitudinal control of suggestion and the means of combating undesirable beliefs.[12] A clearer formulation and one more relevant to human relationships is to be found in these recent records from the study of the psychic surface with its self-concepts rooted in personal needs;[13] and in response to the observation of the words they use and the implications which these words carry many teachers are today transforming their procedures nearer to the heart's desire.

REFERENCES

1. RUDD, W. G. A., *Brit. J. Educ. Psychol.* **XXVIII.** I. 47–60. 1958. *Educ. Res.* **II.** 3. 225–228. 1960.
2. BALES, R. F., *Interaction Process Analysis.* Cambridge, Mass.: Addison-Wesley. 1951.
   See also: RICHARDSON, J. E., *The Active Teacher.* Lond.: Routledge. 1955.
3. On the rating of teachers see: LEEDS, C. H., and COOK, W. W., *J. Exper. Educ.* **XVI.** 2. 149–59. 1947.
   KEMP, L. C. D., *Brit. J. Psychol.* **XXV.** II. 67–77. 1955.
   WRIGHTSTONE, J. W., *J. Educ. Res.* **XLIV.** 5. 341–51. 1951.
   WANDT, E., and OSTREICHER, L. M., *Psychol. Monographs.* **68.** 5. No. 376. 1954.
4. For an early study see: ANDERSON, D. F., *Practical Problems in Teaching Method.* Lond.: Univ. of London Press. 1939.
5. KHAN, Q. J. A., *A Study of the Arithmetical Experience of Certain Groups of Children in an Infants' School.* M.A. Thesis. London. 1953.
6. For different responses to different teachers see:
   LEWIN, K., LIPPITT, R., and WHITE, R. K., *J. Soc. Psychol.* **10.** 11. 271–99. 1939.
   ANDERSON, H. H., *et al.*, *Applied Psychology Monographs of the American Psychological Association.* **6.** 8. 11. 1945. 1946.
   Cf. BIRCHMORE, B., *A Study of the Relationships between Pupils and Teachers.* M.A. Thesis. London. 1951.
7. For different responses to different approaches see:
   LEWIN, K., *et al.*, ibid.
   ANDERSON, H. H., *et al.*, ibid.
   ARBUCKLE, D. S., *Teacher Counseling.* Cambridge: Addison-Wesley. 1950.
   RICHARDSON, J. E., *et al.*, *Studies in the Social Psychology of Adolescence.* Lond.: Routledge. 1951.
   HALLWORTH, H. J., *A Study of Group Relationships Among Grammar School Boys and Girls.* M.A. Thesis. London. 1951.
   HALLWORTH, H. J., *Educ. Rev.* **VII.** 2. 124–33. 1955. Ibid. **X.** 1. 41–53. 1957.
   STAINES, J. W., *A Psychological and Sociological Investigation of the Self as a Significant Factor in Education.* Ph.D. Thesis. London. 1954.

TEACHING: A PSYCHOLOGICAL ANALYSIS

8. For effects on attitude, etc., see:
   LEWIN, K., *et al.*, loc. cit. [6].
   ANDERSON, H. H., *et al.*, loc. cit. [6].
   STAINES, J. W., loc. cit. [7].
   KHAN, Q. J. A., loc. cit. [5].
   RICHARDSON, J. E., *et al.*, loc. cit. [7].
9. SYMONDS, P. M., *Teachers' College Record.* **56.** 5. 277–85. 1955, and **57.** 1. 15–25. 1955.
10. BUSH, R. N., *The Teacher-Pupil Relationship.* N.Y.: Prentice-Hall. 1954.
11. HOURD, M., *Some Emotional Aspects of Learning.* Lond.: Heinemann. 1951.
    MORRIS, B., in *Studies in Education.* 7. Univ. of Lond. Inst. of Educ. 1955.
12. MURPHY, G., MURPHY, L. B., and NEWCOMB, T. M., *Experimental Social Psychology.* N.Y.: Harper. 1937.
    BROWN, W., *Psychological Methods of Healing.* Lond.: Univ. of London Press. 1938.
13. Cf. JERSILD, A. T., *When Teachers Face Themselves.* N.Y.: Teachers' College, C.U.P. 1955.
    See also: BILLS, R., VANCE, E. L., and MCLEAN, O. S., *J. Consult. Psychol.* 15. 257–61. 1951.
    WILKIE, J. S., *A Study of the Self-Picture and its Concomitants in the Period from the last year of the Primary School to the first year of the Secondary School.* Lond.: Ph.D. Thesis. 1962.
    PHILLIPS, A. S., *Brit. J. Educ. Psychol.* **XXXIII.** 2. 154–61. 1963.
    EMMETT, R. G., *An Experimental Study of Personal Interaction in the Classroom with Special Reference to the Self-Concept of Student Teachers.* Ph.D. Thesis. Lond. 1964.
    FLEMING, C. M., in SANDVEN, J., *The Role of Educ. Res. in Social Education.* 107–14. Oslo: Universitets forlager. 1963.

PART VI

THE TEACHER AS EXPERIMENTER

XV

EXPERIMENTATION
AND EDUCATIONAL RESEARCH

A DELIGHT IN doing something not done before is contributory to the fascination which teaching exercises upon both young and old. Most teachers are, therefore, experimentally inclined. 'I can do it.' 'Let me show you.' 'Listen to me.' And, for most, the impulse to 'teach' is followed by an assessment. 'Have they learned?' 'Is there a better way?' Habitual answers may vary with experience and with attitude. The mere existence of the question contributes, however, more often than is admitted, to modifications in method and to differences in approach on another occasion.

By such small unnoticed steps and little nameless unrecorded acts there come the massive changes through which unskilled and hesitant entrants to the teaching profession are transformed into 'experienced' teachers. The same joy in experimenting is, in unacknowledged fashions, to be found in husbands and wives, brothers, sisters, friends, and fellow-workers who reach out as 'teachers' to the modifying of other members in their groups.

Experimentation within schools is an extension of this personal delight. The phrase carries the connotation of the initiation of change – in procedures, in organization, in materials of instruction or in choice of subject-matter – and the changes result from a challenge based on the personal opinion of an innovator. Relatively small departures from tradition on the part of discerning teachers have thus prepared the way for later quite general acceptance of notions whose novelty made them at one time both startling and unacceptable. Infant schools, the introduction of science or mathematics or the mother-tongue to the curriculum, nursery schools, self-instruction, self-correction, project methods, the therapy of art or movement or drama, fundamental education, the community school. Phrases such as these carry echoes of an originality in experimentation which is still probably the most important source of educational advance.

Experimentation in schools is, however, to be distinguished from educational research in which deliberate attention is given to the verifying of hypotheses or the testing of the significance of observable changes. The teacher as an experimenter may be somewhat casual in approach. The teacher as a research worker is pledged to examine any theory in the light of evidence from the most carefully scrutinized and representative body of available facts.[1]

The methods used by educational research workers

The methods of educational research workers may, like those of psychologists, be described under three headings: (a) the making and recording of observations (the study of the obvious in oneself or in others, with or without apparatus of various kinds); (b) the asking of questions (the search for that which is not immediately discernible in a face-to-face interview or a paper and pencil test, and in response to materials and to situations of a variety of types); (c) the analysis and interpretation of findings in terms of statistical concepts (with or without mechanical aid and ranging from the simplest generalizations as to frequency of occurrence to the most elaborate psychometric and sociometric technicalities).

The story of educational research, like the history of psychology, is the record of the changes in these procedures which have followed upon increases in technical skill and upon expansion of the range of the topics studied. From the study of individuals to the study of groups, from the study of the functioning of mental faculties through the study of the physiological correlates of mental processes to inquiries into attitudes, personal attributes and the emotional and social determinants of learning. The same sequence is characteristic of both. It may be traced in the content of books on the psychology of teaching, in the activities required from students in Training Colleges and University Departments of Education, in the questions set in examinations in psychology and education,[2] and in the titles of theses submitted for higher degrees in these fields. In teacher-training studies, for example, in the 1900s the clear statement could still be made that introspection was the only method by which a sound knowledge of psychology could be obtained; and students were asked to examine themselves, to note their states of consciousness, and to investigate their own imagery. By the 1910s miniature psychological laboratories had been set up in many places; and students were being set to test their reactions in mirror drawing, or in tachistoscopic experiments on the rate and accuracy of their perceptions. (They then wrote records of practical work in fashions reminiscent of a physiologist's or a physicist's laboratory.) In the 1920s some of them were invited to co-operate in surveys of achievement in arithmetic, reading, and what is commonly called intelligence. In the 1930s their attention was directed to diagnostic tests and the remedial tuition of children in difficulty; and by the 1940s most of them had been introduced to the painstaking and accurate study of the home life, the attitudes, and the interests of their pupils. Earlier procedures have not necessarily been abandoned. The rich legacy of the past is still relevant to certain present problems; but the changes that have occurred may be estimated from the attention now being given to the social psychology of education in its current sense of the personal-social determinants of learning, sociometry, peer relationships, the contagion of behaviour in groups, and the moulding of a pupil's self-picture through word, gesture, and example in the ordinary contacts of school and playground.[3]

Operational and action research

The techniques of research were first applied in laboratories to human beings (adults or children) brought there for the specific purpose of a research worker. One problem was selected for investigation and attempts were made to study one variable at a time with careful control of details of procedure and exact recordings both of observations made and of responses secured.

By the beginning of the twentieth century a distinction was being drawn between such 'pure' research and so-called 'practical' research – the latter being the activities of those who began by studying a going concern, selected one item for investigation, set up a comparable situation in a laboratory, and, later, transferred a modification of procedure to the practical setting in which the research had had its origin.[4]

At about the same time the phrase 'experimental education' was applied to activities similar to those used in laboratory studies of perception, attention, memory, association, imagination, thinking, and reasoning when these activities took place in the classroom – the chief distinction being in the place of the experiment rather than its nature. By an extension of meaning, the term was also applied to deductions drawn from such investigations as to the learning and teaching of school subjects.[5]

The title 'educational research' was used later (in contrast to 'psychological research') when it was realized more clearly that the observing and interviewing of individuals in the artificial style of a laboratory was less relevant to education than their study in the actual setting of a home or a school.

A similar more recent distinction is now made between operational and experimental research – 'operational' research being the scientific study of a procedure as it normally occurs in practice while 'experimental' research requires the setting up of special conditions. A further distinction within the field of applied research is that between operational or experimental research and 'action' research in which 'action' is taken and a change in normal procedure is introduced, the techniques of research then being applied to the study of the changed procedure.[6]

Mention has already been made of many instances of such operational and action research; and the mutual indebtedness of psychologists and teachers is great. Down the decades the questions of educators and the study of their practices provided fields for inquiry and material for investigation; and the first fruits of 'experimental education' were offered by psychologists who came into the schools as outsiders prepared to organize and to report upon researches in classrooms which were not their own. Herbart, Galton, Stanley Hall, Ebbinghaus, Binet, Meumann, Thorndike, Judd, Claparède. Their studies of memorizing and associated ideas, like their experiments on imagination, inventiveness, and learning, led directly to the refinements of psychometry and perceptual theory as well as to the methods of psycho-analysis and the techniques of projective testing; and in direct succession to their work are the more recent contributions of Moreno, Sherif, Axline or Rogers. Meanwhile, in tentative fashion at first, an increasing number of studies were reported by pioneering teachers, by school superintendents and inspectors, by lecturers in Universities and Training Colleges, and by workers in Child Guidance Clinics. These had all taken the step of acquainting themselves with the procedures required in the collecting and analysing of evidence – a step possible for any trained teacher but necessary for those who would attempt the confirmation or disproof of any claim to educational innovation.

Topics in the field of educational research

Topics for inquiry have been found in many of the issues which concern school life and work. They can usefully be classified under two headings:

(a) the effect of membership of groups – human relationships and their influence upon behaviour and upon the development of personality;

(b) educational guidance.

The study of human relationships in education may be approached in a variety of ways, of which the following questions represent a sample:

What is the relative value of group methods of learning as compared with class instruction?

(What happens when friends are allowed to co-operate in the classroom?)

What is the effect of differing types of social climate upon attitude and attainment?

(What are the differing effects produced by different teachers?)

What are the concomitants of confidence, co-operation, sociability, friendly attitudes, good morale, etc. etc.

(What are the patterns of attraction and repulsion within a classroom?)

What are the interests, preferences, attitudes, opinions, and wishes of selected groups of children or teachers?

What is the relation of such interests, attitudes or ambitions to experiences at home or in school or college?

What is their effect upon susceptibility to learning (in any field)?

What are the therapeutic effects of teaching, of discussions, of reading, of dramatizing, etc.?

What are the personal and social consequences of success (or failure)?

What are the observable differences between teachers when they are succeeding and teachers in situations and with points of view associated with failure and dissatisfaction?

What are the attributes of pupils in situations in which they may be called leaders and what are their relationships (in such situations) to other pupils and to staff?

What are the self-pictures held by pupils under various types of school organization?

Contributions to educational guidance may also take a variety of forms:

analysis of what is involved in appreciation of art and literature, in success in mathematics, science, languages, and the like;

projects associated with test construction – item validation, estimation of reliability, factorial analysis, and analysis of variance (these may be applied to any subject-field);

construction of diagnostic tests and of remedial material (in any subject);

studies as to methods of assessing personality, as to teachers' ratings and the markings of essays and exercises;

inquiries into the personal, social, and intellectual consequences of different types of classification and segregation.

On all of these relevant material is available in learned journals, in reviews of educational and psychological research, and in the lists of completed theses published by many Universities and research councils.[7]

Samples of research

A brief account of some recent inquiries undertaken by independent workers may be of interest here.

In a study of the arithmetical experiences offered to children in their first few weeks at school, Khan, for example, made a careful daily recording over some ten months of the behaviour of five-year-old pupils and their teachers.[8] Her work was in line with that of the reports organized by Lewin and by Anderson; but it was carried out in London as a study of 'operations in progress' with no interference with the accepted practices of busy teachers, each responsible for over forty pupils in a class.

In one school the teacher believed in incidental ways of learning and let the pupils devise their own methods of using the materials and toys provided. She moved amongst them and offered help only where it seemed to be required. David, pretending to be a postman, came to the teacher's desk and knocked at the door of the cupboard. 'Good morning, Mr Postman. Is there any letter for me?' 'Yes.' He gave her a few 'letters' made of used Christmas cards. 'How many letters have you brought me today?' 'Six.' 'Have you any for Mrs Khan?' 'Yes. But she has only two letters. I hope to bring some more for her tomorrow.' Barbara, Mary, Francesca, and Jean gave to the teacher some flour, margarine, and jam they had brought from home. Later they came for them. 'What are you going to make today?' 'Jam tarts.' 'Show me when you've finished and I'll see if the oven is free for us.' When the pastries were baked she brought them back to the classroom. The cooks, who had now washed up and made all tidy, gathered round. 'Which is yours?' 'How many did you make?' 'How many were there altogether?' 'Now you can do some little sums'. 'What do you want to use?' 'You can copy mine if you want to; or you can use the bricks and make another story of your own.'

In another school the teacher did not believe that children could learn much when left on their own. Her methods were formal and little was done to develop the arithmetical uses which could be made of the small amount of material provided. There was a tendency to disorderliness, inattention, and boredom in place of the happy absorption and co-operative activity which characterized the other classroom. 'I wonder if you could go to the sand tray and get me four things out of it. Can you?' 'Yes.' 'Go and get them then.' 'Now we'll see if he's right. How many did we ask?' 'Four.' 'Count them: one, two, three, four, five. Was he right?' 'No.' 'How many did I want?' 'Four.' 'That is simply shocking. Frank, you bring me two shells.' 'Is he right'. 'Let's give him a clap.' 'Look at this. There are three flowers in this picture. This is the figure 3. These pictures are given to help you in counting. We are not doing the rest today.'

From details of this kind Khan obtained evidence both of the range of individual differences in each group and of the difficulties encountered by pupils in writing and reading numbers, in enumerating, in the process of generalization:

$$1 + 1 = 2 \quad \text{so} \quad 100 + 100 = 2\ 100 \ (\text{'two one hundreds'})$$

and the understanding of the meaning of numbers: 'No picture needs to be drawn under the figure nought.' In the observable differences between the two groups there was also support for the finding that instruction requires to be reinforced by the satisfying of primary human needs. Those pupils who were given the more dictatorial type of tuition and received no reward for or recognition of their tentative use of arithmetical concepts showed fewer overt signs of learning and appeared to make less progress than those whose teachers pointed the way past the informal manipulation of material to the discovery, the recognition, and the use of arithmetical concepts of various kinds.

Comparable operational studies of social climates and their effect upon the reactions of adolescents and adults are to be found in the prolonged records made by Basu and by Ansari in Youth Clubs and by Tawadros in a social club for psychiatric patients.[9]

Of similar interest is a study of Edwards in which a series of three mock elections, at something like six-monthly intervals, were held to discover which twelve boys would be chosen by their classmates to act as prefects in a group which had worked together for four years without differentiation of status or any symbolic authority.[10] Along with the second and third elections and at the end of the school year sociometric questions were asked as to their preferred choices and rejections in the sharing of a tent at a school camp. A positive relationship was found between sociometric status and election as a prefect although the latter was not entirely related to personal predilection. The relationship of social status with intelligence was negligible; but academic success was noticeable among those chosen as prefects and, within the range of intelligence covered by the class, social acceptability seemed more clearly associated with good school-work than was initial ability as shown by scores in an intelligence test.

In these studies no 'action' was taken in the sense of an experimental modification of classroom activities or organization. The same is true of an inquiry by Hayes into what appeared to be a relative lack of spontaneity in dramatic improvisations (Spontaneity Tests), group discussions, and creative writing in prose and poetry on the part of groups of girls taking commercial subjects in a Technical School in contrast with the greater social cohesion and greater flexibility of response found among girls following a course in Domestic Science.[11] The supposition with which the investigation began won some measure of confirmation from an analysis of short-hand records of words and actions combined with teachers' assessments for sociability and initiative, along with the results of a Guess-Who? questionnaire designed to discover which girls were in their classmates' opinion most ready to take a share in group life, and a standardized attitude test which permitted each pupil to give an estimate of her own sociability.

234

Action research

Similar carefulness of design and similar indebtedness to the work of Moreno may be traced in another series of studies in which experimental changes or 'actions' of greater or lesser complexity were super-added to questionnaires and observational records. Morgan, for example, undertook an inquiry into the patterns of attraction and repulsion which developed in the course of a school year in a class of thirty-one boys and girls who, at the opening of a session, had met for the first time in a large school new to them all.[12] This socio-genetic study of the birth and growth of a small community of peers began at the end of the first week of term with the invitation to the pupils to make a confidential statement as to those with whom they would most prefer to sit and those whom they would like to avoid. Reseating was arranged to meet their choices and every six weeks throughout the school year they were given a chance to choose again. On the fourth and subsequent occasions they were also asked to rate every member of the class on a five-point scale by putting a cross in one of five columns on a sheet showing the names of all the pupils. In column 1 they were to put a cross against the names of all with whom they very much wanted to sit. In column 5 they were then to show which ones they very much did not want to sit beside. In column 3 they were asked to mark those about whose proximity they were indifferent, while column 2 was for those beside whom they would like to sit, and column 4 for those with whom they would rather not be associated.

From choices recorded in this fashion 'secondary networks' as well as primary patterns of group structure were derived along with indices of sociability (seeking to associate with others), popularity (being sought by others), and reciprocity of regard. Analysis of these showed the development of a preponderance of friendly ratings, an absence of a negative phase, and no direct linear relationship between sociability and popularity.

Similar reminders of the complexity of the interrelations of class-room friendships which are so largely below the level of a teacher's awareness have come from recent experimental work by Pearce and by Wilkie.[13] These compared classes of pupils permitted to work in co-operative fashion in small groups of friends with control groups for whom more formal methods were used; and offered further evidence from a Secondary School (Pearce) and from a Junior School

(Wilkie) of the contribution made to classroom morale by procedures which permit participation and the building of an acceptable self-picture.

Research and educational reform

Educational reforms have, in many cases, had their origin in the convincing advocacy of such workers to whose views power has been lent by their authoritative citation of evidence in support of an innovation. There is, however, a time-lag between certainty on the part of a research worker and subsequent transformation of educational procedures on the part of other teachers. Rice talked of economy of time in the 1890s and demonstrated the futility of long periods of repetitive drill in spelling and other subjects. Further experimentation was needed to commend his views in the 1910s. By 1925 Thorndike, Gray, Gates, and Decroly had proposed better methods of teaching both arithmetic and reading; and a small number of books designed for self-aided study in silent reading and self-corrective instruction in arithmetic had made it possible to demonstrate the effectiveness of individualized work in Winnetka, Dalton or Brussels. Another thirty years were to pass before new textbooks, activity methods, programmed learning and the possible use of teaching-machines became a matter of general interest and concern.[14]

Few research findings have had even so smooth a passage as this. Reference has already been made in Chapter VII to the fact that some research studies have been inadequately reported. Influential among these were the early studies of human development summarized by Stanley Hall in his two volumes on adolescence in 1904. In these, evidence was collected as to averages of groups in height, weight, interest, skills, and the like; but no account was taken of scattering within groups and overlapping between groups. There was, therefore, an appearance of illusory uniformity in his findings; and he talked in what now seem exaggerated terms of the clearly defined characteristics of pupils of different ages, different sexes, and different racial groups.

Some research findings have been misunderstood. Notable among these was the evidence of the late 1900s when attention was beginning to be given to the range of individual differences at every age. The wide variations demonstrated in the first educational surveys of the twentieth century were reported in terms of scores obtained on a single occasion. The progress of pupils was not followed over a period of years; and it was concluded that there were not only types of ability but clearly demarcated types of children. It was thus too readily assumed that those lacking in any present ability were without a corresponding capacity – that they were irretrievably word-blind, number weak, mechanically incompetent or artistically inept. It was therefore expected that initial failure would be followed by ultimate defeat; and proposals for 'aptitude' grouping contributed to the maintenance of educational systems in which classification and segregation were the prevailing pattern.

Some research inquiries have been misquoted. Of these perhaps the most important were those relating to the retesting of pupils – in the late 1910s and after. The figures given in learned journals (whether in the form of differences of averages or of coefficients of correlation between earlier and later testing) were not such as to suggest complete constancy of relative status. The cautious statements of research workers were, however, disregarded by many administrators. Qualifying clauses were omitted from reports of results; and research findings were cited in support of a competitive segregation into groups of initially equal ability which was acceptable for other reasons.[15]

Research findings have met with opposition as well as with indifference, misinterpretation or misquotation. Of this, perhaps the most recent example is the resistance experienced after the Eight Year Study in American schools. In 1933 permission was granted to thirty schools to dispense with external examinations at the stage of transition from school to University. Students were to be admitted in terms of the recommendation of their teachers; and teachers were set free to devise their own procedures. A careful follow-up through eight years in school and University showed that students from the nine-and-twenty schools which had persevered with modified methods and curriculum more than held their own at the conclusion of a University course with graduates of similar age, sex, race, and social background from a control group of secondary schools in which traditional procedures had been followed.[16] This seemed a successful conclusion to an important investigation for which the way had been prepared by several decades of discussion of research evidence contributory to the same general conclusion.

Eight years after the publication of these reports, at a conference representative of more than half the schools, it had, however, to be admitted that in many places the details of the experimental approach had been lost and the teachers had returned to the traditional programme in spite of the unchallenged finding that there is no single school course which alone prepares pupils for later success.[17] Changes in staffing, parental pressure towards more orthodox procedures, lack of confidence between superintendents and teachers, and an absence of consultation between older and newer members of staff. All these appear to have been contributory to the relative impermanence of the educational reforms attempted. What had survived in most schools was a general attitude of co-operativeness between colleagues and more friendly relationships with pupils within the classrooms of many teachers. This in itself is clear gain; but the general disappearance of more detailed changes in methods and in curriculum-content illustrates possible sources of opposition and raises questions as to the means which may be taken to overcome such obstacles to educational reform.

There is a very human unwillingness to admit the inadequacy of familiar procedures when their suitability is challenged by an outsider to one's group; and in an attempt to overcome such resistance, and to make more general use of the skilled assistance of many workers, National Bureaux or Councils for Educational Research have been established in recent years in many countries. These have a prestige, a power, and a financial backing beyond the reach of independent investigators; but the clue to their acceptability probably lies in the complexities of human communication and in those human relationships and social attitudes to which the attention of research workers in education (as in industry) has only recently been turned.[18] The greater the degree of co-operation they have secured and the more obvious the contribution they have invited from teachers, the more rapid seems to have been the infiltration of their findings into routine practice in the schools.[19]

A comparable acknowledgement of the human need for participation may be detected in the collective research efforts organized in some teacher-training departments (McClelland in Dundee, Hughes in Leicester),[20] and in refresher courses and research groups for practising teachers (Corey in New York, Oeser in Melbourne, Moustakas in Detroit).[21] If 'action research' is 'ours' we are more likely to believe in the findings it suggests. If 'operational records' have been made by 'ourselves' it is more probable that we will come to appreciate the significance of 'personal interaction in the classroom'. If 'we' have struggled for months with the attempt to understand and to describe the social and personal repercussions of 'teacher, pupil, and task' it is more possible that lasting changes in our own relationships will be effected.

A similar encouragement of fuller sharing by teachers in the fostering of their own professional growth is observable in the use of dramatizing (socio-drama or psycho-drama) in the training of supervisors,[22] in group discussions in summer schools and international seminars,[23] and in the development of journals directed to the publication of experimental studies by teachers – Research Reviews and Educational Reviews, the *Scottish Educational Journal*, the *Higher Educational Journal*, *Education for Teaching*, and the *British Journal of Educational Studies*. Through agencies such as these the personal delight in experimentation which characterizes all 'teachers' is being disciplined and made more fruitful; and through the more co-operative planning encouraged by the activities they represent it may be expected that the resistance of the 'in-group' to the innovations of the 'out-group' will progressively be reduced.

REFERENCES

1. RUSK, R. R., *Research in Education*. Lond.: Univ. of London Press. 1932.
   FLEMING, C. M., *Research and the Basic Curriculum*. Lond.: Univ. of London Press. 1946 and 1952.
   Cf. MADGE, J., *The Tools of Social Science*. Lond.: Longmans. 1953.
   WISEMAN, S., *Reporting Research in Education*. Manchester Univ. Press. 1952.
2. FLEMING, C. M., *Brit. J. Educ. Studies*. 3. 1. 17–23. 1954.
3. Relevant descriptions of classroom situations may be found in:
   REDL, F., and WATTENBERG, W. W., *Mental Hygiene in Teaching*. N.Y.: Harcourt Brace. 1951.
   WILES, K., *Teaching for Better Schools*. N.Y.: Prentice-Hall. 1952.
   In contrast see: BUCKINGHAM, B. R., *Research for Teachers*. N.Y.: Silver Burdett. 1926.
4. RUSK, R. R., loc. cit. [1].
5. RUSK, R. R., *An Introduction to Experimental Education*. Lond.: Longmans. 1912.
6. Cf. BENNE, K. D., and MUNTYAN, B., *Human Relations in Curriculum Change*. N.Y.: Dryden Press. 1951.
   A slightly different use of the phrase 'action research' is to be found in COREY, S. M., *Action Research to Improve School Practices*. N.Y.: Teachers' College, C.U.P. 1953.

See also: FOSHAY, A. W., *et al.*, *Children's Social Values*. N.Y.: Teachers' College, C.U.P. 1954.

7. See especially; BLACKWELL, A. M., *A List of Researches in Education and Educational Psychology*. (Biennial publication), National Foundation for Educational Research in England and Wales. Lond. 1950, 1952, 1954, 1956, etc.

FLEMING, C. M., and LAUWERYS, J. A., in *Studies and Impressions*. 1902–1952. Univ. of Lond. Inst. of Educ. 1952.

8. KHAN, Q. J. A., *A Study of the Arithmetical Experience of Certain Groups of Children in an Infants' School*. M.A. Thesis. London. 1953.

9. BASU, A., *A Descriptive Study of a Group of Adolescents at a Youth Club*. M.A. Thesis. London. 1950.

ANSARI, G. A., *A Study of Attitudes and Relationships in a Group of Adolescents at a Youth Club*. M.A. Thesis. London. 1953.

TAWADROS, S. M., *A Study of Group Treatment and Techniques with Special Reference to an Experience in a Therapeutic Social Club*. Ph.D. Thesis. London. 1952.

10. EDWARDS, T. L., *A Study of the Social Relationships of a Group of School Prefects with one another and with other members of the School Community*. M.A. Thesis. London. 1952.

11. HAYES, M. M., *A Comparative Study of Spontaneity*. M.A. Thesis. London. May, 1952.

12. MORGAN, A. H., *A Study of Patterns of Attraction and Repulsion within a Classroom*. M.A. Thesis. London. 1951.

13. PEARCE, R. A., *Co-operation in the Classroom*. M.A. Thesis. London. 1956.

WILKIE, J. S., *A Study of Some Effects of the Free Choice of Certain Activities and of Companions for Group Work*. M.A. Thesis. London. 1955.

With this may be compared: BRIDGEWATER, J. M., *A Study of Psychodrama as a Classroom Technique*. M.A. Thesis. London. 1949.

ENDEAN, M. G., *A Study of Reactions to Drama in a Group of Senior Pupils*. M.A. Thesis. London. 1951.

LANGDON, E. M., *An Introduction to Dramatic Work with Children*. Lond.: Dennis Dobson. 1948.

HARTLEY, R. E., FRANK, L. K., and GOLDENSON, R. M., *Understanding Children's Play*. Lond.: Routledge. 1952.

14. For accessible surveys see: *J. Assoc. for Programmed Learning. Passim.*

15. See also: FLEMING, C. M., *Adolescence*. Lond.: Routledge. 1948, 1955 and 1963.

16. AIKIN, W. M., *The Story of the Eight Year Study. Adventure in American Education*. Vol. I. N.Y.: Harper. 1942.

HEMMING, J., *Teach Them to Live*. Lond.: Heinemann. 1948.

17. REDEFER, F. L. *Progressive Education*. **28**. 2. 33–6. 1950.

18. BENNE, K. D., and MUNTYAN, B., loc. cit. [6].

19. Cf. the modifications in the teaching of spelling in Scottish schools after the research inquiries organized by Boyd in the 1920s. See:

BOYD, W., *Measuring Devices in Composition, Spelling, and Arithmetic*. Lond.: Harrap. 1924.

BOYD, W., *The Standard Spelling List and the Longer Standard Spelling List*. Lond.: Harrap. 1926.

20. MCCLELLAND, W., *Selection for Secondary Education*. Lond.: Univ. of London Press. 1942.

HUGHES, E. W., *Brit. J. Educ. Psychol.* **XXV.** II. 99–106. 1955.

HUGHES, E. W., *The Case for Repeated Research with Intact Groups in Education and Sociology*. Leicester Inst. Educ. Univ. Coll. (Mimeograph). [n.d.].

21. COREY, S. M., loc. cit. [6].

OESER, O. A., *Teacher, Pupil, and Task*. Lond.: Tavistock Publications. 1955.

MOUSTAKAS, C. E., *The Teacher and the Child*. N.Y.: McGraw-Hill. 1956.

22. MORENO, J. L., *Psychodrama*. I. N.Y.: Beacon House. 1946.

HAAS, R. B. (ed.), *Psychodrama and Sociodrama in American Education*. N.Y.: Beacon House. 1949.

23. See: LIPPITT, R., *Training in Community Relations*. N.Y.: Harper. 1949.

LERNER, H. H., Bibliography on Leadership and Authority in Local Communities. Supplement to *Bull. World Fed. Mental Health.* **4.** 2.

MCNAIR, M.P. (ed.), *The Case Method at the Harvard Business School*. N.Y.: McGraw-Hill. 1954.

See also *Occupational Psychology* and *Human Relations, passim.*

HUGHES, E. W., *Human Resistance to Change*. Leicester University. 1958.

CLEUGH, M. F., *Educating Older People*. Lond.: Tavistock Publications. 1962.

PART VII

THE TEACHER
AS ADMINISTRATOR AND
THERAPIST

XVI

ADMINISTRATIVE RESPONSIBILITIES

TEACHERS AS ADMINISTRATORS perhaps even more than teachers as craftsmen or as technicians are concerned with their own relationships to other people – as leaders of their pupils, as colleagues or assistants, and as representative adults in contact with parents or prospective employers in the world outside. The social pattern of the school includes all these; and its wholesome functioning is affected by the undertones supplied by each.

Leadership studies

Many references have been made to those relationships between teachers and pupils which can be described in terms of Lewin's analysis of leadership into types which are autocratic, *laissez faire* or democratic, or of Anderson's evidence as to the differing effects of an approach which is integrative in contrast to one which is more completely dominative. Relevant also were the observations made by Sherif and by Redl on the changes in role-playing and in prestige which can take place from day to day.[1] From a teacher's point of view these are both comforting and disturbing. Tomorrow will not necessarily show the same relationships as today.

Group relationships

A fuller recognition of the complexity of group relationships came from these studies of children and young people in informal groups in camps and clubs. It has been enriched also by inquiries into the social structures of groups of adults in industry and in the forces.[2] These may be considered from the point of view of the emphasis which the leader puts upon the task in hand – the target of achievement of the team or the productivity of its members.[3] They may differ with the degree of autonomy enjoyed by the group, the closeness of the

K   245

control it exercises over the behaviour of its members, its informality, its homogeneity, its stability, and its significance in the general pattern of the life of its members.[4] Some groups encourage happiness more than others. Some are more cohesive and show more absence of quarrelling along with greater encouragement of co-operative sharing of responsibility.[5]

The effect produced by groups is also modified by their position within a larger organization.[6] They are 'perceived' in terms of what may be called their inner relationships; but they have meaning also in the setting of what is believed to be the purpose of the whole and the degree of acceptance accorded to that purpose by the smaller groups in which personal and friendly support is found. Co-operativeness among colleagues thus tends to be paralleled by greater willingness to co-operate on the part of pupils; and more independence and inititative is shown both by teachers and by pupils in situations in which more is permitted by those at higher levels in the school hierarchy.[7] In some schools the heads keep quite apart – through personal shyness, disdain or fear. In some they are welcome but occasional visitors. In others they may share their private room with colleagues or seem to prefer staff quarters to their own. Some heads take part in teaching duties. Others are purely administrative. Some delegate the organizing of time-tables or the use of buildings but give full honour to their deputies. Others demand both assistance and subservience. Some make warm contact with their pupils. Others look outwards to committee-work and spend their energies on matters other than the intimacies within the school. In all cases these relationships are circular; and the circle may be either 'vicious' or 'beneficent'.[8] Pupils learn better in contact with adults who give them affectionate appreciation. Teachers co-operate more fully if given trust and responsibility; and the happiness of the whole increases with increased insight into the purposes of each group. Much of what used to be described as the tone of a school can be more readily understood in terms of accumulating evidence of this kind. There is on the part of all a very genuine human willingness to form attachments, to develop loyalties and to accept commitments.

> This is our group (class).
> We do thus and thus.
> We are like this.
> We are not like that.

School discipline

Through such self-pictures reward and punishment, praise and blame reach relative degrees of effectiveness; and in terms of such concepts morale is built and school 'discipline' is ultimately maintained.[9] A certain vagueness of attitude is, for example, characteristic of a situation where morale is low. The 'weak' teacher may show instability of purpose or hesitancy in presentation. Threatenings may alternate with forgetfulness; and concentration upon what is to be taught may be linked with failure to permit the pupils to make their contribution. The 'awkward' class may be one which has come to expect too little to do or it may be one which has memories of a dictatorial handling which was motivated by scorn or by fear. 'Do I accept leadership here?' says the teacher whose role is uncertain in his own eyes. 'What sort of odd teacher is this?' says the unresponsive class. In a more wholesome climate the teacher is, by contrast, more observant, consistent, and hopeful; and the class has as its prevailing opinion a picture of itself as willing to co-operate in the work of the school.

Teachers and parents

The attitudes and the expectations of parents have long been believed to affect the reactions of boys and girls; but in this field also more is now known as to the ubiquity of the human longing to find oneself in the right; and it is more readily admitted that changes can be effected in the attitudes of even the most antagonistic.[10] Associations of parents and teachers have done much to foster an awareness that many parents take an interest in the schools; and as a parallel development there has been an increase in the contributions of psychologists and teachers to journals designed to give education in parent-craft. There is reason, however, to believe that the personal attitudes of teachers are still of greater significance than the organizing of informative lectures, the giving of invitations to participate in the making of school equipment or the provision of guidance through printed booklets. From detailed analysis of questions and comments in parents' conversations over a number of years, Garside, for example, produced evidence of changes consequent on the realization that the teachers had as their primary aim the helping of the children; and to an impressive extent, in the studies of Phillips and Stern, the picture was built up of parents who with a somewhat wistful longing were eager to know what was happening in the schools and interested to see what their children were doing.[11]

A recognition of this is perhaps to be discerned in the custom prevalent in some places of writing end-of-term reports with comments on the progress of each pupil. These are, however, of doubtful benefit not only because of the difficulty which parents experience in making informed judgements on class marks or personal ratings which carry no objective significance but because of the opportunity which such reports give for unwise praise or unskilful disparagement. A personal answer to a direct question by a parent remains a more satisfactory method of effecting changes in relationships than the formal issuing of such documents.

The devising of ways and means by which contacts may be made between parents and teachers requires, however, the highest artistry on the part of the teacher as administrator. One of the fruits of long-term and comparative studies of the development of boys and girls was the realization that the physical setting and the planning of youth clubs and recreational facilities added much to their effectiveness.[12] The permeability of a group is greatly increased if the doorways and the furnishings are so arranged that (without attracting undue attention) newcomers may insert themselves, observe from a distance, approach in a non-committal fashion, and ultimately contribute some gesture or remark which signals their essential suitability as participants in a group. In similar fashion, the wise head of a school shows a certain artistry in the planning of the approach to the teachers' room and in the techniques by which an invitation is given to the parent to pass beyond the ostensible reason for a visit to the real object of concern.[13]

Relationships of parents to teachers, of teachers to heads, and teachers to colleagues are all contributory to the central issue of the educational guidance of pupils. This, like vocational guidance, was formerly thought as a special responsibility which occurred only at points of transition from one class to another, one school to another or one stage of education to the next. It is now, however, recognized that both in industry and in the schools there is need for the continuous exercise of all the wisdom of which administrators are capable.[14]

Some of the technical skills which contribute to the giving of educational advice have been considered in earlier chapters. Survey testing is useful. The observation of personal attributes in their social settings contributes much; and diagnostic testing followed by remedial treatment at all levels is greatly to be desired. All these are most effective in situations in which the self-perception and the aspirations of the pupils are congruent with the purposes and the intentions of the teachers.

Principles of grouping

As a further contribution to this end certain questions have, however, in recent years and with increases in the size of schools, been asked as to the best ways of grouping pupils for the purposes of tuition. Starch in 1916 (faced by the first evidence as to individual differences) suggested that the separation of the brighter from the duller might be desirable; and in the years since then many variants of 'grouping' have been tried.[15]

The problem is found at three levels – within a class, within a school, and within school systems. Proposals as to grouping within a class are closely linked with experimentation into ways of adapting education to individual differences – initiated by Search and others in the 1890s and translated into administrative procedures at Dalton and Winnetka in the 1920s (see Chapter X above). Accompanying this in the 1920s was the alternative proposal that special homogeneous classes should be formed of good, average or weak pupils – X, Y, Z, A, B, or C – with the suggestion that when the administrator had classified pupils in this fashion teachers could with greater efficiency and ease devote their whole attention to the preparation and presentation of lessons. Such 'streaming' or 'tracking' by ability implies a certain rigidity of organization; and it is to be clearly distinguished from the more flexible 'grouping' effected within what is known to be a heterogeneous class or school.[16]

Classifying ('streaming') by ability

Some indication has been given in earlier chapters of the changes in viewpoint which came as a result of the substitution of long-term studies of development for the cross-sectional findings which exaggerated differences between groups and obscured the fluctuations in their membership. A summary of the relevance of this emphasis on classifying is offered in Table VII, p. 250.

Controlled experimentation has failed to establish consistent and significant improvements in achievement as a sequel to segregation or selective promotion.[17] The threat of failure does not of itself

TABLE VII

Streaming by Ability

Origins:
    (*a*) Research findings on individual differences.
    (*b*) Attempts to adapt organization of schools to these.
Discussed and tried out in the 1920s.

Assumptions:
    (*a*) Desirability of class instruction with uniform tasks and timetable for all.
    (*b*) Significance of ability as a determinant of scholastic success.
    (*c*) Approximate constancy of relative status.

Arguments:
    (*a*) Increase in incentive for all pupils.
    (*b*) Decrease in discouragement for less successful pupils.
    (*c*) Production of homogeneous groups for purposes of tuition.

Evidence:
    (*a*) Educational incentives and achievement are reduced for pupils in lower streams.
    (*b*) Discouragement in C streams appears to increase.
    (*c*) Groups after streaming do not remain homogeneous.
    (*d*) Initial ability is not the chief determinant of scholastic success.

make for higher quality of work; and automatic promotion does not inevitably increase the variability of classes, lower their average achievement or reduce incentive within them.[18]

Quite in line with these studies was an analysis made by Rudd of differences discernible within a school.[19] Two groups with about ninety pupils in each were followed over several years. In one, the initial grouping into three 'classes' of mixed ability remained undisturbed. In the other, forty transfers were made from one class to another. Recordings of observed classroom reactions showed more co-operative behaviour, less aggressiveness towards others, and more attentiveness in the groups in which no transfer had occurred. In the other groups there was no consistency of response to promotion or demotion in terms of attainment, of attitude, or of personality as rated by the staff. Attempts to increase the homogeneity of the sub-groups were thus unsuccessful; and the average attainments of the pupils were no greater when the organization was based upon 'streaming' than when it was not.

Whatever the form of classification, boys and girls do not learn in accordance with what can be described as their initial ability, but rather in terms of the learning situation as that is presented to them by skilful teaching and perceived by them and by their group. The significance of the views held by pupils about themselves may also be inferred from Miller's study of the social values and interests of pupils from schools organized in different ways. Where boys were segregated in terms of initial ability, the interests of the less bright were narrower than those in unsegregated schools. Their attitudes to learning were more negative. Their pride in their school was less; and more of them wished to leave at the earliest possible moment. Interests and a sense of belonging were, on the other hand, enhanced for both the duller and the brighter pupils in those schools whose organization was not in terms of segregation by ability.[20]

In the light of these findings it is possible to understand not only the good performance of some pupils in crowded conditions or in single-teacher schools but also the wide fluctuations in scholastic achievement as well as in mental ability which characterize the development of children and adults at all ages and under all types of educational stimulation. Something other than segregation by ability seems to be the vital element in progress.

At the same time, it is to be noted that, on the reverse side of the picture, the uncertainty and sense of inadequacy which follow upon 'segregation' can be recognized as contributory to reduced morale and to an increase in what has sometimes been called the differentiation of ability. Prophesies of incompetence tend to be self-fulfilling and under differentiated educational treatment, differences appear between groups which were not significantly diverse in initial competence.[21] Defeat in one area such as language may be followed by the development of special prowess in another such as art. (This, considered apart from its antecedents, was formerly believed to indicate special artistic aptitude.) Defeat in one area may, on the other hand, be the precursor of an attitude of despondency and disaffection in all.[22] The exact form which personal development will take is not a matter on which prediction can be certain. For reasons such as these, greater support in terms of psychological evidence is available for those more flexible procedures which organize units for schooling roughly according to chronological age with 'setting' or 'grouping' for special purposes and for short periods.

Grouping by friendship

Distinctive among these are the suggestions in terms of classification by friendship to which several references have already been made. Moreno's sociometric techniques were significant in that they provided a more exact method of effecting those friendly relationships to which the happiest classroom procedures have always been

TABLE VIII

Grouping in Terms of Friendly Relationships

Origins:
    (a) Recognition of significance of satisfaction of psychological needs (appreciation and the chance to participate).
    (b) Attempt to utilize these in the organizing of educational activities.
Discussed and tried out in the 1930s and the 1940s.

Assumptions:
    (a) Desirability of group activities in learning in addition to class instruction.
    (b) Significance of attitudes and intentions as determinants of scholastic success.

Arguments:
    (a) Increase in morale of all pupils.
    (b) Better balance of groups in terms of age, social maturity, interests, and physical development.
    (c) Heterogeneity in terms of ability is not, in fact, conspicuous when working partnerships are skilfully arranged in the light of knowledge as to sociometric status.

Evidence:
    (a) No significant difference in achievement has been demonstrated for all pupils.
    (b) Improvement in attitudes, and increased social maturity have been found.
    (c) Increased flexibility of organization appears beneficial to brighter as well as to duller pupils.

contributory.[23] Deliberate use of friendship or the longing for a friend as a means of providing an atmosphere conducive to learning is however a matter of even higher artistry than the administrative skill which establishes good human relations between teachers and adults in the community outside. Such 'classification by friendship' is to be distinguished from a more chaotic 'letting anybody sit anywhere . . .', although it may begin with that on a child's first arrival at a school. Its intellectual affinities are summarized in brief in Table VIII.

Educational stereotypes

Administrative responsibilities of this type must always be undertaken within the framework of contemporary belief; and there is a time-lag between professional research findings and their incorporation into the routine of school life. (See Chapter XV above.) In many countries the most persistent stereotypes – beliefs held with emotional tenacity but without evidential support – have been those of discrete stages of growth, of fixed and clearly defined types of children, and of differentiated types of mental functioning. Acceptance of these is followed by segregation for educational purposes, classifying by ability (or by sex, socio-economic level or race) and limitations in the curriculum offered. Their rejection leads to wider opportunities within systems of comprehensive non-selective schools with grouping for a variety of purposes, and greater flexibility in the curriculum provided. Findings now available show that, while the brightest do not suffer in well-staffed comprehensive schools, the attainments as well as the interests of average and below-average pupils escape the deterioration of quality which characterizes such pupils in schools segregated by initial ability.

Between the assumptions of such contemporary stereotypes and the evidence which is accumulating from experimental, genetic, and social psychology, teachers, as administrators, must find a way for themselves and their pupils. Something can be accomplished through large-scale administrative decisions; but the permanence of the transformations these effect is related always to the degree of acceptance they can win in the thinking of the larger world of adults outside. Even quite notable experiments [24] can be overlaid by more traditional ways and leave little immediate impression if they are not confirmed by the accepting of their hypotheses in the public thinking of other parents and other teachers. More is being done and at a more rapid rate through those intimate changes in attitude and expectation which are reflected in transformed climates of opinion within many schools today. In these the work of teachers as competent administrators is subordinated always to their task as guides who lead both pupils and their parents to better things.

Teachers as purchasers

As a derivative of such changes in interpretation and in methods of promoting learning the responsibilities of teachers as purchasers of educational materials are in many respects more heavy than they were.

The good text-book, like the good film or broadcast, reflects expert opinion on the organization and presentation of its subject. From its author it is reasonable to expect evidence of knowledge of research findings as to what is suitable in level of difficulty and order of development. It is desirable also that the material be such that some degree of individualizing is possible to meet the emergencies of illness, absences, differential rates of progress, or temporary unwillingness to learn. Some provision for the personal activity of the pupil is necessary; and, as a means of winning the co-operation of pupils in the responsibilities of self-correction, a diagnostic test keyed to each section of the work is essential. In some subjects such programmed material is not yet available. The challenge to the expert then lies in its construction rather than its purchase; 'self-instructive,' 'self-corrective,' 'diagnostic' – these three sum up what is being sought when the expert looks past the paper, the illustrations, the printing, and the binding to the making of a decision on the merits of a new series in any subject-field.

In similar fashion, in the purchase of tests the teacher is concerned first with the manual of instructions and norms which accompanies each series. This may be expected to give exactly the words which are to be used – to permit standardizing as far as possible of the conditions of testing. It should show also norms expressed as standardized scores or percentiles and an indication of the methods used in validation and in estimating reliability. (For the latter a figure greater than $+ 0.9$ is commonly found for material to whose making expert knowledge has gone.) When such information is satisfactory the suitability of the test can be admitted in terms of the procedure formulated by Binet long ago. Before testing human beings with a test it is reasonable to ask that the test should itself have been tested on human beings of comparable age and similar background. Good tests still conform to that criterion.

Guidance: educational and vocational

All these things are important. It is well that pupils should have access to the best text-books, that they should be examined in the most expert fashion, and that the use of school buildings as well as their construction, ventilation, and heating should be suitably planned. In similar fashion, it is desirable that the equipment, wages, and material conditions of adult workers should conform to accepted standards; and that boys and girls should find themselves on leaving school in situations in which they can grow towards wholesome physical maturity. More significant than any of these are, however, the human relationships which contribute to the social climates within which tuition or employment is offered. Supervisors who are prepared to act as guides rather than attempt either *laissez faire* or dictatorial control. Teachers who recognize the contribution which their pupils can make, who permit participation, and who believe in the possibility of insight. The presence or absence of such adults and the growth of acceptable self-pictures painted through these and other human contacts form still the essence of the teaching situation; and the provision made for these is the ultimate test of a teacher's administrative skill.

Responsibility for educational guidance has thus passed beyond the choice of materials of instruction or the arrangement of pupils in suitable educational groups to an awareness of the multi-potentiality as well as the variability of human functioning.[25] In the days when the stereotype of 'types of children' was as yet unchallenged by long-term studies of boys and girls and by large-scale aptitude testing in the armed forces of many nations it was supposed that education must necessarily 'vary with ability and aptitude', and in like fashion it was thought that vocational guidance must consist in directing each recruit to a job of a specific kind. In both cases this carried the assumption that only one kind of education and one type of job would be a suitable one and that the 'rightness' of each could be determined at an early age. With fuller understanding there has come in both fields the admission that all human beings have potentialities for success and satisfaction in a much wider range of activities than had formerly been guessed. While patterns of abilities and interests may be discerned among pupils after they have been subjected to differing types of curriculum and among workers trained at different vocational levels there is reason to believe that adjustment is continuous and that development can be guided.

'Aptitude' may sometimes be 'inferred' from initial ability or from immediate interest. It is not determined by these. In the sunny climate of a wisely ordered classroom many pupils have discovered – often to their surprise – that happiness is to be found in tasks which they at first feared and disliked; and many adults have 'discovered' interest in forms of work which to them as outsiders once lacked all human attractiveness. There is in children and in adults a certain measure of flexibility and modifiability; and success for both depends not only on inherited neural and endocrine endowment but upon the opportunity offered by interaction with a social as well as a material environment.[26] The lesson which is today being learned in schools and industry alike, is that while the former remains a hypothesis on which pronouncements are hazardous, the latter consists largely in the roles offered, rejected or accepted by the groups in which human beings meet their tasks.

This sensitivity to the school as a social situation leads very readily to a consideration of the school in its social setting of community and neighbourhood; and to this some attention may next be given.

REFERENCES

1. ROHRER, J. H., and SHERIF, M. (ed.), *Social Psychology at the Crossroads*. N.Y.: Harper. 1951.

   SHERIF, M., and SHERIF, C. W., *Groups in Harmony and Tension*. N.Y.: Harper. 1953.

   REDL, F., and WINEMAN, D., *Controls from Within*. Glencoe: Free Press. 1952.

2. For a collection of relevant studies see: CARTWRIGHT, D., and ZANDER, A. (ed.), *Group Dynamics*. Evanston: Row, Peterson. 1953.

   See also: CARTWRIGHT, D., *Occup. Psychol.* XXIV. 4. 245–8. 1950.

   MARTIN, F. M., *Brit. J. Sociol.* II. 4. 354–9. 1951.

   ARGYLE, M., *Brit. J. Psychol.* XLIII. 4. 269–79. 1952.

   ARGYLE, M., *Occup. Psychol.* XXVII. 2. 98–103. 1953.

   GROSS, N., MARTIN, W. E., and DARLEY, J. G., *J. Abn. Soc. Psycho.* 48. 3. 429–32. 1953.

   BROWN, J. A. C., *The Social Psychology of Industry*. Penguin Books. 1954.

   BERNSTEIN, L., *J. Appl. Psychol.* 38. 5. 324–8. 1954.

FOGARTY, M. P., *Personality and Group Relations in Industry*. Lond. Longmans. 1956.

See also: *Human Relations and Occupational Psychology, passim*.

3. Cf. JENNINGS, H. H., *Leadership and Isolation*. N.Y.: Longmans. 1943.

JENNINGS, H. H., *J. Educ. Sociol*. **17**. 431–3. 1944.

RAUP, R., *et al*., N.Y.: Harper. 1950.

GIBB, C. A., *Austral. J. Psychol*. **2**. 1. 19–42. 1950.

See also: KATZ, D., in DENNIS, W. (ed.), *Current Trends in Industrial Psychology*. Pittsburgh: Univ. of Pittsburgh Press. 1949.

FLEISHMAN, E. A., *J. Appl. Psychol*. **37**. 3. 153–8. 1953.

LAWSHE, C. H., and NAGLE, B. F., ibid. **37**. 3. 159–62. 1953.

4. HEMPHILL, J. R., and WESTIE, C. M., *J. Psychol*. **29**. 325–42. 1950.

STOGDILL, R. M., *Psychol. Bull*. **47**. 1. 1–14. 1950.

See also: JAQUES, E., *The Changing Culture of a Factory*. Lond.: Tavistock Publications. 1951.

5. HOMANS, G. C., *The Human Group*. Lond.: Routledge. 1951.

HALLWORTH, H. J., *Sociometry*. **XVI**. 39–70. 1953.

HALLWORTH, H. J., *Educ. Rev*. **VII**. 124–33. 1955.

See also: TAYLOR, G. R., *Are Workers Human?* Lond.: Falcon Press. 1950.

MEDALIA, N. Z., *J. Abn. Soc. Psychol*. **51**. 2. 207–13. 1955.

ROSENBERG, S., *et al*., ibid. **51**. 2. 195–203. 1955.

6. ARENSBERG, C. M., in ROHRER, J. H., and SHERIF, M. (ed.), loc. cit. [1]. 324–52.

BERNBERG, R. E., II. *J. Appl. Psychol*. **37**. 4. 249–50. 1953.

7. DANG, S. D., A Study of Co-operation in Certain Secondary Schools. M.A. Thesis. London. 1949.

DANG, S. D., *Childhood and Youth*. **4**. 2. 21–6 and 69–71. 1950.

AXLINE, V. A., *Play Therapy*. Boston: Houghton Mifflin. 1947.

THELEN, H. A., *Dynamics of Groups at Work*. Univ. of Chicago Press. 1954.

MACKENZIE, G. N., and COREY, S. M., *Instructional Leadership*. N.Y.: Teachers' College. C.U.P. 1954.

WEBER, C. A., and WEBER, M. E., *Fundamentals of Educational Leadership*. N.Y.: McGraw-Hill. 1955.

PATERSON, T. T., *Morale in War and Work*. Lond.: Max Parrish. 1955.

BIRNEY, R., and MCKEACHIE, W., *Psychol. Bull*. **52**. 1. 61–68. 1955.

8. ANDERSON, H. H., and ANDERSON, G. L., in CARMICHAEL, L. (ed.), *Manual of Child Psychology*. N.Y.: John Wiley. 1946 and 1954.

GROSS, N., and HERRIOTT, R. E., *Staff Leadership in Public Schools*. N.Y.: John Wiley. 1965.

9. HIGHFIELD, M. E., and PINSENT, A., *A Survey of Rewards and Punishments*. Lond.: National Foundation for Educational Research. 3. 1952.

10. Cf. BOWLBY, J., *Human Relations*. **II**. 2. 123–8. 1949.

FLEMING, C. M., *Adolescence*. Lond.: Routledge. 1948, 1955 and 1963.

MOUSTAKAS, C. E., and MAKOWSKY, G., *J. Consult. Psychol*. **16**. 5. 338–42. 1952.

11. STERN, H. H., *Parent Education and Parental Learning*. Ph.D. Thesis. London. 1956.

PHILLIPS, D. J., *Leeds: Researches and Studies*. **10**. 1954.

LANGDON, G., and STOUT, I. W., *Teacher-Parent Interviews*. N.Y.: Prentice-Hall. 1954.

GARSIDE, A., *The New Era*. **38**. 47–51. 1957.

STERN, H. H., *Educ. Rev.* **12**. 2. 103–11. 1960.

TITMUSS, R. M., *Problems of Social Policy*. Lond.: H.M.S.O. 1950.

RADKE, M. J., *The Relation of Parental Authority to Children's Behavior and Attitudes*. Minneapolis: Univ. of Minnesota Press. 1946.

BALDWIN, A. L., KALHORN, J., and BREESE, F. H., *Psychol. Monographs*. **63**. 4. 1949.

SHOBEN, E. J., *Genet. Psychol. Monographs*. **39**. 1. 101–48. 1949.

CUNNINGHAM, R., *et al.*, *Understanding Group Behavior of Boys and Girls*. N.Y.: Teachers' College, C.U.P. 1951.

LORR, M., and JENKINS, R. L., *J. Consult. Psychol.* **17**. 4. 306–8. 1953.

VALENTINE, C. W., and RAWLINGS, G., *Brit. J. Educ. Psychol.* **XVI**. II. 96–101. June, 1946.

WALL, W. D., ibid. **XVII**. II. 97–113. 1947.

12. MEEK, L. H., *The Personal-Social Development of Boys and Girls*. N.Y.: Progressive Education Association. 1940.

13. Cf. GARSIDE, A., loc. cit. [11].

HOPPOCK, R., *Amer. Psychologist*. **8**. 3. 124, 1953.

14. SMITH, MAY, *An Introduction to Industrial Psychology*. Lond.: Cassell. 1952.

SMITH, P., *Occup. Psychol.* **XXV**. 1. 35–43. 1951.

MCMAHON, D., ibid. **XXV**. 3. 200–4. 1951.

RODGER, A., and DAVIES, J. G. W., Vocational Guidance and Training, in *Chambers' Encyclopaedia*. Lond.: Newnes. 1960.

RODGER, A., in MACE, C. A., and VERNON, P. E. (ed.), *Current Trends in British Psychology*. Lond.: Methuen. 1953.

MERCER, E. A., ibid. **XXV**. 4. 217–24. 1951.

LANDY, E., and KROLL, A. M., *Needs and Influencing Forces*. Lond.: Oxford Univ. Press. 1967.

See also: TYLER, L. E., *The Work of the Counselor*. N.Y.: Appleton. 1953.

SUPER, D. E., *Amer. Psychologist*. **8**. 5. 185–90. 1953.

SUPER, D. E., *The Psychology of Careers*. N.Y.: Harper. 1957.

THORNDIKE, 'R. L., and HAGEN, E., *Ten Thousand Careers*. N.Y.: John Wiley. 1959.

STERN, H. H., *Brit. J. Educ. Psychol.* **XXXI**. II. 170–82. 1961.

HUGHES, E. W., *Internat. Rev. Educ.* **XI**. 3. 337–49. 1965.

15. YATES, A. (ed.), *Grouping in Education*. New York: John Wiley. Hamburg: Almqvist & Wiksell. 1966.

On Comprehensive (non-selective) Schools see:

16. FLEMING, C. M., loc. cit. [10].

HUSÉN, T. (ed.), *International Study of Achievement in Mathematics*. Stockholm: Almqvist & Wiksell. N.Y.: John Wiley. 1967.

17. Cf. JEFFERY, G. B. (chairman), *Transfer from Primary to Secondary Schools*. Lond.: Evans. 1949.

See also: RODGER, A., *Brit. J. Educ. Psychol.* **XIX**. III. 154–9. 1949.

18. OLSON, W. C., *Child Development*. Boston: D.C. Heath. 1949.

MURSELL, J. L., *Successful Teaching*. N.Y.: McGraw-Hill. 1944 and 1954.

19. RUDD, W. G. A., *Brit. J. Educ. Psychol.* **XXVIII**. 1. 47–60. 1958.

20. DANIELS, J. C., *Brit. J. Educ. Psychol.* **XXXI**. 1. 119–27. 1961.

MILLER, T. W. G., *Values in the Comprehensive School*. Educ. Monograph V. Edinburgh: Oliver and Boyd. 1961.

On the effect of limitation in the quality of education see:

HUSÉN, T., *Testresultatens Prognosvärde*. Stockholm: Hugo Gebers Vörlag. 1950.

VERNON, P. E., and PARRY, J. B., *Personnel Selection in the British Forces*. London.: Univ. of London Press Ltd. 1949.

WATTS, A. F., PIDGEON, D. A. and YATES, A., *Secondary School Entrance Examinations*. Lond.: Nat. Found. Educ. Res. 1952.

See also: BROWN, W. F., and HOLTZMAN, W. H., *J. Educ. Psychol.* **XLVI**. 2. 75–84. 1955.

HUSÉN, T., *Educational Structure and the Development of Ability*. Paris: O.S.T.P. 1961.

FURNEAUX, W. D., *The Chosen Few*. Lond.: Oxford Univ. Press. 1961.

HUSÉN, T., *Detection of Ability and Selection for Educational Purposes in Sweden*. Yearbook of Educ. Lond.: 1962.

HUSÉN, T., loc. cit. [16].

22. ELLIS, R. S., *Psychol. Bull.* **44**. 2. 1–33. 1947.

WOODS, W. A., *J. Consult. Psychol.* **XII**. 4. 240–5. 1948.

FINCH, I. E., *A Study of the Personal and Social Consequences for Groups of Secondary School Children of the Experience of Different Methods of Allocation within Secondary Courses*. M.A. Thesis. London. 1954.

See also: RIESSMAN, F., *The Culturally Deprived Child*. N.Y.: Harper. 1962.

MAYS, J. B., *The Young Pretenders*. Lond.: Michael Joseph. 1965.

23. JENNINGS, H. H., *Sociometry in Group Relations. A Work Guide for Teachers*. Washington, D.C.: Amer. Council on Educ. 1948.

24. FINDLAY, J. J., *The Demonstration School Record I*. Manchester: Univ. of Manchester. 1908. Record II. 1913.

REDEFER, F. L., *Progressive Education*. **28**. 2. 33–6. 1950.

PIDGEON, D. A. (ed.), *Achievements in Mathematics*. Nat. Found. Educ. Res. London. 1967.

25. SUPER, D. E., *Amer. Psychologist*. **8**. 5. 185–90. 1953.

25. BARNETT, G. J., HANDELSMAN, I., STEWART, L. H., and SUPER, D. E., *Psychol. Monographs*. **66**. 10. 342. 1952.

SMALL, L., ibid., 67. 1. 1953.

XVII

COMMUNITY RESOURCES

No school is a place sufficient unto itself; and none is quite shut off from what is sometimes called the world outside. Even the most private residential institutions have inescapable links with the district in which their buildings stand; and the most monastic hear echoes of the thoughts of other people through the books, broadcasts or newsprint which inevitably form some part of their traditional media of instruction.

Much has been said as to the relations of parents to teachers; and these are admittedly important. It is perhaps not so often remembered that the background of family-friends, of church or club or street carries weight also in the forming of social attitudes and the determining of the 'in-groups' to which 'reference' is made at any point of challenge. 'That is what we do.' 'That is what I am like.' 'My friends think this.'[1]

Earlier evidence is not challenged that the influence of the home tends to exceed that of other groups whose formation is later in time and at a greater physical distance from the first steps of infancy and childhood.[2] More, however, is now known as to the processes by which changes can occur; and when differences are noted by boys and girls between the viewpoint of their home and that of school or college their reactions are now recognized as being more complicated than was formerly supposed. They are not a function of physical age. Still less are they determined by intellectual ability or socio-economic level. They are instead, on this issue also, related to the quality of the inner relationships between one human being and another; and the direction they take depends upon the degree to which the home has satisfied the primary human needs of all its members – not merely by the giving of appreciation and love but by inviting co-operation and permitting an active contribution. 'Mother needs me. I could not do that.' 'Father is a friend of mine. We think the same on that.'

260

The values of the neighbourhood

Influences from other reference-groups reach out in quite comparable fashion; and teachers in their work are thus both strengthened and enfeebled by the secret pressure of the whole community which has wittingly or unawares moulded the self-pictures of the pupils along with those other hypotheses, expectancies or sets which they bring with them to each act of perception.

It used to be supposed that there was, among adolescents, an inevitable awakening of rebellion against all adult standards. The matter is now seen to be more subtle and more challenging. There is in adolescents as in all human beings an upthrust of growth and a trend to self-improvement; but where this is met with courtesy and under-standing its direction is not necessarily antagonistic to the purposes and longings of parents and older friends. Where schools or homes have succeeded in winning co-operative activity their standards gain support from the adolescents in their midst, as well as from younger children and older men and women.

At this point the question may be asked as to how such co-operative activity can be 'won'. The answer seems to be that, like all transmission of attitudes, opinions, and values, its winning is related to the beliefs held by youngsters as to the meaning of the adult behaviour in the interpretation of which they are all the time engaged. A love of gardening is not fostered by telling children that they ought to garden, or by setting them to weed while mother and father sit in the shade. Delight in that pursuit grows little by little through association with others who find in it a source of joy. A lively awareness of religious experience is not promoted by sending boys and girls to Sunday school, or organizing a school service for them every day, while the adults in their group play golf or clean their cars at hours when the children know quite well that people are meeting in the church for worship. 'How can I hear what you are saying when what you are is thundering in my ears?' Only those parents or teachers who by their actions show that they believe themselves to be still learners in the art of living and students of the meaning of human existence can hope to see the commitment of their young people to the ideals and the faith which they (in theory) hold.

In fashions such as these the values of the neighbourhood make entry to the school; and from some such origins there come those idiosyncrasies in perceiving which lend both spice and interest to

L   261

the teacher's task. A letter from a parent in a residential institution. A quarrel before breakfast when the children live at home. A family reason for rejoicing. Tragedies and illnesses. Adventures and excitements. All these enter the classroom with the pupils; and teachers learn to know that in the most unco-operative group there may unexpectedly appear some children who are ready to take another stand, while from the most docile class there may emerge a rebel waiting for the openings given by those unskilled in the management of men.

Accretions of knowledge

Some account must also be taken of those accretions of knowledge which come to schools according to the pattern of occupational and social life in their immediate neighbourhood and in the pupils' homes. The development of a building site. The opening of a factory. A picture at the cinema. Plays broadcast on television. Holidays at the seaside or in the country. Foreign visitors to the town. To some extent these are deliberately used by teachers who are alert to the values of the information which pupils can themselves collect. Whether openly utilized or not, they leave their traces; and their echoes can be overheard in private conversations in classroom or canteen. Through the relative consistency of their range and content there comes also some of the stability of interests discernible among young people as they grow.[3]

Community of interests

It is now recognized that similarities are more remarkable than differences when comparisons are made between the interests of old and young, men and women, boys and girls; and in the congruence of the background of their local knowledge there is to be found some explanation of this. Interest in ideas, interest in people, and interest in things of a variety of sorts – many of these are held in common by all members of a family. Others have their roots in the enthusiasms of a club-leader or a teacher; and in pursuit of these the common humanity of seniors and juniors is of more significance than quantitative differences in their skill. In this sense also the school is linked by hidden ties of preference, experience, and expectancy to the community of which it forms a part.

The world outside

It has sometimes been suggested that life in school is very different from life 'in the world outside'. This can now be seen to be a stereotype comparable to the earlier belief that a child is quite other than a man; and, like that supposition, it assumes a uniformity of functioning for which there is no support in observational records. The social climate of a school, as of a home, a workshop or an office, may be conducive to personal happiness. It may be destructive of human joy. To a greater extent than was formerly supposed there are, however, similarities of structure in all groups;[4] and, while one school is not necessarily like another school, it may be very similar in its personal effect to other institutions in the 'world outside'. Transition from a democratic classroom to a dictatorial and unfriendly factory brings special problems in its train. No less real is the bewilderment of the child who passes from the rigid hierarchies of a formal school to the give-and-take of a workshop run on friendly lines.

Civilian morale

The world comes to the classroom with the pupils. The school goes home at night with them and with their teachers. The joys and sorrows of the day linger in the memory – as the day's triumphs and the disappointments lend flavour to the leisure hours of all other human beings. In this sense also the resources of the community contribute to the strengthening or the enfeebling of teachers.

The responsibility of a home, the confidence of family and of friends, voluntary membership of societies of various sorts, books, hobbies, games, art, music, and the like, all these with their more negative side of distraction, over-pressure, exhaustion or bad manners, provide a background of experience through which teachers, like all adults, struggle towards increasing maturity of outlook and achieve some measure of mental health. In such participatory citizenship, civilian morale has its origin and is maintained;[5] and much of this reaches professional teachers as it reaches all adults – whether they choose it or not. No man is an island unto himself, and even those who elect to work in small segregated groups are continuously under pressure to participate – vicariously through the efforts of journalists or programme producers or directly through their more personal contacts with wives, husbands, relatives, neighbours, and friends.

263

Modern social services

In other senses also the resources of the community are brought to bear upon the work of schools. The social services of a modern state include the provision of probation officers, mental deficiency officers, nursery schools, special schools, child guidance centres, and the like. Details of the functioning of these vary from time to time and from one country to another;[6] but in most places the work of schools is fortified by the efforts of statutory and voluntary agencies directed also to the care and to the educating of boys and girls. These are of special significance in the case of deviating children – the dull, the crippled, the maladjusted or the destitute;[7] but their contribution is so relevant to the aims and purposes of ordinary schooling that wise teachers more and more are setting themselves to discover the facilities available in their districts and at the same time are making personal contacts with those other human beings who act as Youth Leaders, Heads of Recreational Evening Institutes, officials of the National Society for the Prevention of Cruelty to Children, Child Care Officers, Hospital Almoners, and the like. To all teachers these stand as a reminder that behind the school there is the strong arm of the whole community to whose ultimate betterment their special skill as educational experts is continuously directed.

Teachers thus do not work alone. They are never truly isolated from that greater world which occasionally may seem 'outside', but which is in reality always within their classrooms and involved with them in all their tasks.[8]

REFERENCES

1. NEWCOMB, T. M., *Personality and Social Change*. N.Y.: Dryden Press. 1943.
2. MURPHY, G., MURPHY, L. B., and NEWCOMB, T. M., *Experimental Social Psychology*. N.Y.: Harper. 1937.
   HELFANT, K., *Psychol. Monogr. General and Applied*. **66**. 13. 1952.
   COOK, L. and E., *Intergroup Education*. N.Y.: McGraw-Hill. 1954.
   MUSGROVE, F., *The Family, Education and Society*. Lond.: Routledge. 1966.
   DAVIS, C., *Room to Grow*. Toronto: Univ. of Toronto Press. 1966.
3. LEVINE, P. R., and WALLEN, R., *J. Appl. Psychol.* **38**. 6. 428–31. 1954.
   NELSON, E. N. P., *Psychol. Monographs*. **68**. 2. 1954.
   STRONG, E. K., *Vocational Interests 18 Years after College*. Minneapolis: Univ. of Minnesota Press. 1955.
4. HOMANS, G. C., *The Human Group*. Lond.: Routledge. 1951.

See also: KLEIN, J., *The Study of Groups*. Lond.: Routledge. 1956; and ARGYLE, M., *The Scientific Study of Human Behaviour*. Lond.: Methuen. 1957.

5. WATSON, G. (ed.), *Civilian Morale*. Boston: Houghton Mifflin. 1942.
6. See, for example: HALL, M. P., *The Social Services of Modern England*. Lond.: Routledge. 1952.

Social Services in Britain. Lond.: H.M.S.O. 1955.
7. DAVIDSON, M. A., in MACE, C. A., and VERNON, P. E. (ed.), *Current Trends in British Psychology*. Lond.: Methuen. 1953.

DUNSDON, M. I., *The Educability of Cerebral Palsied Children*. Lond.: National Foundation for Educational Research. 4. 1952.

See also: KENNEDY, A., DAVIDSON, M. A., KEIR, G., MCCALLUM, C. M., MOODY, R. L., BANKS, C., and BURT, C., Symposium on Psychologists and Psychiatrists in the Child Guidance Service. *Brit. J. Educ. Psychol.* XXI. III. 167–171. 1951; XXII. I. 1–4 and 5–29, 1952; XXII. II. 79–88. 1952; XXII. III. 155–9, 1952; XXIII. I. 1–7 and 8–28, 1953.

CLEUGH, M. C., *The Slow Learner*. Lond.: Methuen. 1957.
8. For studies reflecting the complexity of the psychological habitat see: BARKER, R. G., and WRIGHT, H. F., *One Boys' Day*. N.Y.: Harper. 1951.

EVANS, J., *Three Men*. N.Y.: Knopf. 1954.

BREWSTER-SMITH, M., BRUNER, J. S., and WHITE, R. W., *Opinions and Personality*. N.Y.: John Wiley. 1956.

On the social background of education see also: *Review of Educational Research*. X. I. 1940; XVI. I. 1946; XIX. I. 1949; XXII. I. 1952.

TRAGER, H. T., and YARROW, M. R., *They Learn What they Live*. N.Y.: Harper. 1952.

FRASER, E., *Home Environment and the School*. Lond.: Univ. of Lond. Press. 1959.

WISEMAN, S., *Education and Environment*. Manchester Univ. Press. 1964.

DOUGLAS, J. W. B., *The Home and the School*. Lond.: MacGibbon & Kee. 1964.

DAVIES, H., *Culture and the Grammar School*. London: Routledge. 1965.

MUSGROVE, F., loc. cit. [2].

XVIII

THERAPIES IN
THE SCHOOL SITUATION

MUCH HAS BEEN written in the field of psychotherapy as to the processes and consequences of interactions within groups; and from Pratt's discovery of many years ago that tuberculous patients benefited from group instruction to the most recent variants of social psychiatry there may be traced a gradual acceptance of the notion that awareness of a common humanity on the part of a patient and some insight into the attitudes and the experiences of others are contributory to the recovery of mental health.[1] The same group processes are operative in the maintenance of mental health wherever opportunities for group intercourse are available in school or church or club.

Indirect evidence on this is to be found in many studies to which reference has already been made.* Spontaneity in grouping, opportunities for leaderless group discussion and the friendliness of attitude and faith in the possibility of improvement which result from 'democratic' classroom procedures have been followed by the re-establishment of shattered confidence, the awakening of hope and the discovery of courage on the part of children of all ages.[2]

Techniques in teaching

The techniques used by teachers to attain these ends vary along as wide a continuum as those exemplified by differing schools of psychotherapy.[3] Gradations in methods may be observed from the inculcation of a specific interpretation (persisted in against resistances almost as strong as those encountered in the process of traditional psycho-analysis) to something akin to the willingness of Rogerian therapists to reflect feeling and await personal insight. Methods differ from teacher to teacher; but they are related also to differences

* For a fuller discussion of group therapy in its relevance to education see: Fleming, C. M., *Adolescence. Its Social Psychology*. London: Routledge & Kegan Paul Ltd. 1948, 1955 and 1963.

among pupils and to differences in subject-matter. Even the hardiest autocrat is affected by the glances and gestures of his pupils; and to classes of higher ability there seems a tendency to accord a more harmonious and 'child-centred' climate.[4] There is also a balancing of responsibility between teacher and class which is a function not only of the age of the pupils but of a mutual acceptance and rejection of adult and child which psychiatrists would describe as transference and counter-transference.

The key problem of teaching, like that of therapy, may be described as one of communication; and it has to be handled within the frame of reference of both teacher and pupil. To the teacher as the professionally active partner there belongs the responsibility of taking steps to secure some understanding of the past life, the expectations, and the aspirations of the child. In this lies the justification for the making of 'case-studies' by students in teacher-training courses and by teachers in active service. From this also comes part of the success which follows friendly attitudes towards parents in their approaches to a school. Much 'information' is conveyed without words; but mutual awareness of the undertones of verbalizations increases the effectiveness not only of direct instruction but also of questioning and the discussion of answers. The therapeutic skill of a teacher is closely related to competence in such matters.

Group work

Membership of groups has sometimes been discussed as if of itself (regardless of the quality of its membership) it were contributory to improvement.[5] There is not, however, reason to suppose that the mere interchange of words among groups of human beings who lack both experience and knowledge can, unaided, result in significant discoveries. Evidence as to the influence of group discussion on the reaching of conclusions has to be read in the light of differences in the type of test, the age of the testees, and the nature of the modification desired. It has been shown that group decisions reached by friendly agreement on an issue on which fresh information has been made available are followed by more effective action than that consequent on the mere hearing of a lecture or the reading of a pamphlet.[6] The light had, however, been supplied. It is known that even so simple a personal contribution as the reading aloud of words advocating a certain viewpoint can exercise greater influence than the same statements read silently or overheard.[7] (A familiar parallel is the singing of hymns or the chanting of slogans.) It is recognized that there is a possibility that a contribution of marked ability may come from a group; but there is reason to believe that its coming is related to the chance that in a group there may be a member of unusual gifts.

There is also no mystical advantage in the mere getting-together in a group.[8] Work in Youth Clubs or residential institutions (boarding schools or colleges) is less wisely handled than it might be if it makes no provision for the fact that certain avocations are best pursued alone. Interest in sociometric status has tended to blind some thinkers to the fact that the information given by sociometric questions is descriptive rather than explanatory or evaluative. It is not to be assumed that either isolation or unusual popularity is reprehensible or symptomatic of maladjustment; but awareness of its existence gives at times a clue to some of the accompaniments of surprising behaviour.[9] Repetition of the same questions after intervals of months also offers some indication of the directions in which relationships between pupils are moving and of the effects of attempts to establish opportunities for friendly contacts where these seem lacking. Neither degree of popularity nor the longing for affiliation is, however, of itself indicative of value. There is a merit in turning aside as well as in being together; and the growth towards social maturity includes a balancing of the issues of similarity-difference, popularity-unpopularity, as well as a coming to terms with one's relative competences in a variety of spheres.[10] The therapeutic values of membership of groups are thus to be looked for in something other than the mere contrast between 'group-work' and 'discussion-groups' on the one hand and 'individual activities' and 'lessons' or 'lecture-courses' on the other.

The content of a course

Of a somewhat different character is the benefit conveyed by the intellectual content of a course. This is partly explicable through the satisfaction it gives to the wish for 'knowledge' which seems an essential human attribute. It is to some extent also a means of reassurance through its reminder of the communality of personal hopes, fears or ambitions. Biblio-therapy – the therapy of books – in a very real sense thus offers at all ages that insight into the lives of others which serves to maintain the awareness of kinship which is one of the ingredients of mental health.[11]

Group belongingness

Attendance at school offers to boys and girls a series of groups to which they may attach themselves. These give a modicum of acceptance. 'I am one of the Willington boys.' They provide an outlet for service. 'I give out the pencils.' 'I can show you where to go.' They answer the need for understanding. 'Our teacher says . . .'

Contributory also to mental health is the blessed anonymity provided by membership of a somewhat large community. There is a certain satisfaction (especially for children from small families) in passing from the concentrated attention of loving friends to a more impersonal setting where as one of a crowd one may observe oneself as well as notice others. There is also a measure of fascination in a heterogeneous group. 'He says . . .' 'She does not . . .' 'They are not like me.'

Much has been said as to the desirability of small classes. It has not, however, been proved that classes of fewer than fifteen are any more conducive to achievement than classes of more than thirty. Something other than the size of the group appears to be the definitive factor. Larger classes probably offer a greater variety of roles in which leadership is possible. They certainly provide a wider choice in friendships. They also permit more extended periods of escape from direct supervision; and they allow more readily for the learning of the skills of self-aided study and self-correction of errors. For the teacher of any group there is a temptation to 'teach' all day long. To the pupils in the larger groups the co-presence of many contemporaries acts in some sense as a buffer against excessive adult pressure or persuasion.

From investigations into the effectiveness of larger as against smaller classes the most valuable outcome has probably been the suggestion that there could be more flexibility in the use of teachers and in the planning of buildings. Classrooms of various sizes are suitable for differing purposes and for different subjects. Teachers vary in their talents and their interests; and pupils differ in their immediate requirements. Team-teaching – the time-tabling of a staff as a team working together – can improve school morale through permitting large classes to encounter enthusiastic teachers while their colleagues are set free for other activities which will prepare them in turn to 'take their subject' another day. The procedure requires a high degree of co-operativeness on the part of all. Where successful, it contributes much to the happiness of a school.

What of the teachers

Teachers, like pupils, are human beings with all human hopes and fears and longings; and the satisfaction of many of their deepest needs comes to them also directly through their work. Like all engaged in 'serving' rather than in 'producing' there is commonly among them a concentration on the requirements of others which conduces to the minimizing of neurotic distress and in itself fosters mental health.[13]

It was formerly suggested that delight in teaching was attributable to the sublimation of a sexual instinct (the Freudian view) or to a lust for power (in Adlerian thinking). It was in some sense a second best to be apologized for and deprecated whenever it was noted to appear. With fuller understanding of the complexity of human nature such interpretations have ceased to be sufficient. Human beings are not fully satisfied by getting pleasure from sex relationships, from the accumulation of possessions, from domination, prestige or status. They require also to give and to participate – to play a role and to understand. The joys of teaching are, for this reason, not confined to professional teachers. They can be studied wherever in an outreaching of deliberate instruction or tuition one human being tries to influence another. In the self-forgetfulness of such endeavours there are to be found the same personal accretions of self-respect and self-understanding which make the work of teachers in the school situation contributory not only to the mental health of many of their charges but to their own development in personal stability and wholesome self-acceptance. It is, in this sphere also, more blessed to give than to receive; and he that loseth his own life does in the most real sense contribute to its saving.

REFERENCES

1. MORENO, J. L. (ed.), *Group Psychotherapy: A Symposium.* N.Y.: Beachon House. 1945.
   BIERER, J., *Proceedings of the Royal Society of Medicine.* 208–9. Dec. 14th, 1943.
   BIERER, J. (ed.), *Therapeutic Social Clubs.* Lond.: H. K. Lewis. [n.d.].
   BIERER, J., *The Day Hospital.* Lond.: H. K. Lewis. 1951.
   EZRIEL, H., *Brit. J. Med. Psychol.* XXIII. 1 and 2. 59–74. 1950.
   SUTHERLAND, J. D., *Psychiatry.* 15. 2. 111–17. 1952.
   EZRIEL, H., ibid. 15. 2. 119–26. 1952.

Cf. SUTHERLAND, J. D., in MACE, C. A., and VERNON, P. E. (ed.), *Current Trends in British Psychology*. Lond.: Methuen. 1953.

TAYLOR, F. K., *Brit. J. Med. Psychol.* **XXV.** 2 and 3. 128–34. 1952.

KLEIN, H. S., and FOULKES, S. H., ibid. **XXV.** 4. 223–34. 1952.

FOULKES, S. H., ibid. **XXVI.** 1. 30–5. 1953.

JONES, M., *Brit. Med. J.* 276–8. Sept. 5, 1942.

JONES, M., *Social Psychiatry*. Lond.: Tavistock Publications. 1952.

BAKER, A. A., *Brit. J. Med. Psychol.* **XXV.** 4. 235–43. 1952.

BAKER, A. A., JONES, M., *et al.*, ibid. **XXVI.** 3. and 4. 222–44. 1953.

2. MOUSTAKAS, C. E., *The Teacher and the Child*. N.Y.: McGraw-Hill. 1956.

JONES, H. E., *Development in Adolescence*. N.Y.: Appleton. 1943.

TAWADROS, S. M., *Internat. J. Soc. Psychiat.* **II.** 1. 44–50. 1956.

DAVEY, A. G., *Education Papers*, Newcastle upon Tyne: King's College Education Society. **VIII.** 3. 45–51. 1956.

FLEMING, C. M., *Acta. Psychotherap.* **7.** Supplement. 117–23. 1959.

3. COLLIER, R. M., *J. Consult. Psychol.* **14.** 3. 199–205. 1950.

BORDIN, E. S., ibid. **19.** 1. 9–15. 1955.

STRUPP, H. H., ibid. **19.** 2. 97–102. 1955.

Cf. GURVITZ, M., 1900–1950. *Brit. J. Delinq.* **II.** 2. 88–102. 1951.

STENGEL, E., *Brit. J. Med. Psychol.* **XXVII.** 4. 193–200. 1954.

4. WANDT, E., and OSTREICHER, L. M., *Psychol. Monograph.* **68.** 5. No. 376. 1954.

SMITH, F. V., SLUCKIN, W., and GRAHAM, D., *Brit. J. Psychol.* **XLIV.** 4. 339–46. 1953.

5. Cf. SHAW, M., *Amer. J. Psychol.* **XLIV.** 491–504. 1932.

MCKEACHIE, W. J., *J. Abn. Soc. Psychol.* **49.** 2. 282–9. 1954.

6. LEWIN, K., in NEWCOMB, T. M., and HARTLEY, E. L., *Readings in Social Psychology*. N.Y.: Holt. 1947.

PRESTON, M. G., and HEINTZ, R. K., *J. Abn. Soc. Psychol.* **44.** 3. 345–55. 1949.

LEVINE, J., and BUTLER, J., *J. Appl. Psychol.* **36.** 1. 29–33. 1952.

HORWITZ, M., and LEE, E. J., *J. Abn. Soc. Psychol.* **49.** 2. 201–10. 1954.

7. JANIS, I. L., and KING, B. T., ibid. **49.** 2. 211–18. 1954.

8. LORGE, I., and SOLOMON, H., *Psychometrika*. **20.** 2. 139–48. 1955.

TAYLOR, D. W., and FAUST, W. L., *J. Exper. Psychol.* **44.** 5. 360–8. 1952.

9. Cf. SHAW, H., *Educ. Rev.* **6.** 3. 208–20. 1954.

10. Cf. JONES, H. E., loc. cit. [2].

FLEMING, C. M., *Adolescence*. Lond.: Routledge. 1948, 1955 and 1963.

11. FLEMING, C. M., *Higher Education Journal*. 23. March, 1945.

WOOD, A. B., *Amer. Psychologist*. **10.** 1. 32–3. 1955.

Cf. ALLPORT, G. W., The Use of Personal Documents in Psychological Science. *Soc. Science Res. Council Bull.* 1949.

RUSSELL, D. H., *Children Learn to Read*. Boston: Ginn. 1949.

12. On size of class see: FLEMING, C. M., *Educ. Res.* **1.** 2. 35–48. 1959.

HASKELL, S., *The Effect of Size of Class upon Class and Teacher*. Lond.: M.A. Thesis. 1959.

MORRIS, J. M., *Reading in the Primary School*. Lond.: Nat. Found. Educ. Res. 1959.

SIEGEL, L., *et al.*, *J. Educ. Psychol.* **51.** 1. 9–13. 1960.

MARKLUND, S., *Educ. Res.* **VI.** 1. 63–7. 1963.

DE CECCO, J. P., *Brit. J. Educ. Psychol.* **XXXIV.** 1. 65–74. 1964.

RUDD, W. G. A., *A Study of Class Size in its Relation to other Variables in the School Situation*. Lond.: Ph.D. Thesis. 1964.

HUSÉN, T. (ed.), *International Study of Achievement in Mathematics*. Stockholm: Almqvist & Wiksell. N.Y.: John Wiley. 1967.

On Team Teaching see: PATTERSON, G. E., *et al.*, *Bull. Nat. Ass. Sec. Sch. Principals*. **42.** 234. 165–7. 1958; and **43.** 243. 99–103. 1959.

JOHNSON, R. H., *et al.*, ibid., 45. 261. 57–78. 1961.

13. See: LINE, W., *Brit. J. Med. Psychol.* **XXIV.** 1. 42–8. 1951.

INDEX TO AUTHORS

273

INDEX TO SUBJECTS

283

University Paperbacks

A COMPLETE LIST OF TITLES

ARCHAEOLOGY

UP 94 Antiquities of the Irish Countryside, *S. O'Riordain*
UP 1 Archaeology and Society, *Grahame Clark*
UP 118 Archaeology in the Holy Land, *K. Kenyon*
UP 150 Industrial Archaeology, *K. Hudson*

ART AND ARCHITECTURE

UP 33 The Architecture of Humanism, *G. Scott*
UP 101 The Classical Language of Architecture, *J. Summerson*
UP 259 Permanent Red, *John Berger*

ASTRONOMY

UP 20 Introduction to Astronomy, *C. Payne-Gaposchkin*
UP 152 Stars in the Making, *C. Payne-Gaposchkin*

BIOGRAPHY

UP 102 An Autobiography, *E. Muir*
UP 300 Disraeli, *Robert Blake*
UP 90 Horace Walpole, *R. W. Ketton-Cremer*

HISTORY

LAW

LITERATURE (see also PLAYS AND DRAMA)

MATHEMATICS AND STATISTICS

MUSIC

ORGANIZATION AND ADMINISTRATION

PHILOSOPHY

PHYSICS

PLAYS AND DRAMA

The Arden Shakespeare

POLITICS

PSYCHOLOGY

SOCIOLOGY AND ANTHROPOLOGY